Fishing
Montana

Fishing
Montana

Michael S. Sample

Revised 1998

GUILFORD, CONNECTICUT
HELENA, MONTANA
AN IMPRINT OF THE GLOBE PEQUOT PRESS

A FALCON GUIDE®

Front cover photo by Michael S. Sample
Back cover photo by Spiker Stock Photography
All black-and-white photos by Michael S. Sample unless otherwise noted.

Sample, Michael S.
    Fishing Montana / Michael S. Sample. — 3rd ed. / revised by Russ
Schneider.
        p.   cm.
    Includes index.
    ISBN 978-1-56044-686-6 (pbk. : alk. paper)
    1. Fishing–Montana–Guidebooks.   2. Montana–Guidebooks.
I. Title.
SH517.S26   1998
799.1'2'09786–dc21   98-18967
                                                                      CIP

Printed in the United States of America.
First Edition/Fifth Printing

 Text pages printed on recycled paper.

To buy books in quantity for corporate use
or incentives, call **(800) 962–0973**
or e-mail **premiums@GlobePequot.com**.

This book is dedicated to the fisheries biologists of Montana Department of Fish, Wildlife, and Parks and the U.S. Fish and Wildlife Service who were so helpful and who work so hard on behalf of our fisheries.

Contents

Montana's Major Rivers and Lakes

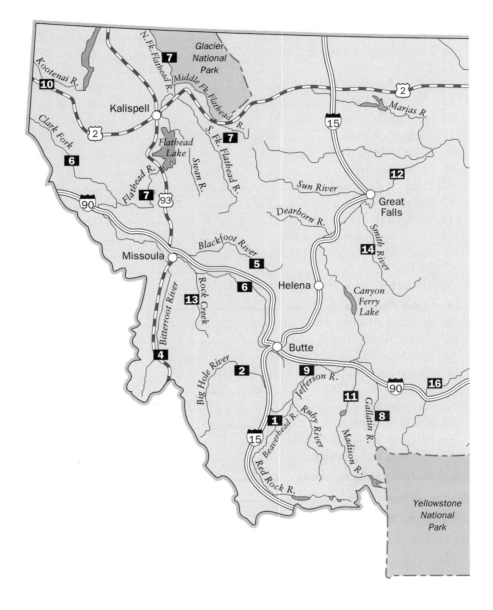

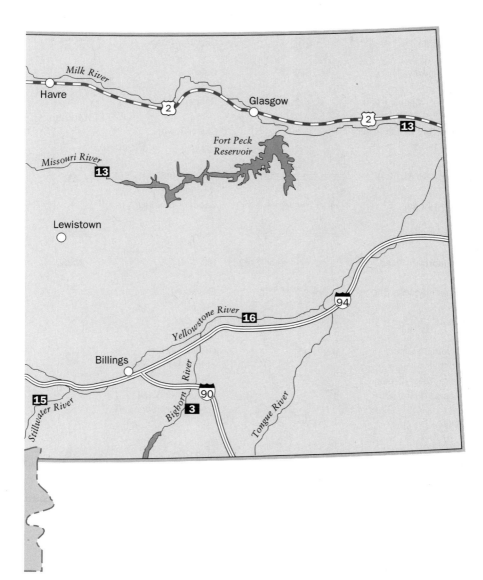

Map Legend

Interstate		One Way Road	One Way
US Highway		Gate	
State or County Road		Ranger Station	
Bureau of Indian Affairs (BIA) Road		City or Town	Standish or Standish
Interstate Highway		Campground	
Paved Road		Cabin or Building	
Gravel Road		Peak	5,281 ft.
Unimproved Road		Hill	
Fishing Access Site	Access here	Elevation	5,281 ft.
Dam		Mine Site	
Diversion Dam		Overlook/Point of Interest	
Lake, River/Creek, Rapids/Waterfall		National or State Forest/Park Boundary	
Bridge			
Marsh or Wetland		Map Orientation	N
Spring		Scale	0 0.5 1
Trail/Route			Miles

Acknowledgments

A book of this scope requires large measures of time, work, and help. One of the joys of researching and writing this book has been working with some very helpful people. My thanks for their efforts are noted here.

Most importantly, three people contributed materially by writing sections of the book for me. In so doing, they saved me considerable time and added their valuable insights on particular waters. Karen Zackheim wrote the Beaverhead, Jefferson, and Rock Creek chapters as well as substantial portions of the Glacier and Yellowstone National Parks sections. Hugh Zackheim penned the Gallatin and Madison River chapters. Wilbur Rehmann did all the writing on the lake section, and Will Harmon created the section on alpine lake fisheries.

Valuable information came from personnel of the Montana Department of Fish, Wildlife, and Parks. Pat Graham, Don Peters, Jim Vashro, Jerry Wells, and Ron Marcoux not only helped tremendously in the research stages, but also kindly reviewed written chapters and gave helpful suggestions. Bruce Rehwinkel, Al Wipperman, Bob Domrose, Al Elser, Joe Huston, Dick Vincent, Dennis Workman, Phil Stewart, Jim Darling, Steve Leathe, Dick Oswald, Ron Spoon, Bill Pryor, Laney Hanzel, Wade Fredenburg, Steve McMullin, Larry Davis, and Steve Swedberg also have my gratitude for their substantial contributions.

I am deeply indebted to Leo Marnell, Ron Jones, and Bob Gresswell, biologists with the U.S. Fish and Wildlife Service, without whom the park sections would be considerably less authoritative.

Fishing guides and purveyors of fishing tackle furnished much of the advice contained in this book. Ray Hurley, Richard Parks, John Bailey, Bud and Pat Lilly, Al Troth, and Frank Johnson bestowed large amounts of time and attention toward making this book more helpful. Fred Tedesco, Mike Brady, Fred Terwilliger, Phil Wright, Curt Collins, Rich Stevenson, Don Alley, George Anderson, Scott Waldie, Tony Schoonen, Fran Johnson, Dave Kumlien, George Grant, Gary Evans, Becky Garland, Hap Jensen, Mike Craig, Ed Curnow, Bob Jacklin, and Mike Mouat were other valuable contributors I would like to thank.

I continue to miss the peaceful, thoughtful presence of Dan Bailey, who kindly shared some of his wisdom with me before his untimely death.

I also continue to be inspired by the memories I hold of the late Joe Halterman, whose courage, intelligence, and drive for excellence have benefited Montana fisheries for generations.

Other people who contributed in one way or another include Hank Fischer, Bill Haviland, Vince Ames, Ridley Taylor, Lou and Bud Morris, Bob Schumacher, Dan Lamont, Greg Zem, Rev. Charlie Gorman, Mark Henckel, Paul Schullery, Paul Roos, Stu Swenson, Jim O'Loughlin, Bob Martinka, and John Varley. A big thank you goes to George Holton of the Montana Department of Fish,

Wildlife and Parks, who gave Wilbur Rehmann much help with the lakes information. Thanks also to Norm Peterson and Larry Peterman for their assistance. I am especially grateful to Bill Schneider, Sanna Porte, Will Harmon, and Helen Ibach for editing, proofreading, typing, and helpful advice on content and preparation.

Lastly, and most especially, I wish to express my deep appreciation to my parents and wife for their long-standing support.

—*Michael S. Sample*

Along with Russ Schneider, Ric Bourie, and Jessica Solberg, the following people were especially helpful in updating the information for the 1998 revision of *Fishing Montana*:

Bill Phippen, Jim Vashro, Phil Wright, Dick Oswald, Don Peters, Steve Leathe, Jim Darling, Ken Frazer, Bill Weidenheft, Kurt Gilge, and Phil Stewart, all employed by the Montana Department of Fish, Wildlife, and Parks.

Al Troth of Dillon, renowned fly tier and guide
George Grant, founder of the George Grant chapter of Trout Unlimited
Tony Schoonen, noted fishing guide
George Anderson, owner of Yellowstone Angler fly shop
Pat Marcusen, author of *Fishing the Beartooths*, published by Falcon
Bill Haviland, veteran fisherman
Hank Fischer, author of *Floater's Guide to Montana*, published by Falcon
Bill Schneider, author of *Hiking Montana*, president of Falcon Publishing
Dave Kumlien of Montana Troutfitters in Bozeman
Eric Hanson, fisherman, of Somers
Curt Collins, the original outfitter on the Bighorn River
Tim Linehan, of Kootenai River Guide Service in Troy

DARRIN SCHREDER PHOTO

Introduction

Why write a fishing guide? The answers to that question tie in closely with the answers to another question—why fish? As with any sport, the purpose of fishing can be reduced to ludicrous simplicity. The goal, at least apparently, is to fool a pea-brained aquatic animal into biting a hook, whereupon the angler cranks the creature in with the help of line, reel, and rod. A definition of this sort is akin to describing the Statue of Liberty as a hunk of copper in a New York City harbor.

In truth, fishing may have as many meanings and purposes as it has participants. As beauty is in the eye of the beholder, so is fishing in the mind, heart, and soul of the angler. An abbreviated list of commonly pronounced reasons for fishing might include: fun, exercise, escape from the pressures of work, escape from the ugliness of city life, the beauty of fish domains, solitude and/ or comradeship, relaxation, the chance to do something wholesome with one's family, the chance to exercise one's creativity, the joy of developing a skill, feeling at one with nature, obtaining food, inspiration, refreshment, celebration of seasons, and the challenge of catching fish.

Catching fish is not the only purpose of fishing, but it does contribute to the experience. Yet it is often observed that a small percentage of anglers catch most of the fish while the large majority catch few or none at all. Fishing guide Ray Hurley once observed, "Fishing must be a wonderful hobby, because so many people have so much fun doing it and yet are so terrible doing it."

There is no such thing as a born angler; people do not come into this world with or without fishing genes. Instead, fishing is a learned skill. Anyone with a modest amount of physical ability and motivation can become a proficient angler. A guidebook such as this can be a valuable aid in the learning process.

Thus, to answer the opening question, *Fishing Montana* was written and published to meet a need for information and education. This book will help anglers be better at something they already enjoy!

Some guidebooks offer the reader the knowledge of one expert; this book cites more than sixty pros. And that is important with a subject as vast as Montana fishing. Not only is there a tremendous amount to know, but also a diversity of opinions helps the angler know there is often more than one answer to questions.

Rather than covering every mountain lake and stream, this book concentrates on Montana's larger fisheries. The bulk of fishing in Montana occurs on the bigger rivers, lakes, and reservoirs, most of which are readily accessible. *Fishing Montana* also contains brief descriptions of the major alpine lake basins and their fisheries. Many of these lakes are remote wilderness tarns, reached only on foot or horseback.

Sooner or later, an angler who really cares about the quality of fishing becomes an advocate. Going to bat for a favorite fishery might mean testifying at a Fish, Wildlife, and Parks meeting, keeping a fisherman's log, or joining an

1

organization such as Trout Unlimited. The Montana Wildlife Federation and the local Rod and Gun clubs have also actively benefited Montana fishing. The professional fishery managers can't do their job alone—they need public input and support. They also need better funding, which can only come when the fishing public pressures state legislators to allocate more money for research, acquisition of public fishing access, and adequate salaries.

Clearly, we in Montana are blessed with some of the best trout fishing in the nation. This is undoubtedly the result of many factors, but certainly one of the biggest is the high water quality which provides an outstanding habitat. Anglers often worry about such factors as fishing pressure, trash fish, regulations, or limits. But in the end, without good habitat, these questions are moot. Protect the habitat, and good fishing will follow.

Rumor has it that when concerned out-of-state anglers call a certain Montana tackle shop to ask how the fishing is, the sales clerks always respond with enthusiastic reports, even when the liars haven't been catching anything. While this may seem an unfair policy, it has its point. As an old saying goes, "Fishin' is always great—it's the catchin' that varies." Here's hoping you have great fishing and tight lines. —*Mike Sample*

THREATENED SPECIES

When this book was first written, many areas in Montana still had excellent fishing for large aggressive bull trout. Bull trout were common in rivers like the Flathead, Swan, and Blackfoot. Unfortunately, bull trout populations are on the decline and deserve special concern. In addition, bull trout are now a "threatened" species under the Endangered Species Act.

The bull trout is a large fish, attaining a length of up to 3 feet and a weight of up to 20 pounds. It is a separate species from the smaller coastal Dolly Varden. Many bull trout are migratory, traveling up to 150 miles through river systems to tributaries to spawn.

The bull trout has been designated threatened because of the restricted distribution of the large migratory form, threats to spawning habitat, competition from non-native species and danger of interbreeding with brook trout. Migratory bull trout for Flathead Lake once spawned in tributaries of all forks of the Flathead River and the Swan River, but Hungry Horse and Bigfork Dams now block about 50% of the original spawning habitat.

It is hard to target the exact reason for the decline of bull trout, especially in the Flathead River drainage, but most people would agree that it is a result of many factors, including the major dams blocking migration routes, siltation of spawning streams from increase development and logging, introduction of competing species such as lake trout, and heavy fishing pressure for the large trophy bulls. Many pictures of old-time fishermen show strings of 6- to 10-pound bull trout. It is hard to say that those fishermen didn't play some role in the decline.

The nature of the predator precludes most catch and release practices. FWP realizes that a predatory fish attacks a lure aggressively, most often swallowing the fly or lure entirely, making it almost impossible to release the fish alive.

As a result, it is illegal to keep bull trout. It is also illegal to target bull trout. Please take care to release all bull trout and maybe someday the population will recover enough to allow widespread fishing again.

WHIRLING DISEASE

Montana's wild and native trout are among the nation's most precious natural resources. Whirling disease, a potentially fatal illness of trout and salmon, has been found in Montana. Unfortunately, fish parts used as bait can spread whirling disease. FWP urges anglers to avoid using anything other than worms and insects for bait. Harmless to humans, whirling disease is devastating to trout: it is a parasite that deforms their spinal cords, forcing them to swim in circles. Eventually, of course, they starve. FWP is currently working to solve the problem. We need your help to prevent its spread.

The tiny parasite that causes the trout illness can survive within live fish, dead fish, and in water and riverbed mud. It can even survive in dry mud.

Montana Fish, Wildlife, & Parks urges anglers to follow these **DOs** and **DON'Ts:**

DO remove all mud and aquatic plants from your vehicle, boat, anchor, trailer and axles, waders, boots, and fishing gear before departing the fishing access site or boat dock.

DO dry your boat and equipment between river trips.

DON'T transport fish from one body of water to another.

DON'T dispose of fish entrails, skeletal parts, or other by-products in any body of water.

DON'T collect or use minnows or sculpins for bait.

DON'T use parts of trout, salmon, or whitefish for bait.

RIVER AND FISHING ETIQUETTE

The following is a list of proper river and fishing practices compiled by the River Recreation Conflicts Group, Ethics and Education Committee.
Boaters:

•Be organized before you approach the launch area.

•Allow space between your boat and others when fishing.

•Watch for wading anglers and plan a path to avoid them and their fishing hole.

•Attempt to travel at a no-wake speed near floaters or wading anglers.

•Kayakers or canoeists "playing the river" should yield to boaters traveling by.

•Do not drag your anchor on streambeds.

Anglers:

- •Don't crowd other anglers—keep out of sight of others if possible.
- •Let others enjoy good fishing spots too.
- •Yield to boats when there in no other channel to navigate.
- •Avoid using the streambed as a pathway.

Using This Guide

The narrative descriptions in this book highlight the experience of many Montana anglers and present a wealth of information about each river, lake, and reservoir.

Overview gives a brief description of each water telling you the type of fishery, where it is, and what the fishing is like.

Key species indicates which species are most commonly caught in the fishery.

Use gives you an idea of the amount of fishing pressure the area received and how that compares with other waters in the state. This information was compiled using angler pressure surveys from 1995.

Key flies and lures offers the suggestions of veteran fisherman for flies and lures for the fishery.

The fishing gives a detailed picture of the fishing experience at each water.

Strategies draws from many anglers to give you the right lures and techniques.

Tributaries provides additional information about smaller waters above the main river, which sometimes have even better fishing for small stream experiences. The names of these waters are in bold for quick look information on a particular stream.

Access includes information on public launch areas and public access points along the river, along with private areas open to the public for either rod fees or asking permission. Remember ask first to hunt or fish on private land.

MAPS

The maps in this book are meant only to help in planning a trip. Once you're headed out to fish, we strongly recommend that you bring along a more detailed map. Montana Afloat, a Missoula company, publishes excellent maps for fishing or floating the state's rivers. The maps are widely available in fly shops, sporting goods stores, and outdoor stores in Montana. The *Montana Atlas & Gazetteer* is a virtual necessity when navigating Montana's highways and backroads. It is available in Montana stores or from DeLorme Mapping, P.O. Box 298, Yarmouth, Maine 04096; (800) 452-5931.

Vacation Planner

(Most lakes in Montana have good ice fishing in winter, but the above are some of the most popular.)

CHOOSING AN OUTFITTER

Make sure your guide or outfitter is licensed with the state and has a permit to guide on the water you plan to float. To report illegal outfitter use call 1-800-TIP-MONT.

For a complete list of fishing guides, contact the Montana Outfitters and Guides Association, Box 9070, Helena, MT 59604, or Fishing Outfitters Association of Montana (FOAM), Box 67, Gallatin Gateway, MT 59730. Also, Travel Montana puts out a yearly Vacation Planner which lists all outfitters, lodges, guides, and resorts. You can obtain a free copy by calling 1-800-VISIT-MT.

Major Montana River Fisheries

1 Beaverhead River

Overview: The Beaverhead River is among Montana's premiere big-fish fisheries, supporting a phenomenal population of large trout in its upper reaches. Each year, the Beaverhead rewards skilled anglers with scores of browns and rainbow over 3 pounds and a few weighing over 10 pounds.

Beginning 20 miles south of Dillon at the outlet of Clark Canyon Reservoir, the Beaverhead River meanders for about 50 air miles to its junction with the Big Hole River north of Twin Bridges. The upper river, the 15-mile stretch between Barretts Diversion and Clark Canyon Dam, winds through a narrow valley with picturesque rock outcrops. The lower river runs through a large broad valley ringed by a series of small mountain ranges.

> **Key species:** Rainbow, brown, cutthroat, grayling, and whitefish.
> **Use:** Ranks 31 Statewide for fishing pressure. Much of the floating pressure concentrates between Clark Canyon Dam and Dillon.
> **Key flies and lures:** Flies—Girdle Bugs, Zonkers, Olive or Black Marabou Streamers, Olive Elk Hair Caddis, Blue Winged Olive, Hare's Ear Nymph, Bead Head Pheasant Tail, Joe's Hopper. Lures—Panther Martin, Rapala Bait—night crawlers.

The fishing: The reason for the Beaverhead's excellent fishery is, in a word, habitat. The Beaverhead differs from the braided-channel, riffle-pool-run pattern of most larger western rivers; instead, the river meanders extensively in a single, smooth-surface channel. The swift current, undercut banks, and thick overhanging willows along the Beaverhead's entire length provide protective overhead cover and the good holding water in which trout thrive.

Typical of most valley rivers draining alkaline western soils, the Beaverhead's water is extremely rich in nutrients. Water flowing from the bottom of Clark Canyon Dam provides nearly constant water temperatures on the upper Beaverhead. This clear, cold water combined with the rich nutrient levels and excellent habitat creates perfect growing conditions for trout and the insects on which they feed. The river supports a variety of insect life, including caddis flies, crane flies, mayflies, midges, and a few small stoneflies.

The combination of habitat conditions on the Beaverhead translates into an abundance of fast-growing trout. According to Jerry Wells, a fisheries biologist, "Growth rates are tremendous on the upper river, some of the best in the state." The more abundant brown trout average 2.5 to 3.5 pounds at 4 years of age and older. Rainbow in that age bracket average 4 to 6 pounds, gaining nearly a pound a year.

The upper Beaverhead also supports one of the best trout populations in Montana. Few rivers can match the 2,000 trout per mile of this remarkable

1 Beaverhead River

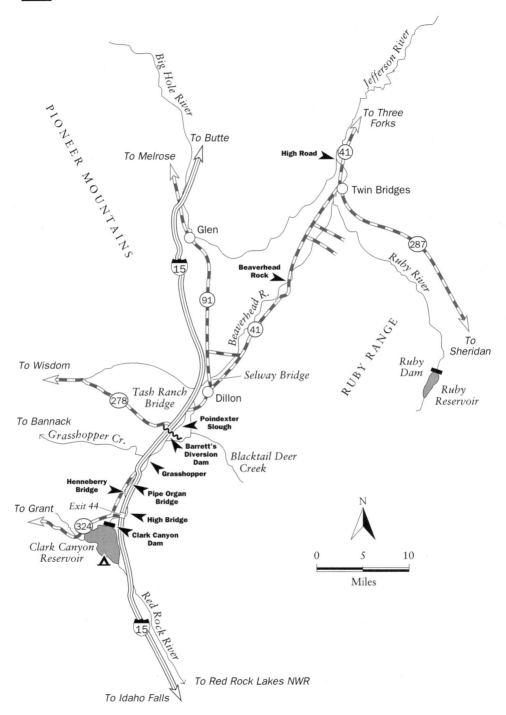

stretch of river. This amounts to nearly 3,500 pounds of fish for every mile of river. Put another way, if you float the river at a normal speed, you will pass by a trout 18 inches or longer every 10 seconds.

Sound good? Now consider the bad news. The habitat that makes such outstanding trout populations has its drawbacks for the angler. Fishing is exceedingly difficult because the river is so narrow and thick with willows. Steep drop-offs along the banks and a swift current make wading difficult on much of the river. The brushy banks limit access for the bank angler, making it difficult to get to a lot of fish.

Floating solves some of the problems but creates others. It allows the angler a better casting angle and room for backcasting. Floating also provides access to otherwise inaccessible waters. But the willows still present a problem to the floater trying to cast a fly tight to the bank. The Beaverhead willows claim many flies and lures. Some guides reportedly augment their supplies by retrieving flies and lures from the bushes.

The Beaverhead is also a tricky river in which to maneuver in a boat. The meandering, swift current puts a premium on oarsmanship. It's easy to be swept into the bank, and at Hildreth's Bridge, 2 miles below Clark Canyon Dam, it's necessary to stop the boat and slowly guide it under the bridge. High profile drift boats don't belong on this stretch of river. Inexperienced floaters would be wise to hire a guide the first time they attempt the Beaverhead.

Outfitters and guides from Dillon and Twin Bridges float various sections of the upper Beaverhead extensively. In fact, one of the biggest complaints about the river concerns the excessive number of boats on the upper reaches. Steve McMullin, a fisheries biologist, says, "This is only an aesthetic problem, not a biological problem. The trout population hasn't been hurt by the pressure yet." Many fishermen release their fish on the upper Beaverhead, and this may prove to be an important factor in maintaining such good populations in the face of the heavy fishing pressure.

Over the past few years, biologists have become concerned about a decline in yearling rainbow trout populations on the upper Beaverhead. McMullin notes, "There is no readily apparent answer or solution to this sudden decline, but it is a high priority research item." Extensive creel surveys proposed for the river may provide some needed information. In the meantime, McMullin encourages anglers to release rainbow and keep only the more abundant 10-to 14-inch browns as a precautionary measure to help protect the rainbow fishery on the Beaverhead. For now, there is a daily limit of one rainbow.

The lower Beaverhead receives very light fishing pressure compared to the upper river, earning it a rating as an untapped fishery resource. In fact, the lower Beaverhead has a much greater reputation as duck and goose hunting water than as a fishery. But there is good trout habitat throughout the length of the river. The thick willow banks and meandering flows persist on the lower river, although the current is slower than on the upper reaches.

The few fishermen that do use the lower river find much of it virtually wild and untouched by human activity. There is an abundance of wildlife along the

Outstanding aquatic habitat such as the upper Beaverhead River makes Montana trout fishing the envy of the nation.

river, including owls, great blue herons, a variety of waterfowl, and white-tailed deer. The wild surroundings contribute to the angling experience on the lower river. If solitude is what you want, the lower Beaverhead is the place for you.

Rainbow disappear downstream from Dillon. Brown trout are the predominant species, averaging 12 to 14 inches. An occasional lunker exceeding 5 pounds is taken from these waters. Anglers generally do well on the lower Beaverhead, even though the trout populations are not as spectacular as those of the upper river.

The exceptional habitat found on the upper Beaverhead progressively declines below Barretts Dam. The beneficial effects of constant water conditions on insect and trout populations are lost rapidly. The waters of the lower river drop to near freezing in winter and can overheat in summer. Irrigation withdrawals below Dillon reduce flows and current, compounding the summer warming effect. The lower river has only about half as much good willow

Cloudy, rainy weather during summer months often improves fishing success on the Beaverhead. AL TROTH PHOTO

bank cover. Together, these conditions mean a smaller trout population because growing conditions are less than ideal.

The lower Beaverhead has another problem that has probably affected trout populations adversely. Water turbidity has become a major concern for anglers and fisheries biologists over the past few years. Spring runoff is only a short-term contributor. Erosive banks and return irrigation flows contribute silt to the river throughout the year but especially in the summer. The result is usually murky water, where visibility of less than six inches is not uncommon. Rarely is visibility better than a few feet. Long-time residents of Twin Bridges still remember when the Beaverhead's water was clear as it ran through the town. In summertime, the Beaverhead is a phenomenal fishery, though it is very difficult to fish. Because of serious landowner-floater problems, anglers should be ultra-careful not to aggravate the situation. If anglers abuse their privileges, fishing certain sections may become impossible.

Strategies: It takes an experienced angler to be consistently successful on this river. The Beaverhead is without question one of the most difficult rivers in Montana to master.

With its excellent trout populations and large numbers of big fish, the Beaverhead River can provide exciting fishing for the determined angler. But the fish are wily and have all the advantages a river can offer—good bank cover, swift current, and an abundance of readily available food. With all the odds in favor of the trout, it takes skill and patience to outsmart them.

Fishing the Beaverhead requires techniques suited to its tough conditions. The foremost consideration is getting the fly to where the fish are. This means casting under willows and tight into the banks. It pays to be a gutsy caster on this river, but it can be expensive.

At one time, most of the fishing was done with large patterns, but things have changed. Fly selection requires small subsurface patterns in sizes 12 to 22, with 14 and 16 being the norm. Girdle Bugs, named for their rubber legs originally made from old girdles, are black-bodied, plain-looking flies. A size 14 or 16 Bead-Head Girdle bug can be quite effective.

According to Al Troth, nationally renowned fly tier and resident expert on the Beaverhead, "Fast, accurate but short casts are very, very important on the Beaverhead, because you have so little time to adjust your line when floating." With the boat moving quickly down a narrow, meandering river, the angler is rarely in perfect casting position and must learn to read the water rapidly. Troth also believes a good backhand cast is important in order to take advantage of both banks. Presentation of the fly is critical on the Beaverhead. Troth suggests that anglers "make the fly swim as slowly and deeply as possible" to be successful. He suggests stopping the boat and wade fishing.

A local favorite, the Zonker, is a silver-bodied fly with a rabbit hair strip down the back. Other good flies include black or olive Matukas and Marabou streamers.

Generally, the idea is to imitate the action of sculpins and other small fish. Lures can be effective at this and do work well on the Beaverhead within the limitations of such a narrow river. The Panther Martin and Rapala are reported to be especially good. Flies on spinning gear can also take fish.

Float-fishing is the best method of fishing the Beaverhead when there is plenty of water because it provides access to so much otherwise inaccessible water. The thick willow banks and deep, swift water make wading difficult in all but a few spots. The banks are mostly private land, further limiting good access to the river.

Bait fishing is predominately done from shore due to the need for slower water and more time to drift the bait in deep water. Limited bank access means few opportunities to find good fishing spots. Night crawlers are the most popular bait.

Although the Beaverhead is not noted as a dry fly stream, there is some good action on top. Caddis flies provide the bulk of the surface fishing throughout the summer. Size 12 to 18 imitations will do the trick. Early summer mornings witness a good hatch of size 14 to 18 mayflies. A few small stoneflies, size 10 to 18, hatch in the riffles around midday in July and August. Small nymphs, hares ear nymph, are worth a try before and during a hatch in the widely spaced riffles along the Beaverhead.

The crane fly provides a unique hatch on the Beaverhead. Crane flies live in riffles in clean gravels. Crane fly larva are like juicy, pastel caterpillars. Hatching in late August and September, the adults resemble giant mosquitoes. Over an inch long with giant wings, they dance high on the water's surface. Fish rise explosively to feed on these giant flies, even climbing the bushes to grab one. For best results, skate a well-hackled, slender-bodied, high-floating imitation on the water's surface. Fish will often take the fly on their way down, so don't be too quick to set the hook or you may pull the fly out from under the fish.

Salmon flies are not among the trout's fare on the Beaverhead. Unlike most southwestern Montana rivers, the Beaverhead does not have the rocky substrate necessary to support this notable insect. The river bottom is too silty and lacks the high spring runoffs that normally cleanse river bottoms.

Fishing on the Beaverhead heats up with the water. Because the Beaverhead taps the cold waters from the depths of Clark Canyon, it takes warm summer air to heat the water sufficiently for fish to get active. Fishing stays good into the fall.

The best time of day to catch fish is when they're feeding in the mornings and evenings. But midday on a cloudy day can prove highly productive. Mid day can also be excellent for nymphing.

A problem that occasionally interferes with fishing on the upper Beaverhead is the irregular fluctuations in water flow from the dam in response to irrigation needs. While river flows rarely fall below minimum levels necessary for the fishery, due to excellent cooperation with the East Bench Irrigation District, sudden rises in flow can make the trout inaccessible to anglers. The current becomes too fast and deep to get a fly or lure to the fish. When water levels suddenly drop, the trout get spooked and rarely hit a fly or lure.

Fishing the lower Beaverhead generally requires the same skills and techniques as the upper river. However, because the character of the river changes below Barretts Dam, there are some differences worth noting.

The stretch from Barretts to Dillon provides the best conditions for bank anlgers. Reduced river flows and slower currents make wading possible in this stretch. The river flows through hay meadows with fewer willow banks, making bank access easier. Fishing is very good for good-sized browns and rainbow. Ask permission for access to private lands along here.

Float-fishing provides the best opportunity to explore the Beaverhead River downstream from Dillon. However, because the current is fairly slow unless the water is high, travel can be very slow. This end of the river is strictly brown trout fishing, so work the banks hard.

On the lower river, north of Dillon to Twin Bridges, water conditions often dictate angler success. Water turbidity presents the biggest problem because visibility becomes so poor. Fish can't see the fly or lure unless it lands right in front of them. Dry fly fishing is only good when the water is relatively clear, with visibility at least a foot or better. When turbidity is high on the lower river, don't even bother fishing it. Head for the river upstream from Dillon, where conditions are always much better.

When visibility is good, fishing can be excellent on the lower Beaverhead for 1- to 2-pound browns. There are bigger browns here, too, but they are tough to catch.

Weighted streamers, Girdle Bugs, and lures cast tight to the willow banks are the best methods for success. A few hatches provide occasional good dry fly fishing. Caddis hatch in the evenings all summer long, and crane flies hatch in the late summer, although in fewer numbers than on most upper sections. Late in the summer grasshopper imitations work well, especially in areas with grassy banks.

Bait fishing opportunities are better on the lower Beaverhead than the upper river. Slow current and occasional deep holes provide excellent conditions for drifting nightcrawlers and grasshoppers.

Water temperatures on the lower Beaverhead rise substantially during the summer due to lower flows and slow current. As a result, fishing quality declines during August. Trout get sluggish in the warm water and aren't very active during the day. When the days are warm, it's best to be out fishing in the early mornings or evenings when the water is a little cooler.

TRIBUTARIES

Red Rock River, the Beaverhead's major tributary, has its headwaters in the Red Rock Lakes National Wildlife Refuge. Running through swamplands and a series of picturesque lakes, these waters provide one of the last trophy grayling fisheries in the state. Unfortunately, the upper lake is silting in, threatening the survival of this remnant native population.

There are some cutthroat in the Centennial Valley portion of the Red Rock, but fishing is not very good. Also, private land makes access difficult. The river has been altered and the banks overgrazed, causing a severe silting problem. Trout populations are depressed.

Below Lima Dam the river has little water most of the year, and fishing is poor. Despite some good hatches, whitefish seem to be the dominant fish in these waters.

As it picks up spring waters along its length, the last 15 miles of Red Rock is an excellent fishery. Rainbow and brown trout are abundant, with browns reaching 2 pounds plus. The fall brings good spawning runs of very large browns out of Clark Canyon Reservoir. Ted Turner owns most of this section of land and it is not too floatable.

The river meanders through a cottonwood bottom and has lots of deep holes and good bank cover. The water is never crystal clear, but it has good visibility. Small mayflies and caddis provide most of the surface action in midsummer. Wet flies and streamers achieve the best success, however.

The Red Rock River receives little fishing pressure because it is surrounded by private land. The ranches are huge in this area, so getting permission to fish from one landowner will provide access to a lot of river and a full day of fishing, but Al Troth reports that access to this section is almost impossible because of private holdings.

Grasshopper Creek, another tributary, is still suffering from the effects of gold dredging in the early 1900s. The first big gold strike in Montana was in this creek near Bannack, Montana's first territorial capital. Violations of heavy metal water quality laws have been fairly well cleaned up. If current conditions can be maintained, stream quality and its fishery should gradually improve. FWP is monitoring the stream and is already seeing some improvement. Trout populations are depressed below Bannack, but the stream still supports 10- to 15-inch brown trout in small numbers.

Fishing gets much better above Bannack. There is excellent trout water in this stretch, and it receives only light pressure. But because the surrounding land is all private, access is difficult.

The upper reaches of Grasshopper Creek have a good population of tiny brook trout. Access is provided through Forest Service land.

Poindexter Slough, just south of Dillon and running roughly parallel to the Beaverhead, is a spring-fed creek that supports a good population of 12- to 15-inch brown trout. Poindexter can provide some excellent fly fishing for the experienced angler, but it's not easy fishing. Weed beds, willow banks, and extremely wary trout limit one's success here, and an overabundance of large mosquitoes during the summer severely dampen the pleasures of fishing.

The roughly 25 miles of **Ruby River** below Ruby Dam resemble a small-scale version of the Beaverhead River. This river provides the same prospects and problems that characterize the lower Beaverhead. Thick willow banks make casting difficult. Fluctuating water levels and eroding banks make the water muddy until mid-summer. In wet years, such as 1982, large water releases from the reservoir in fall turn the river muddy again in September. But most years, the lower Ruby offers good fishing for 1- to 3-pound browns in the early spring and again in the fall when the water is clear and low.

The Ruby River recently garnered statewide attention for its history of lack of fishing access and angler-landowner conflicts in early 1997. After the real estate boom in Montana, a group of private landowners bought up all the land along the Ruby River, blocking most access points. This caused some strife among locals and access was limited to bridges where Montana's Streamside Access Law mandated public access. Fortunately, the landowners bent over backwards in gestures of goodwill to the public to fix this problem. Between FWP, anglers, and many good gestures from landowners, by the late summer of 1997, FWP had several new fishing access sites on the Ruby. Remarkably, these were later vandalized. If you ever see vandalism at any public access or on superfluous private land site, call 1-800-TIP-MONT to report it.

Bill Phippin of FWP reports that all access sites will continue to be maintained and should offer excellent angling opportunities. With these changes in access, pressure has increased. Look for regulation changes in the future.

The Ruby drains into the Beaverhead 3 miles upstream from Twin Bridges. The lower reaches are also bounded by private land, so permission is required to fish on lands not accessed through public fishing access sites. Fee fishing has been instituted on some ranches.

Above Ruby Reservoir there is good fishing for 10- to 14-inch rainbow trout. It's a small river at this end, and access is difficult until you get up into the Beaverhead National Forest lands. The upper Ruby is a good stream for beginners. Ruby Reservoir's popularity is on the rise. After being almost totally drained, the fishery has recovered to produce 13-to 18-inch rainbows regularly.

ACCESS

Almost the entire length of the Beaverhead runs through private land. A number of bridges and public access sites provide access along the river, although there are still extensive stretches of relatively inaccessible river downstream from Dillon. You'll need permission from landowners to get into many remote areas.

The farthest upstream access point is at the river's source at the base of **Clark Canyon Dam**. Take Exit 44 on Interstate 15 to access this area. There is a public access and campground site here that is very popular during the summer. About 2 miles downstream, just off Interstate 15 from Exit 44 on the frontage road, is the **High Bridge** access. This spot is one of the most popular sites for launching float trips. **Henneberry Bridge**, also reached from the frontage road, has been rebuilt after a wash out, and FWP developed a fishing

Fishing from a boat gives anglers a better casting angle to the trout hiding under the willows. AL TROTH PHOTO

access site (FAS) here for boaters. **Pipe Organ Bridge**, named after a unique rock formation along the river, provides the final access from the frontage road before the river crosses under I-15 again. This is a good take-out spot for floaters.

East of the highway downstream from Pipe Organ, FWP maintains **Grasshopper FAS** across from the mouth of Grasshopper Creek. Use the Grasshopper Loop Exit 52 from I-15. The Bureau of Reclamation maintains a good fishing access site at **Barretts Diversion Dam**. There is also a picnic area and small campground here. Boats must be taken out of the water here and walked around the diversion. Towards Dillon, FWP has another fishing access site at **Poindexter Slough**. It's an easy walk to the Beaverhead from here. Many local floaters enjoy the "Tash-to-trash" section of the Beaverhead, putting in at the **Tash Ranch Bridge** downstream from Poindexter Slough and running down to the road to the city dump west of Dillon. Floaters also use the dump road as a put-in to continue downstream of Dillon. At the north end of Dillon, Highway 91 crosses the river via **Selway Bridge**, where there is limited access to the river.

Downstream from Dillon access is more limited and float times tend to be longer. Low water can further prolong an outing on this reach of river. The **Beaverhead Rock**, just off Highway 41 about halfway between Dillon and Twin Bridges, is owned by FWP and provides the last public access until the highway bridge in Twin Bridges. Two bridges, about 7 miles in either direction from the Beaverhead Rock, cross the river, but you should ask landowner permission for access.

Available access sites are generally adequate for float fishermen willing to put in a long day on the river. Bank fishermen, however, must seek permission from landowners along much of the river's length, particularly to gain access to more remote reaches. FWP is currently interested in acquiring new access sites between Dillon and Beaverhead Rock to help remedy this situation. Please ask permission where necessary and be considerate of the private landowner's property and rights.

2 Big Hole River

Overview: "If you were going to make trout streams, the Big Hole is what you would use for the model." So says George Grant, a veteran fisherman of the Big Hole for more than fifty years. He may be prejudiced, but thousands of anglers share his opinion.

The free-flowing, "blue-ribbon" Big Hole River flows 150 miles through one of Montana's most scenic valleys to join with the Beaverhead River. Along the way, the rich, diverse waters foster bountiful aquatic life, including river otters, grayling, salmon flies, and trophy trout.

Two controversies cloud an otherwise bright picture of Grant's ideal trout stream. First, in dry years, irrigation diversions almost completely drain the lower river, resulting in substantial fish mortality. Second, heavy fishing pressure, especially during the salmon fly hatch, may be reducing the population of big rainbow, although populations thus far show no negative signs of fishing pressure. The biggest negative effect of heavy fishing may be reduced quality of fishing experience not reduced quality of fishing.

> **Key species:** Rainbow trout, brown trout, brook trout, arctic grayling, and mountain whitefish.
> **Use:** Heavy, heaviest between Divide and Melrose. The section from Divide Creek to the confluence with the Jefferson Ranks 17th statewide for angler pressure.
> **Key flies and lures:** Flies—Sofa Pillow, Fluttering Stone, Elk Hair Caddis, hoppers, Matuka Sculpins, Wright's Royal, Bitch Creek Nymphs. Lures—hammered brass, Thomas Cyclone, Rapala, and Mepps. Bait—worms, and hellgrammites.

The fishing: Prior to 1910, when high water washed in rainbow stock from a private pond, the Big Hole contained native cutthroat, eastern brook, and grayling. In the succeeding 20 years, rainbow up to 19 pounds rewarded anglers.

Brown trout were planted in the lower Big Hole in the 1930s. The remnants of a dam at Divide blocked the browns, locally known as Loch Levens, from ascending into the upper river until another high runoff removed the barrier in 1966. Today, browns are common upstream to Fishtrap Creek and a few individuals roam as far as Wisdom. Divide no longer marks a dramatic division of two separate fisheries.

Brookies, cutthroat, and grayling still survive in the upper reaches of the Big Hole. An eagle soaring high over the upper watercourse would see innumerable creeks from the Bitterroot and Pioneer Mountains mingle in the immense upper valley, or "Big Hole," as it was known to trappers and Nez Perce Indians.

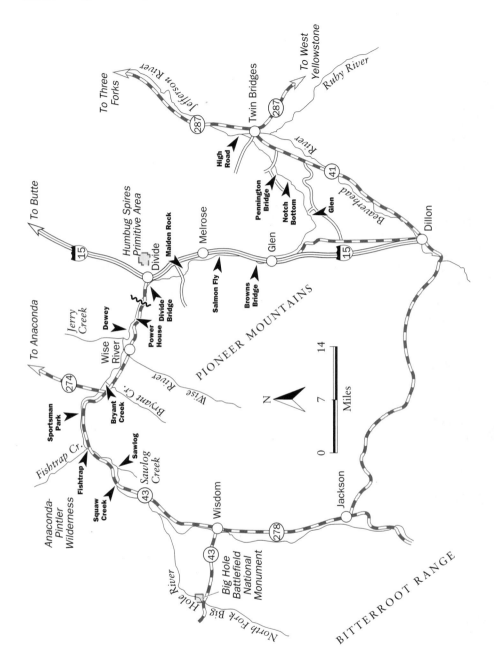

Phil Wright, a former fly fishing guide who operated out of Wise River, thinks the alkaline chemical balance in the upper basin benefits the rich aquatic life of the river. He backs up his argument by pointing out that Kentucky thoroughbred owners once shipped hay from the Big Hole because of its high nutritional value.

Grayling in the upper Big Hole represent one of the last important river-dwelling populations in the lower forty-eight states. This brightly colored fish, with its generous dorsal fin, does not compete well against some introduced species. Once found throughout the Big Hole, the grayling now hold out principally in the stretch from Jackson to Wisdom and in some tributaries. Fishing for grayling is catch-and-release only throughout the Big Hole.

The native cutthroat did not compete well either and now make up an insignificant percentage of the fish population. Brookies, on the other hand, thrive above Ralston, with "lots of fair-sized fish in tributary streams up to 500 brookies per 1,000 feet of stream," says Dick Oswald, fisheries biologist for the Montana Department of Fish, Wildlife and Parks (FWP). Oswald says the brookies could stand more harvesting and that they provide a relatively easy catch.

From Ralston downstream for several miles, the rainbow rule has shocked a few big rainbow up to 8 pounds, but Jerry Wells, a fisheries biologist, fears they won't be found there much longer because they are "very vulnerable" out in the riffles. The banks in this section have been heavily grazed for decades and offer little cover.

The meandering, relatively flat water of the upper river picks up speed and changes character near the settlement of Wise River. Boulders now punctuate the cobble streambed as the river enters a series of canyons. The canyons mark a transition zone: the number of browns increases in these waters, while the number of rainbow drops progressively. Rainbow are still the dominant fish all the way to Melrose, however. Demonstrating the drop in altitude here, cottonwoods increasingly provide streambank cover along with the willows from this point on.

From Melrose to the mouth of the Big Hole, the river returns to a meandering pattern, throwing its current first one way against the thick brushy bank, then sweeping to the other side. Long riffles and pools characterize this last 30 miles of the river. The Big Hole frequently braids into two channels here. The jungle growth on the banks grants superb cover for the dominant brown trout.

On an August evening in 1935, the late Butte fisherman Charlie Cook floated a number 8 Dr. Mummy beneath the overhanging willows near Melrose. He knew this water harbored some large trout and therefore "was on edge and alert when I felt a heavy strike." Cook fought the fish up and down a long pool and successfully turned the fish's runs without losing the last few loops of line on his reel. His arm was tiring at the wrist, but with the help of his companion, the fish was finally netted. Fourteen hours later, the "beautiful specimen of the Loch Leven variety" still weighed 11.25 pounds.

Cook's account appeared in *Field and Stream*, which awarded him first place in a national contest. As George Grant says in his book, *Big Hole River*

The Big Hole—definitely one of the most beautiful, undammed rivers left.
AL TROTH PHOTO

Memories, the fish was "undoubtedly one of the largest brown trout ever taken from the Big Hole on an artificial fly."

Jerry Wells, a fisheries biologist, reports that he still finds a rare brown of that size when electrofishing from Divide to the mouth. The chances of catching a 3-pound brown, though, are fairly good. Of over two thousand fish examined in a creel census, the average size was an impressive 14 inches. Oswald adds that above Divide there are still respectable numbers of browns in the 5-pound range and up, including a 15-pounder. He also notes reports of a 16-pound brown below Glen and a goliath 20.5-pounder pulled from the river below Melrose.

Nevertheless, long-time anglers and river guides worry about the Big Hole's big fish. Tony Schoonen, a guide for many years on the Big Hole, says, "Certainly, there are lots of fish, but not as much size to them." Grant, who may have fished flies in the Big Hole more days than anyone, reports, "From my own experience, the average size of the trout is diminishing. The fishing of the 1930s, 1940s, and 1950s was far superior to what it is today."

Wright describes hatchery fish as "three-year fish," because they grow rapidly the first three years, then slow down sharply as they achieve sexual maturity. Hatcheries discourage other genetic strains of fish, some of which mature late, perhaps not for five or six years. Some of these strains eventually grow to great size because they convert food to growth instead of reproductive energy. Wright's reasoning follows that killing the lunkers will soon deprive the fish population of the best genetic strains, leaving only fish of smaller size. "You can't kill the goose that lays the golden egg," he warns.

Wright, Grant, and Schoonen need only point to the Madison River and Rock Creek as examples. The mortality of large fish was so high in those two fisheries that the average size of trout caught declined sharply until the crisis was recognized and FWP instituted regulations reversing the trend.

At least for the brown trout, no crisis now exists on the Big Hole, in the opinion of Wells and Oswald. Oswald stands by his records showing the continued presence of decent numbers of lunker browns, as noted above. He also cites a number of factors that would account for any apparent decline in the population of larger fish: fishing pressure has increased; stream flow has decreased on average in recent years, a situation made worse now that many ranchers continue irrigating into October; and the number of browns per mile has gone up. Fish biologists are fond of pointing out that as fish density increases, size tends to decrease because a stream can support only a given amount of biomass. Oswald notes that FWP ceased stocking the Big Hole in 1974, allowing the wild strains to better compete for food and space, but that these same fish tend to grow more slowly than hatchery strains.

On the plus side, the annual mortality of older browns currently runs forty to fifty percent, which is much less than it is on the Madison. "It's the rainbow that are getting annihilated," Wells reports.

"We don't want to wait for a crisis to happen," say some anglers and guides. And they don't want to lose the rainbow. One fisherman at a Trout Unlimited meeting in Butte added, "I don't know what those rainbow were made of, but they were really something." Another pointed out that 12-inch trout abound in numerous rivers, but only a few rivers can support trophy fish.

The outgrowth of this debate is that some of the Big Hole is managed for larger trout. Under trophy fishery management, anglers can keep the better-tasting, smaller fish, but should carefully return most larger fish.

Will anglers be willing to bring home a photograph instead of a bragging-sized fish? Perhaps the question should be this: when a fish attains such a great size, why not save it to reproduce and to thrill several anglers instead of just one?

On another front, the Big Hole drainage, lush though it usually is, periodically suffers drought just as much of the rest of Montana does. During dry years, ranchers whose livelihoods depend on the Big Hole to irrigate their hay fields and pastures drain much of the river's water. The toughest time usually comes about mid-August. "They nearly dried it up two or three years that I've seen," says Schoonen.

Jerry Wells, in his study of the Big Hole between Melrose and Divide, found that the controlling factor for the fish population was the level of flow. "Without sufficient flow, we found fewer numbers of fish. They're simply gone from the population."

And where they go is not entirely clear. Wells wonders whether anglers don't take a greater number of fish because their hiding places are so exposed in low water. Add to this the stresses of less living space and the low oxygen content in warm water. The result is higher mortality. "It takes a long time to come back from a low water year, " testifies Schoonen. "We need to have water adjudicated for trout."

A possible solution is to have one or several off-stream reservoirs to hold some of the spring runoff until it's needed later in the summer. But ideal sites are difficult to find, and who would fund such a project?

Another solution lies in allocating some water for use in the stream to benefit the fishery. FWP is currently pursuing several methods of maintaining such "instream flow" on Montana's rivers, either through obtaining a legal water right, or by leasing water from other, willing, water users.

Streambank stability is another concern associated with irrigation diversions. Schoonen maintains that he finds the big trout where the streambanks have been stable for long periods of time. Conversely, stretches where the streambed has been gouged and the river's current changed by wing dams have been shown repeatedly by studies to be poor water for trout.

"I hate to say it, but bulldozers are the worst thing that ever happened to the Big Hole," said the late Fran Johnson, whose fishing shop served anglers in the Butte area for many years. Ranchers used the dozers to divert water from the river for irrigation.

"But," points out Wells, "there has been incredible improvement compared to the way things were years ago, when guys just took their cats out in the stream and tore it apart." The Streambed Preservation Act requires a permit before anyone can physically alter the bed or banks of a stream, and this has encouraged more responsible action. Under the auspices of the River Restoration Act and the Big Hole River Foundation, FWP has also pursued funding for special projects to replace the bull-dozed diversions with more efficient— and less disruptive—channel alterations on the Big Hole.

In the conversation of anglers, one other problem surfaces: is the Big Hole being loved to death? Except at peak runoff, the Big Hole is a small river, yet it receives tremendous fishing pressure. In recent years, FWP has estimated that as many as 66,000 fisherman spent days on the Big Hole.

Grant thinks that the Big Hole just can't handle these numbers, especially with the Madison regulated now. So many boats and anglers have taken some of the fun out of fishing the river, Schoonen admits. "A lot of the old-timers have given up on it."

The greatest influx of anglers coincides with the famous salmon fly hatch. Wells remembers when seventy boats passed one point on the river in one day. In such a flotilla, a social problem develops. Johnson thinks, or at least hopes, that problems will be self-regulating; many boats will keep the fish from biting; fewer bites will keep the number of floaters down.

Anglers take about thirty percent of the year's catch during the three-week salmon fly hatch in June. For anglers preferring more solitude, the river is less crowded prior to the hatch, a favorite time for Wells who notes that the trout are really active then. Some of the crowd departs right after the hatch, but perhaps the best time for prime fishing with little company is mid-September to mid-October. A bonus of autumn is the golden beauty along this blue-ribbon stream.

Like the nearby Beaverhead, the Big Hole attracts anglers in search of trophy trout, especially during the late-June, early summer salmon fly hatch.

Strategies: Throughout most of the Big Hole, in late summer, an angler can stand in the middle of the river and reach either bank with proficient casting. Anglers like this size of river. The river is not so large that it intimidates, yet it's large enough to support trophy fish.

But don't stand in midstream during the spring runoff, at least not without concrete shoes and steel girders to keep from being swept down into the Jefferson River. The Big Hole swells in May and stays that way until mid-July. Especially in the lower reaches, the river is up into the willow thickets, making it almost impossible to fish extensively from the banks. Most anglers float in inflatable boats.

Happily, the Big Hole rarely gets so muddy that it is unfishable. The water, the color of strong tea, allows visibility of a foot or two. In such conditions, anglers should work bait in the eddies and along the banks. Johnson suggests nightcrawlers and hellgrammites. Grant doesn't fish with bait, but if he did, salmon fly nymphs would be his choice. All of these work throughout the season, not only during runoff.

The Big Hole does not lend itself to lure fishing. A few anglers skilled in the use of hardware do reasonably well, but guides such as Schoonen generally steer spin anglers to the Jefferson, where their chances will be better. For those who still want to try lures, Thomas Cyclones, hammered brass, Mepps, and Rapalas are good bets.

The Big Hole is one Montana river where fly fishers comprise the majority of anglers. Because the river is small and rarely reaches depths of 6 feet, the water is naturally more suited to fly fishing. Fly rods sprout like weeds during the salmon fly hatch. Depending on the weather, the 2-inch bugs commence crawling out of the river and up the banks and willows in the Twin Bridges area about June 10. In a normal year, the hatch progresses upriver several miles each day and peters out near Ralston about the first of July. However, as Schoonen points out, the game does not always go according to plan. Hard frosts may snuff out the hatch completely. Or a hot spell may bring out the hatch the length of the river in just four or five days, instead of three weeks.

"The salmon fly hatch is one of the world's greatest crap shoots," says Phil Wright. "When you hit it right, it's tremendously exciting. But it can be a complete bust." Wright thinks the hatch is vastly overrated, but it is a dramatic event. "The water is high, and you're just bombing down the river," he says.

"Your chances of catching any salmon fly hatch just right aren't very good," Wells explains, "unless you're there ten days. But even then, you might hit it hot for only twenty minutes." Wells recommends fishing just before the hatch.

Undeniably, most large trout are caught during the hatch. As Grant explains it, the big fish follow the nymphs to the river's edges and then wait near the surface for the clumsy insects to fall in from the willows. When the conditions are right, anglers using sofa pillows, fluttering stoneflies, and squirrel tails find exciting surface action.

Besides scenery and trophy trout, the Big Hole offers good family fun.

The salmon fly hatch is not, of course, the only hatch of consequence. Several species of smaller stoneflies hatch through mid-summer. In addition, caddis in tremendous clouds hatch throughout the summer. Grant explains that the Big Hole does not have many mayflies because larva are eaten by the stonefly nymphs.

The choice of which flies to buy and use often troubles neophyte fly fishers. However, Wright advises that "the perfect fly presented imperfectly will not catch fish, while an imperfect fly presented perfectly will take fish." He also believes matching the hatch works occasionally, but generally the angler is after more of an impressionistic effect, especially when water is high and fast.

A well-stocked fly fishers, in Wright's mind, would have elk hair caddis, Henryvilles, a hopper imitation, Matuka sculpins, his Wright's Royal, and some sort of big Marabou streamer. For the salmon fly hatch, he likes both a high floater and a low floater imitation plus, for the nymph, something "big, black, and ugly," such as the Bitch Creek fly.

Tony Schoonen takes a somewhat different tack. He finds Royal Wulffs and Joe's Hoppers useful, but doesn't think much of matching the hatch. If the trout are feeding, Schoonen reasons, they rarely pass up a hellgrammite or minnow imitation. He cautions not to use too big a fly, though.

George Grant recommends the water above Wise River to the angler who wants to fish exclusively dry. On the lower river, most anglers who take big trout are nymph anglers. The typical riffle-pool combination has an open side with a rocky beach; the other side will be overgrown with willows and slightly undercut. Grant stands on the open side casting across or quartering upstream. The idea, he advises, is to keep the nymph drifting without imparting motion to it for as long as you can along the undercut area. Trout may hit it either when it shows up in their window or as it arcs across the stream on the drag.

In the more broken water of the canyon section, the trout's food factories are in the riffles. The pools serve generally just as resting areas. When the trout are feeding, they move up into the fast, foamy water. "Look for the dead spots. Watch the bubbles and see where they slow down," advises Wright. "One needs to develop the sense of current speed, of where a trout can hold."

What time of day is best? Ask four experts, and you'll end up fishing from daybreak to sundown. Johnson prefers summer fishing in the morning and evening. When the real hot spells come, the angler should be on the stream at first light. Schoonen maintains that the most consistent time is about 10:00 AM to 2:00 PM—"God's time, not the funny time," he says, in reference to daylight saving time. Wells likes the "gentleman's hours" from 8:00 AM to 10:00 PM. Grant thinks the angler who is really serious about catching fish starts at daybreak, but he considers mid-day to be better suited for leisurely enjoying the river than for fishing.

Grant also feels certain that there are days when the finest angler in the world couldn't catch a fish on the Big Hole. "That darn Big Hole," Schoonen agrees, "when it shuts off, you can't catch them on flies or lures anywhere on that river." He feels a full moon and an east wind make a very tough combination for the fishing. "That east wind just kills the fishing nine times out of ten."

Boulder-studded runs like this one on the Big Hole have excellent pocket water where trout like to hang out. AL TROTH PHOTO

One last note on the heavy pressure the Big Hole receives: George Grant and Tony Schoonen would like to see some special regulations on the Big Hole to maintain the quality of the fishing experience. Grant suggests non-floating or wade-only days on certain sections of the river, especially during low water times when there is not much room for boats to get around wade-anglers. However, the actual fish populations do not appear to be suffering, according to Dick Oswald at FWP. The fish are still there, but it is harder to catch them.

TRIBUTARIES

The Big Hole has countless small creeks flowing into it in the upper basin, but only a handful below the mouth of the **Wise River**. Fishing at the mouths of these little tributaries is often productive, and some of the larger creeks provide terrific fishing for unsophisticated, pan-sized trout miles from the main river. For young anglers with short attention spans, these creeks might be just the ticket.

Prior to 1927, the Wise River enjoyed a reputation as a fine fishing stream, but in that year the Pattengail Reservoir had a disastrous washout. The streambed has not yet recovered from the gouging of that flood. Dewatering due to irrigation withdrawals doesn't help it much, either.

Still, a side trip up the Wise River makes a scenic and cool retreat from the mid-summer heat, and the fishing can be lively for rainbow and brookies.

ACCESS

Considering that the Big Hole flows through private land almost its entire length, the river is astonishingly accessible.

To gain access to the confusing myriad of springlets, brooks, forks, and branches of the Big Hole between Jackson and Wisdom (and above), explore the ranch roads off the highway and inquire locally. Families with youngsters will love the fast action the throngs of brookies provide here even when the rest of the river is skunking the pros. Be sure to ask permission before fishing from this private land.

Downstream from Wisdom, the river brushes Montana Highway 43, granting the first point of casual access to the main river. The road then moves away for a couple of miles before coming back at a bridge that provides a commanding view of two big bends of gentle water. Some of the land on either side of the bridge is public, even though it is fenced.

Three developed accesses follow, each with an appreciable amount of river frontage. **Fishtrap Creek, Sawlog,** and **Sportsmen's Park** all receive heavy use. Downstream from Deep Creek and the highway from Anaconda, MT 43 again crosses the river. A nearby dirt road gives access to the other side of the river for a couple of miles. You can no longer access the river at Dickie Bridge. The new **Bryant Creek Bridge** is an important access because you can turn off the highway and access the river from the east side. Halfway between Bryant Creek and Wise River is a boat launch just off the right of way.

The next access (aside from one spot where the river briefly bends over to the highway shoulder) comes just after the little town of Wise River, when a gravel road off the highway quickly bridges the river on its way to **Jerry Creek**. The Bureau of Land Management (BLM) maintains an access site here, and there is also easy access from the highway for the next 6 or so miles downstream for wading or bank fishing. FWP has two new access sites—one at **Dewey**, about 5 miles downstream from Jerry Creek, and another just upstream from the Butte water intake dam.

Below the remnants of the old Divide Bridge and another BLM access, the highway and river part company. The next access is off of U.S. Highway 91, south of the town of Divide. A gravel road leads to **Maiden Rock Bridge**, which has an FWP boat launch. The bridge itself is private, but by walking either up or down the railroad tracks a short distance, the wading angler can reach some eminently fishable sections of river.

Another road (not to be confused with the road to Maiden Rock Bridge) leaves Melrose, immediately crosses the river, and winds up and down to the **Maiden Rock** Fishing Access. Bank anglers will like this spot, especially upstream.

There is a large campground and boat launch at Melrose Bridge (**Salmon Fly** Access). You can also access the river via **Lower Maiden Rock** Access about 7 miles upstream from Melrose.

The deep holes of the Big Hole produce trout in the 10-20 pound range—for those anglers good enough to catch them. AL TROTH PHOTO

Following that is a quick succession of three more bridges each with good access, (the last at Glen), and some more casual access via the railroad tracks between Melrose and Glen. There is some walk-in access just downstream from Glen and the **Notch Bottom** access some 5 miles downstream. From Glen, one can travel a cantankerous old ranch road almost all the way to Twin Bridges. At times this road strays far from the river, but anglers who drive on will find a couple of places where the river brushes the roadside and **Pennington Bridge** with its FWP access site (boat launching can be difficult here). Just outside Twin Bridges, FWP has a fishing access site at the **High Road.**

As the access comes a little harder between Glen and Twin Bridges, fewer anglers venture to try this section of classic brown trout water. Those who do generally find the fishing worth the extra effort. Floating makes good sense through this section.

As numerous as all these developed and informal accesses are, still more numerous are the cooperative landowners who will grant anglers access if they ask permission. However, only respect and careful consideration for landowners and private property can keep it that way. For additional information on floating the Big Hole, pick up a copy of *Montana Afloat #8, the Big Hole River.*

3 Bighorn River

Overview: Prior to 1968, a fishing guide probably would not even mention the Bighorn River, but the building of the Yellowtail Dam created an exceptional tail-water fishery. Today, outdoor writers label it as possibly the best trophy trout fishery in the lower forty-eight states. And the word is out. Even on an early spring day in April, there might be over 100 boats on the upper 13 miles of river in one day. The consistent good fishing provided by stable cool water flows from the dam bring anglers in large numbers to the Bighorn year-round.

> **Key species:** Brown trout, rainbow trout, mountain whitefish, golden eye, burbot, smallmouth bass, catfish.
> **Use:** Heavy, with a concentration on the 13 miles below the dam. The upper section ranks 8th statewide for fishing pressure.
> **Key flies and lures:** Flies—Sow Bugs (soft hackle), Scuds, CDCs, Pale Morning Duns, Midge Clusters, Adams, Light Cahill, Midge Pupa, Olive Woolly Bugger, Yellow Bighorn Special Lures—Mepps, gold brass, Rapala Bait—worms.

The fishing: The building of Yellowtail Dam changed this silt-laden river into a clear, superb tailwater fishery. By flooding the 71-mile canyon, the dam not only trapped the silt, but also created a giant heat sink which moderates the temperature extremes of Montana weather. Trout grow in temperatures between 44 and 66 degrees Fahrenheit. The water in most trout streams comes between these two temperatures only about three months of the year, but in the Bighorn River where the water comes from 200 feet below the surface of Bighorn Lake, the growth period doubles from mid-June to mid-December.

The limestone watershed adds its rich minerals to the temperate water. Trout food, sow bugs, scuds, caddis larva, mayflies, midges, and baitfish, flourish in such salubrious conditions. The clarity of the water allows sunlight to reach the bottom, giving rise to a profusion of moss and long, stringy weeds. In short, the conditions are terrific for browns and rainbow.

Numbers normally make for boring reading, but the Bighorn numbers are so impressive they cannot be ignored. The river has not been planted with rainbows since 1983, but the Bighorn averages over 2,900 trout over 13 inches per mile. Consider John Navasio's Bighorn record 16-pound, 2-ounce rainbow. And note that the average fish captured measures better than 15 inches long. The Beaverhead, itself a tailwater fishery, has even better statistics. But, as anyone who has fished both rivers can testify, an angler has a much tougher time coaxing trout from under the willow jungle along the Beaverhead's banks than from the open riffles of the Bighorn. George Anderson, who runs the Livingston fly shop and guide service called Yellowstone Angler, writes that ". . .when the fishing is hot on the Bighorn, it is possible for a good fisherman to catch and release more than 50 trout in a day, most of which will be in the 15"-20" class. Rainbows and Browns up to 22" and 4 pounds."

The average angler catches one rainbow for about every four brown trout on the Bighorn, but FWP electrofishing surveys show that in some stretches browns outnumber rainbow by a whopping nine to one ratio. Browns started dropping out of the tributaries and populating the main river as soon as the

Casting downstream in slow water is a good technique for fast-growing Bighorn River trout.

3 Bighorn River

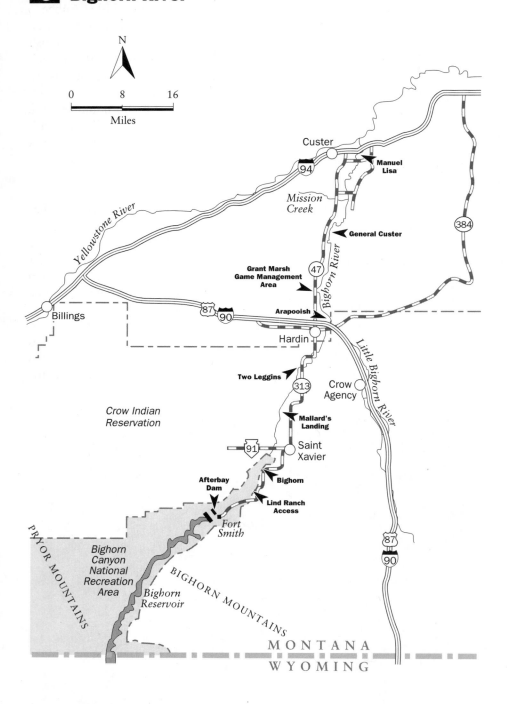

dam made the Bighorn suitable. Now, thanks to the regulated temperature of water flows in November and December, the browns' spawning success is nothing short of phenomenal. Pat Marcuson, a fisheries biologist and author of *Fishing the Beartooths*, wondered if too much of a good thing might not end up being bad news. "If we have two successive years of strong recruitment, we might have lots of snaky browns chasing a limited amount of food."

Marcuson's words proved prophetic when, in 1986 and 1987, the brown trout population rocketed to a record high of 8,459 fish per mile. As more browns crowded into the river, mortality rates for the larger fish (four years and older) reached 99 percent. The reason for this was clear. A riverine ecosystem will only produce so many pounds of trout food, which in turn will feed only so many inches of trout. Intense competition for food by smaller browns seriously hurt the condition and numbers of the large brown trout.

Ironically, it took a drought to rescue the big browns from their own kind. As flows in the Bighorn dwindled during the dry years of 1988 and 1989, water temperatures also decreased, and the number of brown trout per mile plummeted to 4,601—a reduction of nearly 46 percent from the 1987 population. In recent years, high water flows have had an affect on both fishing and hatches. Flows of up to 15,000 cubic feet per second (cfs) and higher result from trouble coordinating spring runoff and irrigation needs between Wyoming and Montana. Despite this dramatic decline, the number of big browns that are 18 inches or longer actually increased to about 400 fish per mile. Unfortunately, this boom and bust scenario may repeat when aquatic conditions once again favor brown trout reproduction.

The Bighorn's rainbow fishery was once supported almost entirely from state hatcheries. Anglers, and especially commercial guides, loved the hatchery fish because they could catch the showy trout more easily than the browns, and the bows put on weight faster than the browns, becoming what are known locally as "Bighorn swimming pigs," fish with small heads and big, deep bodies. These stocked fish grew up to 24 inches.

But the planted rainbow quickly became successful spawners, and the last of the hatchery fish were planted here in 1983. Today, the rainbow population is gaining on the browns, and these wild rainbow are a more durable, if slightly smaller, fish than their hand-fed ancestors. Currently, the average rainbow in the Bighorn measures a plump 18 inches long.

One fish that is usually conspicuous in the cast of characters on other Montana trout streams rarely shows up in the Bighorn—the whitefish. Perhaps the browns eat whitefish fry and the generally unpopular fish has never established a good foothold in the Bighorn. FWP speculates that nitrogen supersaturation from the operation of Yellowtail Dam may help suppress any whitefish recruitment. Nevertheless, anglers now report catching whitefish where they were previously unreported. Curt Collins thinks this may be due to the increased nitrogen problem which has worsened in recent years because of higher flows.

Another fish that has shown up recently in big numbers is the golden eye. These are primarily warm water fish, living in the lower reaches of the Bighorn, but as the summer water temperatures rise, schools of golden eye move into the upper stretches.

The Bighorn runs at an average of 3,000 cubic feet per second, which makes it considerably larger than the Big Hole or the Madison. Except in a few of the wider riffles, anglers find they cannot wade across the river. Fluctuations in water levels for power purposes do not pose a threat to safety as they do on the Flathead or Kootenai. Because the streambed is made up of small rocks and gravel, anglers have good footing. In fact, the bottom seems almost cemented in place because of the lack of a spring runoff which would loosen up the aggregate.

The river heads from the afterbay to the Yellowstone in relatively straight fashion. Bill Haviland, who worked for the Park Service's Bighorn Canyon National Recreation Area, estimates about 20 islands braid the course of the first 13 miles. The river has no whitewater to speak of, but moves at a moderate clip between its relatively stable banks. Here and there, cottonwoods have fallen in making a hazard for boaters. Also watch for the whirlpool about 1 mile downstream from Afterbay Dam and the short set of rapids below the gray bluffs, about 9 miles downstream from the afterbay.

Haviland calls attention to another hazard. Because of the reservoir-caused time lag in the spring, the water remains very cold even in mid-June. On hot June days, Haviland wears a T-shirt, while adding long underwear under his trousers and waders to protect against chilling. Neoprene waders with insulated boot feet can solve this problem.

Between the afterbay and Hardin, the river flows through the Crow Indian Reservation. While the Crows have historically shown little interest in fishing, they have contested the right of non-Indians to float and fish the Bighorn. The state diplomatically closed the river until the Supreme Court ruled the water belonged to Montana and not exclusively to the tribe.

When the state reopened the river to fishing in 1981, there was some initial tension between Crows and non-Native Americans. While the bad feelings have since calmed down, anglers should be aware of the sensitivity of the situation. In particular, anglers must stay within the high water marks unless they have permission from the landowner. FWP defines the high water mark as "the continuous area where vegetation ceases."

With all the publicity of the Supreme Court case and enthusiastic reviews of the subsequent fishing, anglers have predictably flocked to the river, and angling pressure has become a problem. FWP figures show that use peaks in mid April through May and then again in mid August through September. Weekends and holidays bring by far the largest crowds.

Angling pressure has certain predictable results. First, trout become more educated and selective. On the Bighorn, FWP studies show that only one of twenty fish caught on average will be kept. The returned fish reassume their feeding stations with an increased skepticism of feathered and metallic offerings.

Outfitters George Anderson and Curt Collins both acknowledge that the fishing is far more difficult now than immediately after the river was reopened.

Second, social problems develop. Anglers put their boats in and float down the river only to find their favorite holes already occupied. Anglers who have already staked out a spot get miffed at other anglers floating through their fishing water. On the Bighorn, FWP has tried to alleviate this problem by purchasing additional access sites. It would also help the situation if more anglers utilized the lower half of the river. This section holds somewhat fewer fish and the water is often too cloudy for fly fishing, but those fish see far fewer hooks than their upstream brethren.

Third, some anglers become concerned about how many fish are being taken out of the river. Those anglers push for more restrictive limits or "catch and release only." Other anglers who like trout on their tables protest. FWP biologists sit in the middle, listening to both sides and working to determine what would be best for the resource.

Shortly after the Bighorn River re-opened to fishing in 1981, a meeting was held by FWP to air such differences of opinion. Don Tennant strongly supported a return to a more liberal limit, or no limit at all. He argued that a river can only support so many pounds of trout. Trying to "stockpile" extra fish by tightly limiting the creel limit only results in more but smaller fish. As a corollary, Tennant rejected regulations which discriminate against anglers who wish to use bait. Tennant suggests such regulations unfairly treat older anglers and kids, who are most likely to depend on bait to catch their trout.

Anderson and several others countered that the limits should be imposed to protect the larger fish. "What we're seeing is a real reduction in trophy class

Evening fishing is often best for brown trout on the Bighorn.

fishing. It's a shame that such a great fishery is being pounded down." Anderson added that "the rainbow in the 4- to 6-pound category are really getting wiped out." Almost a decade later, Anderson notes that, "the big rainbows did get nearly wiped out in just a few years. Even a one fish limit on rainbows didn't help." As for Tennant's suggestion on bait, the fly and spin sponsors point out that a trout usually swallows bait deeply and will die whether or not the angler puts it back in the river or in the cooler.

In 1988, FWP reached a compromise between the two points of view by establishing a relaxed limit on browns, which seem able to hold their own under intense fishing pressure, while protecting rainbow, particularly larger ones. Current regulations split the Bighorn into three sections. In the uppermost 12 miles of river, from the steel cable below Afterbay Dam to Bighorn Fishing Access Site (FAS), there is a five trout limit, only one of which can measure over 18 inches. Rainbows are catch-and-release only, and no bait-fishing or motor boats are allowed. From Bighorn FAS downstream to the Interstate-90 bridge at Hardin, bait-fishing and motors are permitted, and anglers may keep one rainbow. The five-trout limit, of which only one can be over 18 inches, also applies to this reach of river. Downstream from I 90, motors and bait-fishing are allowed, and the limit is ten trout with no restrictions on species or length.

Other than the difficulties with access and fishing pressure, anglers may have one other, less immediate, problem to worry about. The Bighorn's proximity to Montana's coal fields may make it tempting to extract water for a slurry pipeline. While not currently a threat, this possibility would prove a nightmare for the fishery if it became a reality.

Until such a disaster befalls the Bighorn, anglers will continue to try for the trophy fish. Success does not come easily, but many anglers feel the fun is mostly in the chase and not the catch. Haviland remembers one haunting day with great enjoyment. On this particular day, he was having little success until he tied on a shrimp imitation and cast up in a riffle. "All of a sudden the line stopped and wouldn't budge. I was just starting to think I'd hooked a log when it took off. In one run, it took out my 40 yards of line and 70 yards of backing. I ran after it, but it straightened the hook and got off."

Instead of getting depressed about losing a lunker, Haviland relishes the experience. His parting words: "Ain't fishin' great!"

Strategies: As with almost all trout streams and rivers, a small percentage of anglers catch most of the fish on the Bighorn. What do these successful anglers know or do that other anglers don't? A number of factors figure into the answer, but several experts suggest that adaptability makes the biggest difference.

Successful Bighorn anglers are willing to change their strategies, methods, and offerings if their first try of the day doesn't produce fish. If trout don't take dry flies, try a nymph down deep. If a brass spoon hasn't produced a strike in half an hour, put on a lure with a different color or action. Six great-looking riffles and not a strike? Try the banks and the deep pools.

Vince Ames fishes the Bighorn frequently. While he would modestly argue that he is not an expert, other anglers note that Ames catches many more fish than the average angler. Ames tries to arrive at the riverbank without preconceptions. "Be open-minded and keep loose" until observations show the angler what to try first. Is there any surface activity? If so, are the fish actually feeding on the surface, or are they nymphing just below the surface film? If Ames sees no surface activity, he then decides either to fish a nymph deep or to try a streamer. If he decides on nymphs, he tries to figure out by observation whether to use a mayfly nymph, which swims, or a caddis larvae imitation, which should be presented on a dead drift.

Anderson suggests that his clients bring along two outfits, one a 8.5-9 foot number 3 or 4 line rod for fishing dry flies and the other a number 5 or 6 line rod with a floating line for fishing nymphs. In the fall a number 7 line rod with sink tip line is a useful tool for fishing Woolly Buggers and streamers. For fishing dries, 5x and 6x tippets on 9 to 12 feet of leader is the norm while 4x and 5x will work fine for fishing nymphs.

Collins points out that from November to the first of May, the fly fishers use mostly nymphs and streamers, while from May to November the angler can add dry flies to the arsenal. Midge hatches that begin in February do provide some good early season dry fly fishing, especially on cloudy windless days. Small Adams, midge clusters, and many other midge patterns in size 22 to 16 work well. Towards summer, Collins also recommends CDC patterns, pale morning dun parachutes and in 1996 he noted that there was a good golden stone hatch.

For mayfly imitation, Collins likes patterns such as Adams, Blue Duns, and Blue Quills in size 14 to 18; Blue Wing Olives and Light Cahills 16 to 20; Mosquitoes; and CDCs are a good choice throughout summer and fall. Collins ties his own version of the CDC and notes that the oil gland feather off a duck keeps it dry and you can tie it to be very visible. For caddis, Collins rates the Elk Hair Caddis as a "great fly" and adds that both tan and black can be successful, with black being the better choice. Collins adds some terrestrial patterns for hoppers, ants, and spiders. Anderson does not pin any hopes on hoppers. Only occasionally does the hopper fishing on the Bighorn become important on years when there is an infestation of grasshoppers.

In the nymph department, Scud and Sow Bug patterns get high marks for effectiveness any time of the year. Collins notes that the best pattern has become the Sow Bug. High flows in the 1990s made the Sow Bug the rivers number one food source. Scuds still work year-round and a San Juan Worm may also take fish. Anderson's "hot nymph patterns" include Soft Hackle Sow Bug patterns, Gray Sparkle Scuds, Flashback P.T.'s and a variety of Midge Pupa.

When fishing nymphs deep, Anderson often uses a buoyant indicator placed 7-to 9-feet up on a 12 foot leader. One or more BB size split shots are placed on the leader above the tippet knot 18 inches from the nymph. Anderson often uses two or more nymphs tied in tandem fashion, from the bend of the first fly to the second with about 12 inches separating the nymphs.

The Bighorn has some outstanding streamer and spin fishing waters. Some of the streamers mentioned by Anderson and Collins are Olive Woolly Buggers, light and dark Spruce Flies, brown Matukas, Zonkers, black Nose Dace, and white Marabou Muddlers. However, a yellow streamer called the Bighorn Special might be the most popular fly of all on the river. Streamers for the Bighorn should be of the larger variety such as a size 2.

The Bighorn's moss can hamper spin fishing from April to mid-October. Otherwise, spin fishing can be dynamite. Haviland recommends Mepps, sometimes with feathered hooks. He thinks the smaller sizes are best. Brass is most effective; gold can be good, while silver, in Haviland's experience, does not do as well. However, the lure that tops most recommendation lists is the gold number 5, 7, or 9 Rapala. "It's just awesome what they can do," says Collins.

Bait anglers plying the lower river almost always use worms. Navasio's record rainbow was taken in by the standard nightcrawler. As mentioned before, bait anglers should be aware of special regulations.

Haviland has two strategies for anglers to consider. The first is a dropper rig. At the end of his leader Haviland ties on a Muddler Minnow or a Bighorn Special. 2 or 3 feet up the leader, he ties on a separate 6-inch strand of leader with a black hair fly dangling at the end of it.

This dropper rig does not just present the trout with a choice of flies. The real intention is to make the hair fly look like an egg-laying caddis fly as it dips to the water's surface. The large streamer acts as an anchor. With a little practice, the angler can play the tension in the line so that the dropper fly will bounce, skitter, and tease any trout that is keying in on one of the Bighorn's prolific caddis hatches. The dropper rig has become the preferred way to nymph fish. Using two flies allows you to prospect with two different patterns to see what the fish are biting.

The dropper rig method may sound complicated and too tricky to skeptical anglers, but it is a proven producer. In 1935, Charlie Cook caught an 11-pound-plus brown on the Big Hole in western Montana employing this same tactic. When anglers see caddis flies fluttering just above the river surface, they might do well to try the dropper fly.

Haviland's other unconventional method will not appeal to the weak of heart nor to those who like to catch a suntan while they fish. Mature trout, especially browns, are notoriously nocturnal in the summer. Almost all anglers have witnessed the voracious feeding which so often takes place as the light dims after sunset. While most anglers head home at this time, Haviland finds nightfall a good time to start his fishing.

Haviland explains that as the light level drops, the big browns feel safe enough to come out of their deep pools and into the shallow riffles. With the help of a full moon, he has seen big fish practically on the rocks, fins out of the water, looking like a pack of hungry sharks. Haviland feeds them something substantial like a Muddler Minnow on the end of stout, 10-pound test leader. He stresses that the night is a smaller world where you can catch fish right up to your feet. There is no need for 90-foot casts at night, provided a stealthy approach is made.

Because of the shortage of access, most Bighorn River anglers use boats.

Obviously, it helps to know the section of the river very well from past experience. Falling into a river over the top of the waders at night could be scary, even dangerous. And there can be little surprises, such as one night when a startled beaver slapped his tail right next to Haviland. But the fishing can be prime; in a two-hour stand in one pool, Haviland once caught eleven fish between 18 and 22 inches long.

What kinds of water do the experts fish on the Bighorn? Guide Mike Mouat likes the inside corners and the deeper banks. Anderson looks for tailouts for sight fishing nymphs. Deep flowing water along banks or weeds are prime dry fly spots. Collins fishes just off the heavier water or where the heavy water hits the slack. He notes that trout are very opportunistic and follow the hatches feeding in different areas of the river depending upon the food source. This sometimes means fishing with nymphs in the riffles or below the riffles with sow bugs. Collins also keys in on the rare spots with gravel because the fish really seem to like it there. Haviland notes the drift lanes between the moss beds.

The Bighorn remains ice-free and open for fishing year-round. January and February rate as the slowest months, but even they can be good. Summer and fall are the most popular times, but warmer winter days also bring local anglers to the river to cure their cabin fevers. Water releases are more constant now in comparison to earlier years, and water levels remain at a given level for several weeks. Some higher releases may occur in spring in anticipation of heavy snow melt.

Rivers with giant reputations sometimes have a way of disappointing anglers, especially neophytes. Collins sees lots of beginners with these "delusions of grandeur." Even though the Bighorn is an open river full of trout, it is not easy pickings for those who will not take the time to study its subtleties and learn the water. The fishing here especially favors the adaptable angler who, if he fails in his first try, goes on to try a different fly or lure or a different way of fishing them. While other anglers continue to flail away at the water uselessly in the same ineffective way, for the adaptable angler, good things can happen at any time.

TRIBUTARIES

The Montana section of the Bighorn has one tributary of note to anglers, the **Little Bighorn River**. This river carries a heavy silt load at times, but the upper reaches in particular have some good fishing. However, the Little Bighorn runs entirely within the boundaries of the Crow Reservation and access to it is next to nil.

ACCESS

"It is unlawful to go upon tribal, trust, or allotted lands on the Crow Reservation for the purposes of hunting, fishing, or trapping." (18-USC 1165) Thus it is imperative that anglers wishing to fish the Bighorn from Hardin to Yellowtail Dam reach the river either through FWP's fishing access sites or National Park Service land.

The uppermost of these is just below the bridge across the river from Fort Smith and immediately downstream from the **Afterbay Dam**. Next, about 3 float miles down, is NPS **Lind Ranch Access**. Twelve more miles down is FWP's **Bighorn Access**. These three sites currently receive the brunt of visitation.

A very long day's float (about 19.5 miles) down from Bighorn puts the angler at **Two Leggins Access**. From there, an 11-mile float past Hardin to the edge of the Crow Reservation ends at **Arapooish Fishing Access**, just off I 90.

Below the Reservation, there are two more developed sites on the west side of the river. Grant Marsh Game Management Area is about 7 miles north of Hardin. And at the mouth of the Bighorn near the Interstate 94 bridge is the **Manuel Lisa Fishing Access**. Anglers can, of course, reach the river north of the Reservation by crossing private lands with permission. A map of the river and detailed information for floaters is available in *Montana Afloat #14, the Bighorn River*.

Power boats are currently prohibited on the Bighorn from the steel cable below Afterbay Dam downstream to Bighorn FAS. FWP has added two access sites, **Mallard's Landing** and **General Custer**, to disperse fishing pressure more evenly along the river.

4 Bitterroot River

Overview: Rumor has it that Joe Brooks, the celebrated angler, world-wide traveler, and prolific writer, once penned his ten choices for the best trout streams in the world. The Bitterroot was one of the chosen few. Notwithstanding, the Bitterroot has not attracted the national publicity other Montana streams have. Unfortunately for them, there are a lot more locals in the Bitterroot Valley than there used to be.

> **Key species:** Rainbow trout, brown trout, brook trout, cutthroat trout, bull trout, mountain whitefish, largemouth bass, squawfish, and northern pike.
> **Use:** Heavy to moderate as you go upstream. The lower section from Big Creek to Missoula receives most of the pressure and is ranked 9th statewide for fishing pressure.
> **Key flies and lures:** Flies—Muddlers, Royal Wulffs, Yellow Humpies, Woolly Worms. Lures—Panther Martins, Marabou jigs, Mepps. Bait—worms and bottom insects.

The fishing: The Bitterroot, unfortunately, has not been treated as a treasure. Subdividers and developers carve the land along its banks into ever-smaller lots. Up to the time of this writing, the river has accommodated these and other demands and still holds forth with some excellent fishing. A prime reason for this is the use of sportsmen's dollars to buy water from Painted Rocks Reservoir; releases and agreements with irrigators keep water flowing in the river through the summer. During the severe droughts in the 1980s and 1990s, the Bitterroot actually fared better than the Big Hole.

"Outstanding. And just amazing that it is so outstanding." That's the fishing assessment of Hank Fischer, veteran floater and fisherman of most Montana trout streams. Fischer enjoys fishing the Bitterroot so much that he has practically patented a three-day float trip, starting from the confluence of the East and West forks. In late June and July he's thinking rainbow as he canoes past riffles and down runs.

Rainbow and browns make up the bulk of the fisherman's quarry, but his creel may also contain brookies and cutthroat. Illegal plants of northern pike provide another game fish. And, much to the surprise of anglers who have never encountered them, some sizeable largemouth bass lurk in the backwaters. The chance of catching such a mixed creel is just one reason for the Bitterroot's popularity. Cutthroat numbers have increased with catch and release regulations.

High on the list of reasons why people enjoy fishing the Bitterroot is its scenic beauty. From the confluence of the forks near Conner until it joins the Clark Fork just west of Missoula, the Bitterroot flows on a northerly course along the base of the handsome Bitterroot Mountains. These mountains rise at so sharp a vertical angle that they appear to stand straight up from the river's west bank. They also seem to protect the valley from the high winds and severe weather that haunt other valleys such as the Yellowstone and Madison.

In the protective lee of the mountains grows a mixed forest of ponderosa pine and tall, craggy cottonwood. When floating the river, the fisherman rarely sees the nearly solid swath of human occupation that stretches most of the way up the valley. This vegetative screen grants a feeling of isolation. The beautiful

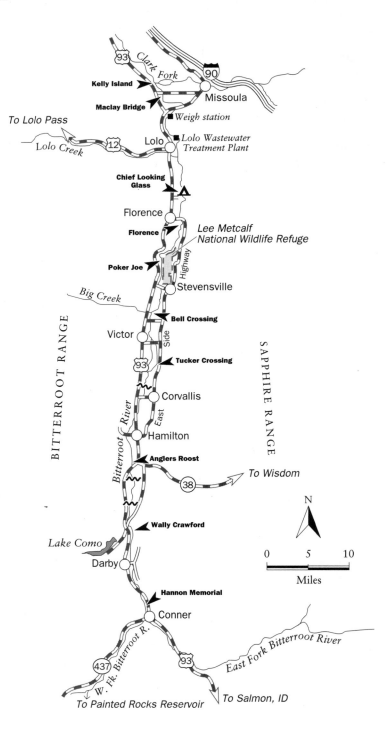

riparian greenbelt harbors amazing amounts of wildlife—deer, beaver, osprey, mink, even an occasional moose.

But it is the river itself that pleases the angler's eyes. Following the brief, but horrendous, runoff in late May and early June, the water becomes transparent. Every pebble and rock can be seen plainly, even in a 6-foot column of moving water. Many an angler has snatched away his fly prematurely after seeing the start of a rise. Summer thunderstorms cause a quick show of muddy color, probably due in part to the logging in the watershed and poor streambank adjustment practices, but the water soon returns to cerulean blue.

The water of the Bitterroot is not only clear for the most part, it's also very readable. The fishy spots are obvious.

The Bitterroot is a pool-riffle river with well-defined fish habitat. Between Darby and Missoula, the angler can choose from big, heavy water; small side channel; riffle; or pool. Washed-down trees and cut banks and roots along the way, attract fish beautifully.

Don Peters, a fisheries biologist for the Montana Department of Fish, Wildlife, and Parks (FWP), describes the river in a similar fashion, "The Bitterroot has a lot of slack, dead water which is really clear and offers no cover for fish, especially when the river is really low." He advises avoiding these "glassy sections." He also recommends fishing old river channels, eddies, and oxbows. Here, among the log jams and debris, is excellent brown trout habitat. "Oftentimes these old river channels receive primarily ground water and have the appearance of a spring creek. These are haunts for big fish," Peters advises. These swampy-looking places are often bypassed by anglers who never guess what they may be missing.

In selecting the better places in the Bitterroot to fish, the angler would be wise to watch for what Hank Fischer terms "the intact sections," where the river has not recently altered its course. As anyone who has built within its floodplain knows, the Bitterroot is a very unstable river. Surviving the spring runoff is tough when most of a winter's worth of snow whooshes down the river in three weeks. Banks fold in and gravel bottoms shift radically. Peters describes this as a "bed load movement, where the bottom moves just like it's on a conveyor belt." Standing on the bank, one can almost hear the river grinding its teeth.

Peters suggest that, while brown trout spawners key into the raw gravel beds of the new channels, the best fishing generally is in areas with good overhead cover, which generally are the established channels with trees and brush along the banks.

"Trout populations are greatest in the upper river, yet the largest trout appear to prefer the haunts of the lower Bitterroot," Peters says. For western Montana, the growth rates are excellent—about 4.5 inches a year, half as fast as the growth rate of Rock Creek trout.

How big do trout eventually grow in the Bitterroot? No one has definitive figures about the biggest one percent of the fish population, but there are some

Bitterroot trout have a faster growth rate than the famous Rock Creek, with more trout in the upper river, but larger trout in the lower river.

big ones. A 4-pound brown certainly wouldn't shock most local fishermen. There are hushed mentions of some big brook trout in certain places. Don Peters remembers a newspaper account of a 15-pound rainbow caught in one of the irrigation ditches off the main stem of the river.

Anyone assessing fishing in the Bitterroot eventually confronts a question: How can this river, which by all accounts suffers from heavy fishing pressure, horrendous runoffs, and then sediment and other environmental problems, still provide such enjoyable fishing?

The answers vary. Hank Fischer cites the superb riparian habitat. Don Peters explains that the high rough fish population means the river "temperature and nutrient loading favors good trout growth."

Strategies: When the river is running bank-full in the spring, the best places to fish are along the banks and in the side channels. When the runoff subsides and the water drops away from the banks and retreats across the gravel bars to the main channel, the riffles are the hot spots. That, in a nutshell, is the advice of the experts who fish the Bitterroot.

As the river approaches peak flows, the currents in the main channels are powerful and unrelenting. Attempting to hold its position against such an onrush would be exhausting or even suicidal for a fish. The trout seek quieter water. Any place out of the main sweep of the current should be a favored place for both the fish and the angler.

Watch for the places where obstructions such as logs and boulders slow the water. Try the eddies where the water turns around. Check out the mouths of the numerous tributaries—fish often congregate there to eat the plentiful feed.

When the water has the consistency of chocolate pudding, the avid fly angler in this area will be testing their skills in the clearer waters of Rock Creek, just west of Missoula, or if they can gain access, in one of the choice spring creeks along the Bitterroot. Those people devoted to lure fishing are probably better off casting their shiny hardware into lake waters until the river flushes some of the mud out. However, anglers with worms can take trout from the cloudy waters. Using bait in the slower spots should bring success, but the fisherman's patience may be tested by the Bitterroot's incredible population of squawfish and suckers.

Once the river begins to clear, lures and flies become useful again. Whichever piece of foolery the fisherman uses at the end of his line, the strategy is about the same. "Fling it to the banks," says Fischer, who catches good numbers of brown trout up against the banks.

Those places where the angler is most concerned about hanging up his line and losing his lure or fly are precisely the best places to find brown trout—fallen trees, tangled roots, and undercut banks. Naturally, fishing those places calls for accurate casting, some patience, and a few extra hooks, but the rewards are waiting around those hazards.

When the water comes down and retreats from the bank cover, the angler's attention turns to riffles. The urgency of the spring runoff is long gone in August and September. The Bitterroot becomes a slow stream, dropping an average of only 12 feet per mile. Clear, quiet water does not give enough protection to trout of catchable size. They seek a place where they can remain hidden from above.

The riffles offer just such protection. The bouncy, fractured surface of riffle water makes it difficult to see fish even in the shallows. The better oxygenated water in riffles grants trout some relief from the oxygen-poor water created by summer heat. During warm months, trout find most of their food in the riffles.

The lower end of the Bitterroot from Lolo to the Clark Fork River has very slow water and few riffles. The areas just downstream from the major irrigation diversions, such as those near Victor, are almost completely dewatered in later summer; trout die, stop feeding, or migrate to more hospitable sections. Thus, go upriver in times of low water.

The section from Conner to Hamilton, for example, has plenty of riffles and usually adequate water. Patient anglers await the first couple of frosts, when irrigating slows and water rises. Curiously, the river is almost deserted at this time, when the weather can be most hospitable and the fishing terrific. "It's amazing how ravenous the rainbow are at this time of the year," Fischer testifies. "They're storing up for the winter."

When wading, work each riffle carefully. In fast water, trout almost always face upstream. Approach from below the riffle and slightly to one side or from well above the riffle to avoid detection.

Work the fly or lure along the edge of the fast water. There is often a telltale, visible line between the fast and slow water to guide the angler. Trout wait just out of fast water, ready to dart at food as it tumbles by.

The same kind of feeding station exists around boulders in a riffle. A boulder buffers the current and provides a resting place for trout even while whitewater cascades all around it.

For bait and spin anglers, traditional Montana baits and lures work well in the Bitterroot. In addition to worms, Peters suggests trying bottom insects which can be found in ample supply beneath stream rocks. Marabou jigs sometimes prove effective when worked along the bottom. Mepps and Panther Martins have also passed the test of time. If the silver hardware doesn't work, try the gold.

The fly fisher has plenty of bugs to imitate—good caddis hatches in early summer or late spring followed by the mayflies in mid-summer. Johnson gets roused just thinking of the stoneflies, which aren't as big as salmon flies but still make a good mouthful for big square-tailed trout. Although terrestrials may not be as important on the Bitterroot as some other rivers, grasshopper imitations still catch their share of trout in late summer.

In August and September fishing the riffles with attractor flies is productive. Fischer likes to use big attractors such as Wulffs, which he casts downstream into the riffles and fast runs from his canoe. He also uses streamers about the time the leaves begin to fall. But perhaps his favorite, and that of many other anglers, is the Muddler, that sculpin imitator. Whether or not trout think the Muddler is a sculpin is a topic of debate, but most anglers who have given it a fair try will not debate its effectiveness.

Logjams and other obstructions slow the flow and produce excellent hiding places for trout.

Fishing the most productive places in a stream and presenting the fly well is more important than hair-splitting decisions between nearly identical feathered hooks.

A final suggestion: those backwaters warrant investigation. Whether it's with a bobber and worms, a copper spinner, or a big black Woolly Worm retrieved with a twitch, give it a try. There are some tackle-busting lunkers in those swamps.

TRIBUTARIES

The **West Fork of the Bitterroot** starts near Horse Creek on the southwestern edge of Montana and flows in a northerly direction through Painted Rocks Reservoir to its confluence with the East Fork near Connor. Above Painted Rocks, the West Fork supports nice populations of pan-sized rainbow, cutthroat, and brookies. Below the reservoir, anglers find a few browns and bull trout mixed in with the above cast of characters. Fish sizes run larger in this lower section. Some anglers float down from the reservoir, especially during high water when wading can be hazardous to one's health. Anglers gain access mainly through asking permission from private landowners, but also through some Forest Service land and in places where the stream runs right next to the road.

The **East Fork of the Bitterroot** curls around the southern end of the Sapphire Mountains and joins the West Fork at the Hannon Memorial Fishing

Access, one of FWP's most beautiful streamside sites. The East Fork runs quite a bit smaller than the West Fork but has much the same size and species of trout. Peters finds that some sections have excellent numbers of fish while other stretches hold fewer. Access is nearly all private.

Besides these two forks, the Bitterroot gathers its water from dozens of small streams, springs, and irrigation returns. Some have colorful names like Sweathouse Creek and Jack the Ripper Creek. The Burnt Fork and Blodgett, Lolo, Rock, Skalkaho, Rye, and Sleeping Child Creeks, as well as a host of others, serve as important local fisheries and, in some cases, spawning areas. None of these would stand up long under increased fishing pressure and therefore are not hot-spotted here.

Most of these small tributaries suffer heavy irrigation demands during the summer months. Anglers generally do better heading upstream to Forest Service land, where irrigation withdrawals have not yet subtracted water from these streams' normal flows. Peters notes that the east side streams drain from a sedimentary rock watershed, which imparts more nutrients to the water than the igneous rock watershed on the west side. Thus the east side tributaries tend to have more productive trout water. The exception to this rule of thumb comes when irrigation water sinks in on the west side's benches, then reappears down by the river in the form of very fertile springlets.

ACCESS

Anglers currently have a choice of six FWP developed access sites on the main stem of the river. **Hannon Memorial fishing access site** (FAS) enables anglers to enjoy the river where the east and west forks come together near Conner. Between Hamilton and Lolo, the next four are **Bell Crossing, Poker Joe, Florence**, and **Chief Looking Glass**. At the mouth where the river joins the Clark Fork just west of Missoula, **Kelly Island** FAS gives anglers access to this interesting area of many channels.

To supplement these formal accesses, anglers utilize at least eight bridges crossing the 80 miles of river. These include **MacLays, Stevensville, Victor, Woodside, Hamilton**, and **Main Street** bridges as well as a couple of unnamed bridges along U.S. Highway 93. Several other spots, including the **Lolo Wastewater Treatment Plant**, widen the choice. Actually the river never gets very far from U.S. 93; anglers can reach almost any section they wish if they take time to ask permission. Anglers can also arrange float trips lasting anywhere from two hours to two days. Pick up a copy of *Montana Afloat #1, the Bitterroot River*, for a river map and more information on floating the Bitterroot.

5 Blackfoot River

Overview: Made famous by Norman Maclean's *A River Runs Through It*, the Blackfoot is a national treasure. Winding its way through tall, dark timber in western Montana, the Blackfoot River beckons anglers to over 100 miles of unspoiled, free-flowing water. With six species of game fish, the "Big Blackfoot" offers much more variety than most trout streams. Variety also marks the course of the river. Anglers can choose to fish meandering meadow stretches, dancing riffles, transparent pools, log-jammed stretches, and boulder-pocket water in the midst of thrilling rapids.

> **Key species:** Cutthroat trout, brook trout, rainbow trout, bull trout, and mountain whitefish.
> **Use:** Moderate. A section from Clearwater River ranks 36th statewide for fishing pressure.
> **Key flies and lures:** Flies—Grizzly Wulffs, Humpies, Red Ants, Muddlers and Yellow Stimulators. Lures—Eagle Claw two-way spinners, Panther Martins, Mepps, and Thomas Fighting Fish. Bait—worms, maggots, and grasshoppers.

The fishing: The Blackfoot tells a comeback story that is bound to become more familiar across the state as management techniques are refined and fisheries rise in the list of the state's priorities. The river's fisheries were in decline until recent efforts—primarily new regulations and habitat repair and protection—began to pay off.

A forward-looking coalition of private landowners, corporations, government agencies, and concerned individuals has blessed 30 miles of the Blackfoot with a "recreation corridor" that provides anglers, floaters, and campers with accesses, campsites, and conveniences while protecting both river and landowners. Such cooperation and intelligent management has been hailed nationally as a landmark project. The continued success of the corridor depends on how responsible the public is in observing the special regulations. As this type of arrangement is obviously vastly preferable to the locked-up, fenced-off, posted waters of some other rivers in the state, anglers are urged to be especially conscientious here. Hopefully, the concept will spread.

The Blackfoot begins as a small stream, populated mostly by cutthroat above the town of Lincoln. As with much of the Blackfoot River and its tributaries, the headwaters were hit hard in the flood year of 1964, but with the passage of time, the signs of the scouring are fading.

Paul Roos, nationally known guide and outfitter, does not recommend fishing from Lincoln up to where the Landers Fork joins the Blackfoot, as that stretch is characterized by poor fish numbers and habitat. But just below Lincoln, the Blackfoot receives an influx of water from several tributaries—Keep Cool Creek, Poorman Creek, Beaver Creek, and several others—which starts what Roos describes as one of the best fishing sections of the whole river. It is not, however, one of the best floating sections due to a profusion of logjams, some of which span the river like sieves to strain out unsuspecting floaters. Basically brown trout water with excellent bank cover and undercuts, the Blackfoot here, as elsewhere, also harbors at least a smattering of brookies, cutts, rainbow, and bull trout.

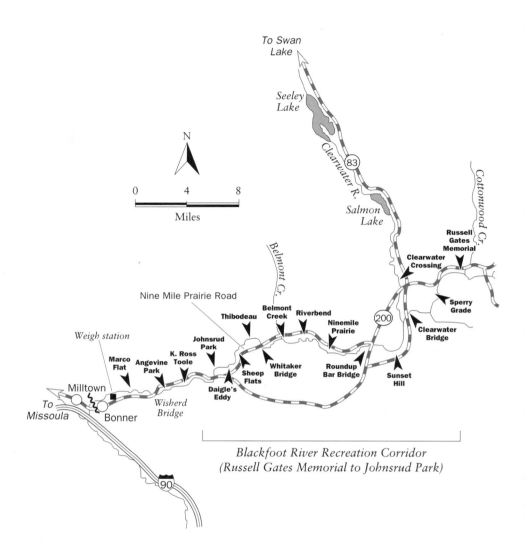

To Swan Lake

Seeley Lake

Clearwater R.

(83)

Salmon Lake

Cottonwood Cr.

N

0   4   8
Miles

Belmont Cr.

Russell Gates Memorial

Clearwater Crossing

Nine Mile Prairie Road

Sperry Grade

Thibodeau

Belmont Creek

Riverbend

Ninemile Prairie

(200)

Clearwater Bridge

Johnsrud Park

Weigh station

Marco Flat

Angevine Park

K. Ross Toole

Sheep Flats

Whitaker Bridge

Roundup Bar Bridge

Sunset Hill

Daigle's Eddy

Milltown

To Missoula

Bonner

Wisherd Bridge

(90)

Blackfoot River Recreation Corridor
(Russell Gates Memorial to Johnsrud Park)

From the Helmville bridge down to the confluence with the North Fork of the Blackfoot (a distance of 9 miles by air, 27 by river), the current flows very slowly over the mud-lined streambed and around uncountable bends. Some nice caddis hatches feed the resident brown trout, but Roos finds this section unappealing to most anglers and "sort of like trying to float a lake."

Below the confluence with the North Fork, the current and the fishing both pick up. Rainbow predominate. Some salmon flies, caddis, and mayflies along with plentiful terrestrials make for well-fed fish. Scenic values are exceptional, especially in the Box Canyon just below Scotty Brown Bridge.

Anyone wishing to float any section of the river between the County Line Fishing Access Site (FAS) and Johnsrud Park should consult Hank Fischer's *Floater's Guide to Montana*. This rock-studded stretch has eaten more than its share of boats over the years. Even bank anglers find this section challenging. The fast and powerful current makes wading a chancy enterprise in places, especially when the water is still high. Moreover, anglers have more difficulty fishing pocket water around boulders than they do fishing standard riffle-pools. Because of the popularity of floating, anglers must put up with occasional disturbances. Nevertheless, the refreshing splash of whitewater, good numbers of trout, and the chance of hooking into a very rare lunker attract many anglers.

The last 10 miles from Johnsrud Park to Bonner has much less hazardous water. Fishing that the Montana Department of Fish, Wildlife and Parks (FWP) rates as good to excellent comes mostly in the bends, at the mouths of little tributaries, and, especially, below the broad riffles.

Each year has its own peculiar flow pattern, but on average the Blackfoot produces a dramatic runoff starting in late April, peaking in late May, and dropping off sharply late in June and early July. As the water comes down, it usually clears remarkably fast. By August, it looks like the distilled water generally associated with Glacier National Park's pristine streams.

Those anglers who relish getting out in the winter to catch whitefish find the Blackfoot to their liking. The lower river grows lots of whitefish, some of them very large. In 1977, the Blackfoot rewarded an angler with a mountain whitefish, a 4-pound, 9-ounce fish. Although not generally thought of as a trophy fishery, the river has, in Roos's memory, produced 5-pound rainbow and 8-pound browns.

Aside from some concerns about siltation from logging practices and the slim (but possible) chance of dam construction, the Blackfoot has remained relatively healthy. Irrigation withdrawals are negligible. Recreational cabin sites have not sprouted along the banks in any large numbers. Indeed, the Blackfoot is an intact trout stream, producing trout near its potential, harboring abundant wildlife along its floodplain, and dazzling visitors with its scenic beauty. Angling use has seen a 125 percent increase in the last five years, and catch rates are up as well.

A large part of this good fortune is due to the combined funding and efforts of state and federal agencies, conservation groups such as Trout Unlimited, and the Blackfoot Legacy, and strong citizen participation. Together, they have

Although not as noted a trout fishery as some other Montana rivers, the Blackfoot River offers more than 100 miles of unspoiled, free-flowing water, much of it filled with trout.

cleaned up and protected more than 200 main-stem and tributary miles in the Blackfoot watershed. this was a model watershed restoration project, probably one of the finest efforts occuring in the west. Cutthroat trout numbers are rebounding and bull trout numbers are on the upswing.

But much of this good work is now overshadowed by the Seven-up Pete Mine, a propsed gold venture east of Lincoln where the Landers Fork joins the upper Blackfoot. The site boasts a "substantial body of ore," says one FWP biologist, and mining it will be "a huge undertaking that can't help but have some major effects on the river." Mining has historically been hard on fisheries in Montana, so patrons of Blackfoot trout are understandably concerned. Anglers and friends of the river can help protect the Blackfoot's future by joining TU or the Blackfoot Legacy, and by contacting the Montana Department of State Lands to get on the mailing list as the project continues.

Strategies: Each river has its own physical makeup, its own flow characteristics, its own seasonal patterns, and its own type of trout food. These variables often weigh to the advantage of some fishing techniques while weighing to the disadvantage of others.

The Blackfoot is open to all comers. The big Blackfoot will accommodate just about any trout fishing technique yet devised. Wherever an angler feels most comfortable operating, whether pool, run, riffle, boulder pocket, in a boat, from the bank, or wading mid-stream, the angler will find plenty of those friendly places somewhere in the Blackfoot's 100-mile length.

Because the Blackfoot has a relatively cold drainage, which stays in the grip of winter longer than most streams on the other side of the Divide, the trout are slow to become active. All methods of fishing can be intermittently good in April until the river muddies up, whereupon the river becomes the exclusive domain of the bait angler until July.

Becky Garland from Garland's Town and Country Store in Lincoln has been stocking and selling fishing tackle for years. Her customers who use bait usually go with earthworms and maggots (for whitefish). She also sells Eagle Claw two-way spinners, small lures with colored beads or flashy metal pieces onto which the angler attaches a morsel of bait. As another alternative, some anglers use stonefly nymphs or grasshoppers with split shot.

As the river starts to clear, spinning gear becomes useful. Listening to her customers and noting what they purchase, Garland suggests that the smaller lures work much more effectively than the big hunks of metal. To stock a tackle box, she recommends Panther Martins (silver and gold), Mepps, Thomas Fighting Fish, and red and white Daredevles.

Depending upon the vagaries of a particular year's weather, the river may start to drop and become less turbid just as the salmon flies begin to emerge. It is rare to find a a good hatch of salmon flies under fishable conditions. The smaller golden stoneflies hatch out a little later. The hatches start at the lower end of the river and progress upstream to the mouth of the North Fork, above which the hatch peters out due to heavy sediment on the riverbed.

Once the water clears, fly anglers watch for hatches of mayflies and caddis plus some terrestrials. Garland suggests trying red Ants, Mosquitoes, Humpies, and Grizzly Wulffs in sizes 12 or 14. Johnson observes that, when fishing the riffles and pocket water "you can do better with attractors and larger-sized flies." Late in the summer, hopper patterns work well near the banks.

The late Joe Halterman once observed that one of the distinctive aspects of fishing the Blackfoot was the consistent surface action in the middle of the day, even during the heat of the summer. Dry fly anglers will generally do best working the shaded banks and places where trees and brush overhang the water.

One other fly pattern deserving attention here is the classic Muddler Minnow. Although the Muddler baffles outdoor writers who search for reasons for its success, clearly this fly works very well. Fished either wet or dry in the summer, the Muddler seems especially effective for autumn browns when kept under the surface.

While the Blackfoot has plenty of good trout water, it also has two types of places which could best be skipped by anglers. One of these typically shows up in the very slow stretches such as around Mineral Hill, where heavy deposits of sediment give the streambed a uniform color and consistency. Trout rightfully avoid these places because they are so easily spotted and thus vulnerable to predation. Anglers fishing these long, glassy slicks must analyze where the trout would feel safe.

For the same reasons, Paul Roos recommends skipping places where the river crosses large slabs of bedrock, such as in several spots in Box Canyon. Trout do not find protective cover here, nor do they find much food.

One final suggestion comes from Larry Davis, the FWP warden stationed in Lincoln: "When everyone is off chasing elk and deer in the hills during the hunting season, that's the best time to fish the Blackfoot." He sees very few anglers in the fall, but those he checks often report excellent angling. As a bonus, the brilliant fall colors along the Blackfoot would please even New Englanders.

TRIBUTARIES

Landers Fork lost much of its best holding water and vegetative cover during two recent flood years. Davis notes that few anglers do well in the bottom stretches of this geologically unstable stream, but as the anglers go upstream several miles from the highway, the fishing improves. **Copper Creek,** a tributary of Landers Fork, yields some nice cutthroat.

In the vicinity of Lincoln, a half dozen small streams and a few ponds sometimes provide exceptional fishing for those who can gain access, but that access is not always easy to come by. Make friends locally.

The **North Fork of the Blackfoot** has some of the most beautiful water in the state, thanks in part to its wilderness watershed. Several miles past the end of the road, a waterfall marks the top of the bull trout water. Above the falls, cutthroat and a few rainbow make up the fishery. Below the falls, larger cutts and rainbow mingle with bull trout up to fifteen pounds. The North Fork has its own access site, "Harry Morgan," not far from Ovando, as well as many miles of Forest Service access upstream.

Monture Creek is a long, rather small stream flowing through mostly private land, but with a nice FWP campground just off Highway 200. Most of the trout fall into the pan-sized category, but occasional larger fish provide pleasant surprises.

Cottonwood Creek has bushy banks and lots of undercuts, features which anglers find difficult but which brown trout relish. This small stream flows for about two miles through the Blackfoot-Clearwater Wildlife Management Area. Tedesco remembers an eight-pound brown which rewarded one diligent angler here.

When springtime runoff has most area streams looking like chocolate pudding, the **Clearwater River** is a sight for sore eyes. With a chain of lakes to settle out the sediment, the Clearwater runs high but clear from the foot of Salmon Lake to its junction with the Blackfoot, living up to its name beautifully. Although tough to fish because of innumerable willows and alders along undercut banks, the Clearwater provides some excellent fishing for sizeable browns before summer temperatures heat up.

The Blackfoot has more than a dozen other, smaller tributaries where adventuresome anglers sometimes try their luck at catching not only resident trout but also spawning lunkers.

ACCESS

Anglers wishing to fish between **Mineral Hill** (where Helmville-Avon road—#141—crosses the river to join Montana Highway 200) and the headwaters depend on casual access along the highway and county roads.

If interested in fishing the river from Mineral Hill downstream to Bonner, anglers would be wise to obtain a copy of the pamphlet *Montana Afloat #2, the Blackfoot River.*

"**Aunt Molly**" refers to a block of FWP land covering about 5 miles of the river frontage 6 to 13 miles downstream from Mineral Hill. Road access is a county road leaving from Montana Highway 141 about two miles south of the Mineral Hill bridge.

Cedar Meadow, downstream from the Blackfoot's confluence with Nevada Creek, is more a boat launch spot than a place to fish extensively.

River Junction is an extensive camping and fishing spot that has no road access and thus is of use only to floating anglers.

Scotty Brown Bridge has no public land around it, but less than a mile downstream the recreation corridor begins, so some floaters launch here. County Line, just off the highway, has campsites. Sperry Grade, two miles downstream, has good fishing above a series of rapids.

Clearwater Bridge is at the top of a 2-mile section with two accesses and some casual road access.

The **Roundup Bar Bridge** marks the top of a 16-mile section loaded with access and including seven campgrounds. Anglers need to travel the gravel road which leaves the highway on the north end of the bridge and closely parallels the river down to Johnsrud Park, the end of the recreation corridor.

Below Johnsrud Park, the river and MT 200 rarely part company. **Angevine Park** is the last formal access site, but anglers can pull off at a number of spots. Floaters should not venture past the Bonner Weigh Station or risk loss of life or limb as water runs into the Mill town dam system.

6 Clark Fork

Overview: Think of the sure-fire titles for best-selling novels about this river: For those who love to cheer for the underdog, *The Comeback Story of the 1970s*. Romantics will swoon over *A Red River Goes Blue*, while Zane Grey devotees will surely snap up *Tough Trip From Hellgate to Paradise*.

No doubt about it, the Clark Fork is a river of many faces. An angler in the upper river who must drag his canoe across gravel bars might be skeptical, but the Clark Fork at Thompson Falls holds the undisputed title as Montana's mightiest river. If the angler were to canoe from Warm Springs all the way to Thompson Falls, he would paddle almost every conceivable kind of water, from a meandering, brush-choked brooklet to a powerful, full-fledged river with deep runs, fathomless pools, and whitewater.

> **Key species:** Brown trout, cutthroat trout, rainbow trout, bull trout, squawfish, suckers, northern pike, and whitefish.
> **Use:** Moderate to heavy. The section below Missoula ranks 7th statewide for fishing pressure, but the upper section does not receive as much pressure.
> **Key flies and lures:** Flies—Muddler, Woolly Worms, hoppers, Montana Nymphs, Henryville Special, Bucktail Caddis, Olive Stimulators, and any small brown caddis imitation. Lures—gold Daredevles or Mepps. Bait— nightcrawlers and hoppers in season.

The fishing: Prior to 1973, no angler in his right mind would launch a canoe in the upper Clark Fork. A sickening mixture of municipal sewage and acidic and heavy metal wastes from the Anaconda Company's operations painted the river red and delivered a lethal blow to all aquatic life in the upper Clark Fork. Jim Vashro, Montana Fish, Wildlife, and Parks (FWP) biologist, remembers fishing the river above Deer Lodge and doing quite well in 1966, when a "red tide" swept through and made the river look like tomato juice.

Once the Anaconda Company instituted an effective pollution abatement program and the river had a chance to cleanse itself, insects and fish slowly repopulated. At first only a marginal fishery, the upper Clark Fork now shows potential for becoming a first-rate trout stream. Vashro says that by 1982 he saw one of the most dramatic recoveries first hand.

Still standing in the way of complete health is an oversupply of nutrients, heavy metals in the floodplain, and an undersupply of instream water. Mines in Butte, Anaconda, and Opportunity discharge sewage effluent into Silver Bow Creek, which then flows right through Anaconda Company's settling ponds.

But Jim Vashro reports that, incredibly, the settling ponds function "almost as well as a tertiary sewer system," resulting in almost complete removal of even nitrates and phosphates from the water. Preliminary tests have shown that the liver and kidney tissues of fish in the Warm Springs area contain some heavy metals, but well below the federal Food and Drug Administration's suggested limits.

Vashro urges anglers not to overlook the Warm Springs Ponds (Hog Hole) or Job Corps Ponds. They offer challenging flatwater fishing for 5- to 10-pound browns and rainbow, catch-and-release. The presence of these magnificent fish give hope that no matter how badly we screw up some waters, ecosystems can recover if given the chance.

Just below the settling ponds, Silver Bow Creek combines with Warm Springs Creek to inaugurate the Clark Fork. From this point down for about 20 river miles, the stream supports bountiful numbers of brown trout. Short riffles separate a succession of deep pools and cavernous undercuts. Willows crowd the banks and lean over the water. Browns relish such cover.

Just below Deer Lodge, heavy local fishing pressure plus some pollution problems take their toll. Fish numbers and size drop off. The last few miles to Garrison, the water "seems to grow tired," in the words of FWP biologist Don Peters.

Tributaries are the keys to the rivers' health and where to fish. For example, when the Little Blackfoot River adds its clean, clear water at the junction, the dilution rejuvenates the Clark Fork and another good stretch of fishing ensues. Red-barked dogwood, aspen, and water birch create a distinctive riparian habitat here; foliage enthusiasts revel in autumn's red and yellows.

One of the Clark Fork's best fishing sections runs from Gold Creek to Drummond. Former fishing guide, Frank Johnson, ascribes this to "incredible, incredible habitat." Deep pools, eddies, and undercut banks, some 100 yards long, present almost continuously ideal housing for browns.

Below Drummond, anglers begin to find a few rainbows and an occasional cutthroat. Trout populations in general decline severely, however, especially from Bearmouth to Rock Creek. This is due to critically high summer temperatures in the stream and to extensive channel alterations to accommodate the freeway.

The Clark Fork benefits once again from its cooler, cleaner tributaries when Rock Creek adds its superb water. From the mouth of Rock Creek to Milltown Dam, trout abound again in impressive numbers and the aquatic life shows more diversity. Browns still predominate, but rainbow amount to 30

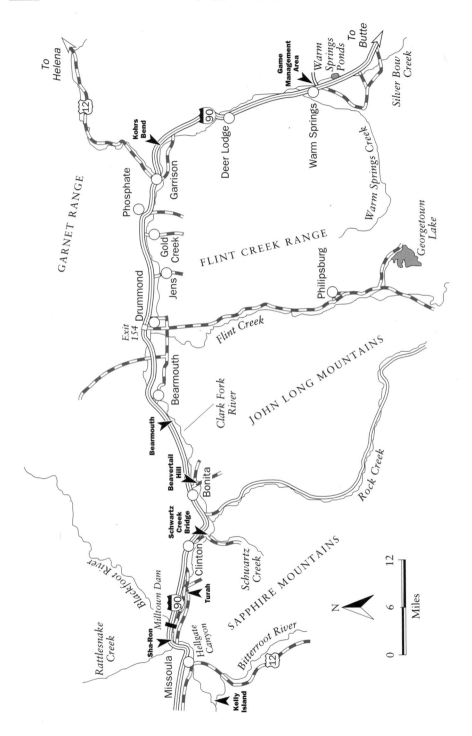

To Helena

12

Kohrs
Bend

90

Phosphate

Garrison

Deer Lodge

Warm Springs

Game
Management
Area

Warm
Springs
Ponds

To
Butte

Silver Bow
Creek

Warm Springs Creek

Georgetown
Lake

GARNET RANGE

Gold
Creek

Drummond

Jens
Creek

FLINT CREEK RANGE

Philipsburg

Exit
154

Bearmouth

Flint Creek

Clark Fork
River

JOHN LONG MOUNTAINS

Bearmouth

Beavertail
Hill

Bonita

Rock Creek

Schwartz
Creek
Bridge

Clinton

Schwartz
Creek

SAPPHIRE MOUNTAINS

Blackfoot River

Milltown Dam

90

Turah

Rattlesnake
Creek

Sha-Ron

Hellgate
Canyon

Bitterroot River

12

Missoula

Kelly
Island

N

12
6
Miles
0

6 Clark fork River (lower portion)

percent of the population. In contrast to the stream above Rock Creek, where relatively few anglers venture, many try their luck downstream to the dam.

Vashro and Peters think the condition of the brown trout in the upper Clark Fork has improved recently, but when the biologists electrofish, by stunning the fish with electric current for census purposes, they still find some fish with large heads and skinny bodies. These are usually browns that spawned the previous fall. They don't recover very rapidly in the stressed system. These "snaky" trout demonstrate that not all is right in the stream.

Insect populations are incredibly abundant, but limited to a few pollution-tolerant species. Mayflies and stoneflies that require very clean water are still in short supply. Caddisflies, especially *hydropsychidae*, can be extremely abundant because they are more pollution tolerant.

Curiously, the biologists also find an occasional large cutthroat, almost always in excellent condition. Peters thinks the cutthroat drop out of some tributaries when the fish reach such a size that the smaller water no longer seems secure. Yet cutthroat have a reputation for being finicky about water quality. As Hank Fischer says, "the Clark Fork's story doesn't add up quite right. No one has quite put the whole story together."

Unquestionably, the upper Clark Fork has a concentrated nutrient load. Municipal sewage plants, mining, and farming contribute an overly rich chemical balance to the water, which, in turn, triggers profuse algae growth.

During a sunny summer day, the algae (what most of us call moss) produces so much oxygen that the water can't get rid of it; oxygen can build up to 150 percent of saturation. Then at night, algae and bacteria consume the oxygen so quickly that it drops to 50 percent of saturation. Peters notes that oxygen supersaturation has many of the same effects on fish as nitrogen supersaturation. "Moreover," he says, "the fluctuations are very hard on the trout."

Add yet another problem: summer water temperatures commonly reach critical levels, such as 76 degrees Fahrenheit at Bonita. Even the tolerant brown trout keel over during extended periods of such high temperatures.

Fish biologists and anglers agree that if the fishery on the upper Clark Fork is to improve, more of the stream's water must be kept within its banks, not siphoned off for irrigation during the summer. More water would not only dilute the nutrients but also keep temperatures at a healthier level. More efficient use of irrigation water would result in less leaching of minerals from the soil; this would be a benefit to ranchers as well as the fishery.

The confluence of the Clark Fork and the Blackfoot marks not only a major transformation of the Clark Fork but also an interesting spot to compare the two rivers. While the Clark Fork above this juncture drains nearly twice as large a basin as the Blackfoot, the Clark Fork's flow is actually slightly less on the average than the Blackfoot's. While the Clark Fork carries a rich load of nutrients, the Blackfoot's water looks distilled by comparison. While both rivers generally reach peak flow near the end of May, the Blackfoot has much the more spectacular runoff.

Below the confluence, the Clark Fork goes through a rapid transition. The water flattens. Riffles become more isolated. Deep pools alternate with runs. Instead of brush, boulders stud the shoreline.

Hordes of rough fish populate the river from Milltown Dam down through Hellgate Canyon. Peters reports that in all his electrofishing experience in rivers, he has never seen such a concentration of big suckers and squawfish. When the electrodes send their current across the section, the water turns white with rough fish, and the FWP crew has to hunt hard for the scarce trout.

The objects of much angling effort, a few brown trout and bull trout lunkers lurk in the big pool below the dam. Downstream, the trout population continues the shift from brown trout to rainbow. Below Kelly Island and the mouth of the Bitterroot, the browns practically disappear and rainbows rule the roost.

From Missoula to Superior, the average trout Johnson catches measures about 16 inches. Peters concurs with this impressive estimate. Unfortunately, these big fish do not inhabit the river in big numbers. "The fish seem to be just in pockets," says Johnson. Peters describes the fishery as "real spotty in distribution, with lots of water between good spots." Fischer advises anglers to spend considerable time on the river to recognize "the subtle differences" between those places which house trout and those that prove to be empty residences.

Perhaps not by coincidence, the only truly fine tributary to the lower Clark Fork flows into the most productive section of the river below Kelly Island. Fish Creek joins the Clark Fork just after the river begins its way through Alberton Gorge (sometimes called Fish Creek Gorge), known primarily to whitewater rafting enthusiasts. Boulder-strewn rapids make hazardous boating for all but the most experienced rafters.

Anglers find it difficult to gain access to this section; even when they reach the banks, they still find the swift water a tough proposition to fish. But the effort may have its rewards, as good numbers of big rainbow find the gorge to their liking. Peters notes that the gorge marks the only section of the river below Kelly Island where electrofishing crews find more than spotty populations of trout.

An electrofishing survey near Superior turned up some cutthroat and bull trout as well as rainbow. While it may not appear to be classic cutthroat water, Johnson catches "some big and heavy natives" around Superior.

Joe Huston, a fisheries biologist, agrees that the section from St. Regis to Paradise, known locally as the "cutoff section," used to get very little fishing pressure, primarily due to its distance from large population centers. Jim Vashro reports that the section is starting to get discovered, particularly by anglers from Idaho and Washington. In Huston's mind, the cutoff section should be termed a "real sleeper," because it holds good numbers of rainbow and bull trout as well as some browns, cutthroat, and whitefish. FWP's census shows about 400 fish per mile on this stretch, with an average size of 16 inches.

Once nearly wiped out by pollution, the Clark Fork trout population has come back strong.

Anglers occasionally catch trophy-sized trout here, either in the riffle water of the upper section or in the pools of the last 10 miles. The entire section is scenic, easily floated, and readily accessible from the highway, which means it probably isn't undiscovered anymore.

At Paradise, the warmer water of the Flathead River mingles with the Clark Fork. Immediately a tendency toward more rough fish and few trout develops. Huston recommends one last productive area, the Weeksville rapids, and a 5-mile stretch west of Plains where some big rainbow enjoy the faster water. Other than that, the Clark Fork below Plains interests anglers primarily for its northern pike, some of which weigh over 30 pounds. Pike are found in a few backwater sloughs or in Thompson Falls Reservoir upstream to the Eddy Island area.

Strategies: Like most fish biologists, Vashro enjoys spending some of his leisure hours in pursuit of trout, not with the electrofishing gear, but with a fishing rod. In friendly competition with anglers he knows who fish from Warm Springs to Garrison Junction, he often compares notes on successes and failures.

Vashro acknowledges that bait users do well, generally with nightcrawlers and hoppers in season. Anglers with gold Daredevles or Mepps catch fish here, as they do in most Montana waters. Anglers using flies also do well, although they have a terrible time casting in close quarters with all the brush. He corroborates reports of massive caddis hatches ("just like a snowstorm") and tells of finding 2,000 caddis nymphs per square yard of streambed. Montana nymphs and small, green Wooly Worms catch more than their share of fish; any small brown caddis imitation works nicely during a hatch. As an afterthought, Vashro suggests trying a Muddler or Woolly Worms under the banks.

Any effective strategy on the upper river takes into account the scourge of moss. By mid-summer, both the green filamentous type of moss and the floating brown algae have bloomed in profusion. Bait and spin anglers quit in despair. Even those who fish dry flies spend a frustrating amount of time unwrapping the stuff from their feathered hooks. Some summers seem worse than others do. Vashro suggests wading the middle of the river and casting to the edges with hopper patterns and Muddlers. "Fish them wet," says Vashro, "twitching them out into the current. And hang on—you'll get explosions." He can recall several fifty-fish days taking brown trout with this method in the Gold Creek area.

Hank Fischer and Frank Johnson try to avoid the floating gunk altogether, preferring to fish either early in the spring before runoff or immediately after the river comes back into fishable shape. Once the cold nights return in the fall, moss no longer presents a problem, and the fishing heats up.

Above Rock Creek, only a few mayflies and a handful of salmon flies struggle to continue their life cycles. Johnson reports that each year he sees a few more of both of them. But basically, this is caddis country. Like Vashro, Johnson recounts seeing clouds of caddis so thick that in a time-exposure photograph he took, he could hardly see the water. Standard adult caddis patterns that should work well here include the Henryville Special, the Bucktail Caddis, and the Elk Hair Caddis. To boost the angler's arsenal, add a few hopper imitations as well as some Muddlers.

Jim Vashro explored some undercut banks with a probe and found caverns going back under the banks as much as six feet. The current undercuts the stream banks much of the way from Warm Springs to Rock Creek. Brown trout favor the undercuts and the pool-eddy combinations; anglers should follow suit. Cast dry flies close to the bank; sinking flies, lures, and baits should go under the bank, if possible. Fishing is often better early and late in the day when dim light lures the browns from under cover.

More anglers wet their lines between Rock Creek and the Milltown Dam than in any other comparable length of the river. Cold, fresh water from Rock Creek jolts the much warmer Clark Fork back to life. Insect life proliferates. Mayflies ride the breezes. Salmon flies, powerful magnets, both for trout and anglers, crawl out of their cases and spend their short adult lives airborne before dropping to the water's surface as potential mouthfuls for waiting trout. The much-awaited hatch comes up the river from Missoula soon after peak runoff; the exact timing depends on the weather and water temperatures.

The river below the dam provides a tough test for the average angler. Instead of easy-to-read riffles, anglers will find long runs and pools that make fish habitat indefinite. Few places permit wading. The immense size of the river means the angler can only fish a small portion of any given stretch. Frank Johnson comments, "There isn't a lot of character to it until you gain some experience. The inexperienced fisherman won't do as well here as on the Bitterroot."

Almost like a Florida angler cruising in search of a school of tarpon, Johnson either floats or drives in search of rising trout. He points out that between Missoula and Superior, about twenty places offer good lookouts not far from the highway. If one spot shows no hatch or feeding fish, he moves to the next one.

Johnson thinks matching the hatch is unnecessary. Feeding trout in the lower Clark Fork tend to be unselective and very active. "But," he says, "they may be in 4-inch slots, and if you don't get your fly in that slot, they'll totally ignore it."

"It's a challenge on a really huge river," says Johnson, "to use techniques and flies which normally would be used on a spring creek."

Hank Fischer also puzzles why some places hold fish while others don't but says that if you fish it enough, you find places where fish rise regularly. He cites an example, a place where the river speeds up and cuts into a bank. "It doesn't look any better than other banks," Fischer admits, "but I caught a fish there the last five times I've tried."

Fischer also recommends fall fishing. Fischer finds some large mayflies coming off the river in the afternoons and uses a big Wulff on the surface to fool the trout. Fischer thinks that the trout move into the shallow water with the advent of cooler weather. He especially likes a stretch that parallels a leaky irrigation ditch; the breaks in the ditch seem to aerate the water and make a good spot for trout.

Whether an angler chooses bait, lures, or flies, the same type of spots should hold his interest. Watch for deep banks, gravel riffles dumping into deeper water and tributaries where they enter the main river. Work the pocket water around boulders. Try to spot underground springs bubbling into the river. And skip the long, flat runs.

This river requires experience. Anglers unfamiliar with the river should not expect instant success. Try floating some sections; no other way provides such a fast education.

Bank anglers should enjoy the confusing channels around Kelly Island or the boulder-filled reaches in Alberton Gorge. For the adventurous that like to search out far away, relatively unknown water, the cutoff section between St. Regis and Paradise promises a chance for a lunker. Jim Vashro said, "early Spring fishing is picking up in the cut-off section. There is a golden stone hatch just before runoff starts."

TRIBUTARIES

Four major tributaries to the Clark Fork have chapters devoted to them in this book: Rock Creek, and the Blackfoot, Bitterroot, and Flathead Rivers. The lesser tributaries are described here.

Warm Springs Creek provides very important spawning water, but nearly runs dry in late summer. A number of other small tributaries (which shall remain nameless because they could not withstand much increase in pressure) support a surprising number of trout. Peters recalls finding one that could be crossed in places without getting the ankles wet, yet harbored a three-pound brown and quite a few 15-inchers in the pools between the shallow riffles.

Peters rates the **Little Blackfoot** as "a fine fishery, even though it has been abused by channel alterations." An FWP study found thirty catchable trout in a bulldozed section, but more than ten times that number in a comparable, but unaltered, section nearby. In addition to some good-sized browns, the Little Blackie also fosters some cutthroat and rainbow in its deep pools, undercuts, and logjams. Vashro suggests fishing from Elliston to Avon or below Avon in the intact sections. Quite a few local anglers, especially from Helena, already fish this stretch. The river flows through private land here; be sure to get permission from the landowners before crossing their property. Russ Schneider of Helena prefers to fish this section in the winter when the water is nice and low. He recommends a #16 Bead-Head Pheasant Tail fished directly upstream. But, he notes, even in winter you are likely to see other anglers.

Excessive withdrawals, sediment, and some pollution problems hurt **Flint Creek**, but the stream still manages to support some nice browns. Peters says the access is mostly on private land, but the landowners normally grant permission. When electrofishing the lower section, Jim Vashro turned up some of the densest populations of browns he'd ever seen. The canyon section below Phillipsburg is usually turbid, but holds a surprising mix of a very nice sized browns, rainbows, and brookies.

Rattlesnake Creek is closed to fishing from its headwaters down to the Missoula water supply dam. From the dam to the mouth, local anglers work for spawning trout during the runs. Because the Clark Fork does not receive enough population recruitment from its tributaries, Peters thinks even the lower Rattlesnake may someday be protected for the spawners.

Most of **Fish Creek's** watershed lies within undeveloped public land, which makes for outstanding water quality. "I consider it the best potential cutthroat water in the region," exclaims Peters. Rainbows also favor the lower reaches.

"Someone has always been mucking around with the **St. Regis River**," notes Peters. After some mining, two railroads, and a superhighway ripped up the stream bottom, few fish remain, although current efforts to improve the stream habitat may help in the future.

The upper reaches of the **Thompson River** attract Kalispell anglers for pan-sized brookies, rainbow, and cutthroat. The Thompson River holds about 400-600 trout per mile, but only a small percentage exceed 12 inches. "Ready access and high fishing pressure are the problems and the stream is overdue for more restrictive fishing regulations," Vashro said. The middle 20 miles hold mostly rainbow up to 20 inches plus some brookies and whitefish.

Occasional browns and bull trout run with the predominant rainbow in the last 15 miles. Huston finds some trout up to 5 pounds, probably out of the Clark Fork, in the lower reaches. He rates the salmon fly hatch on the Thompson "second only to Rock Creek." The hatch comes earlier here than on other streams, usually in mid to late May. Almost the whole length of the river below Thompson Lakes runs close to roads.

ACCESS

Much of the Clark Fork runs just a cast or two from a highway. Because the river intertwines so much with the highway and railroad tracks, anglers have a wide choice of pull-outs. In many cases, the highway right-of-way includes the thin strip of land between road and river, providing undeveloped but convenient public access.

Because Interstate 90 makes it hard to access some major stretches of river, anglers who innovatively use farm roads, railroad right of ways, etc., can fish relatively unfished water. But remember: don't leave your car in a place the highway patrol may ticket it.

In addition to the informal accesses, passage to the river is granted by FWP fishing access sites (FAS), bridge crossings, and corporate landholders such as Champion International. Of these, some of the most important are mentioned below.

Leaving I 90 at Warm Springs, anglers can reach the top of the river through FWP's **Game Management Area** around the Warm Springs Ponds. FWP has another access, **Kohrs Bend**, reached by the Beck Hill exit off I 90 east of Garrison. Vashro reports that the landowners between these accesses usually grant permission to fish.

Floaters and anglers also utilize several bridges between Warm Springs and Garrison.

Floating in a canoe from the Gold Creek Bridge to Drummond allows the angler to fish the most remote section of the Clark Fork, but at least one landowner along this stretch has some pronounced unfriendly feelings towards outsiders. Stay off the banks and watch for a strand of electrified wire stretched across the river.

Below Drummond's municipal park, anglers may wish to pull into the **Bearmouth Rest Area** for I 90 westbound travelers. River fishing here is poor so it doesn't receive a lot of pressure. The river borders the rest area beside a beautiful stand of quaking aspen. Also try the pond for some fair-sized stocked trout.

The fishing access at **Beavertail Hill** just above Rock Creek would best be used during the cooler portions of the fishing season. Below Rock Creek, water temperatures do not present such a problem. A private landowner allows fishing around the Schwartz Creek Bridge just upstream from Clinton, and FWP maintains an access site at the northeast corner of the bridge. FWP has another access near the tiny community of Turah.

"The big water of the lower Clark Fork —big trout, but hard to fish."

The bridge at Milltown makes a good starting point for a float to the **Sharon FAS** in East Missoula, which also has a boat ramp. Anglers can reach the river almost anywhere in the city of Missoula.

Just below Missoula, FWP has a major fishing access site, **Kelly Island**, which can be reached from either side. The boat ramp is on the south side of Kelly Island off Spurgin Road.

Other accesses between Missoula and St. Regis include Council Grove, the Champion land at Big Flat, Harpers Bridge, Petty Creek, Cyr Bridge, and Forest Grove (upstream from Superior on the northside road). Access below St. Regis rarely presents a problem.

Almost all of the Clark Fork grants easy floating, but a few diversion dams (such as those around Missoula) and some big rapids (as in Alberton Gorge) demand considerable skill and caution. For more thorough information on floating, see *Floater's Guide to Montana* by Hank Fischer (Falcon, 199?) and the pamphlet, *Montana Afloat #4, the Clark Fork River.*

7 Flathead River

Overview: The Flathead is truly a cosmopolitan river. It flows from a foreign country, Canada, past the Glacier National Park, gathering water from the Bob Marshall and Great Bear Wildernesses, passing through Flathead National Forest, many state lands, private lands, and the Kootenai Nation on its way to the Clark Fork.

Anglers talking about "the Flathead" may be referring either to the magnificent lake, the mighty river that feeds it, or to the big valleys and basin that surround these waters. (Flathead is also the name of a county that is one of the state's fastest growing, experiencing a flood of new residents.)

Together the lake and river make a complete system; the lake supplies many of the fish while the river supplies the spawning grounds and summer feed. The mighty bull trout used to be the focus of a nationally renowned fishery, but today bull trout are illegal to target or take. Quite a change occured in only a few years.

> **Key species:** Cutthroat trout, whitefish, rainbow trout, bull trout, lake trout, and northern pike.
>
> **Use:** Heavy. No section of the Flathead River ranks in the top 50 of state fishing pressure, but the Middle Fork receives very heavy rafting pressure from Moccasin Creek access to West Glacier on the Whitewater Section.
>
> **Key flies and lures:** Flies—Elk Hair Caddis, Stimulators, Wulffs, Humpies, Hoppers, Ant patterns, and the Royal Trude. Lures— gold Daredevles or Mepps. Bait—nightcrawlers and hoppers in season.

The fishing: The Flathead River and its forks make up a unique fishery in Montana because many fish are nonresidents traveling from Flathead Lake. Compared with some of the nutrient-rich rivers in southern Montana, the Flathead's pure, nutrient-poor water supports less aquatic life. Tough winter, cold water, and low chemical content combine to make water gorgeous to look at but less than hospitable for fish.

River anglers have Flathead Lake to thank for providing quarry on a seasonal basis. The lake acts like a giant heart, pumping pulses of fish into its arteries. In spring, cutthroat and bull trout start their spawning runs; in fall, major pulses of lake whitefish follow.

For the bulls and cutthroats, the eventual destinations are the tiny headwater creeks that branch off the Middle and North Forks. Some travel up to 130 miles before stopping to make their redds and deposit their eggs. The lake whitefish generally run as far as Blankenship Bridge and above.

The South Fork of the Flathead

Hungry Horse Reservoir gobbled up much of the South Fork, and the dam cut off upstream migration from Flathead Lake. The short section of the South Fork below the dam holds few fish because of a lack of fish food and severe fluctuations in the volume of water released by the dam.

However, for the hardy angler who can solve the access problems, the upper 50 miles of the South Fork above the reservoir have much to offer. The river there not only has a spawning run of bull trout and resident cutthroat trout, but also a handsome setting in the pristine Bob Marshall Wilderness. As with most of the Flathead River system, the pleasure of being out in such beautiful country adds an extra dimension to fishing the South Fork.

Jim Vashro said "the South Fork is incredible. Cutthroat range from 400 to 1,000 fish per mile. At Big Prairie, 30 percent are over 12 inches." However, the South Fork, along with the entire Flathead River drainage, has gone catch-and-release for all cutthroat. Many anglers catch an average of ten cutthroats an hour; 10 to 30 percent of these fish range from 12 to 18 inches.

The best fishing on the South Fork is at Big Prairie, about 30 miles into the wilderness. Fishing is also good just below the Meadow Creek Gorge or 2 to 4 miles beyond the Meadow Creek wilderness portal. Don't expect to have the South Fork to yourself. Recent national publicity in fishing magazines has increased the number of outfitted and private anglers on the river. You may see up to twenty rafts float by you in a day of fishing in August.

The Middle Fork of the Flathead River

The Middle Fork originates deep in the Bob Marshall Wilderness. Officially designated a "wild river" for the first half of its length, the Middle Fork plunges swiftly from the confluence of Strawberry and Bow Creeks to Bear Creek. From Bear Creek, U.S. Highway 2 parallels the river for the second half of its course to the mouth of the North Fork.

The upper section of the Middle Fork provides fishing, floating, and spectacular backcountry experiences; the lower section offers floating but only marginal fishing. Pat Graham of the Montana Department of Fish, Wildlife and Parks (FWP) rates the fishing on the lower section "poor."

The Middle Fork marked the epicenter of the infamous 1964 flood. On an annual basis, the Middle Fork averages a discharge of less than 3,000 cubic feet per second (cfs), but on June 9, 1964, the river gushed 140,000 cfs and scoured its streambed so badly that the results will be obvious for years to come. Fortunately, such a flood should occur only once in about 200 years.

Much of the upper Middle Fork runs through steep-walled canyons with big, deep pools. After a muddy runoff in May and June, the river drops and clears rapidly. Anglers who want to float from Schaefer Meadows to Bear Creek try to time their trip to include the brief period when the water has substantially cleared but still runs in sufficient volume to carry rafts over the rocks. Each year has its own weather patterns, but this period generally comes between June 20 and July 15.

Because of the area's remoteness, the upper Middle Fork receives little fishing pressure. In the earlier part of summer, anglers work primarily for westslope cutthroat.

The North Fork of the Flathead River

FWP director Pat Graham likes a description he heard of the North Fork: "a baby thrashing around in a cradle." He explains that, in the spring, the river runs high, throwing rocks and trees all over, while in the fall, the North Fork is a tiny river meandering through a big floodplain. The sides of the cradle include the Whitefish Range to the west and the awesome peaks of the

7 Flathead River (South Fork)

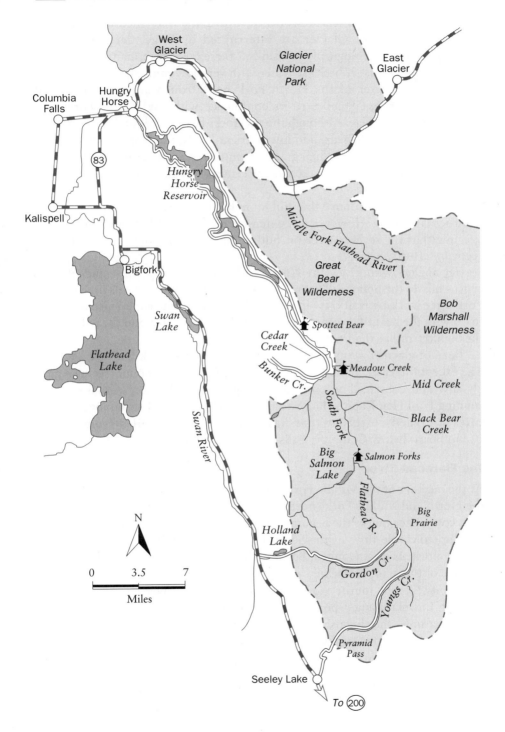

Livingston Range to the east. Mid-Stream in the North Fork marks the western boundary of Glacier National Park.

One of the unusual features of the North Fork watershed is that five of the drainages out of Glacier are interrupted by large, deep, fjord-type lakes. Referred to geologically as "sinks," these lakes trap many biologically important chemicals and release water with very low nutrient levels.

The first quarter of the North Fork hails from Canada. The United States portion runs 59 miles to its confluence with the Middle Fork near the Blankenship Bridge. Although the two forks have some similarities such as size, wilderness watersheds, and low nutrient levels, the North Fork drains a larger area, has a more gradual gradient, and faces more serious environmental threats. The environmental concerns center on logging and residential development.

Threats of a Canadian Mine still loom but may be at least ten years away from actual mining. However, any extensive mine in the Flathead River Drainage may have a severe effect on bull trout and westslope cutthroat trout recovery efforts.

Yet anglers who know the North Fork will think that this kind of creel census misses the point. Bill Schneider, who liked to cool his heels in the North Fork after working trail crew in Glacier Park, thinks the experience has more to do with the beautiful scenery, exceptional water quality, and the wildness of the country rather than with the fish numbers.

Born of glaciers, running free and wild, the North Fork has lore about it. The exceptional can, and often does, happen. An angler recounts seeing a grizzly sow and cubs feeding on camas along a bank. A rafter enthuses about running Fool Hen Rapids. In a stroke of unbelievable luck, a biologist recaptures a tagged cutthroat that has just traveled 70 miles from British Columbia to below Columbia Falls in under 24 hours.

The Flathead River

At the meeting of the Middle Fork and the North Fork at Blankenship Bridge, the North and Middle Forks normally carry about the same amount of water. This confluence marks the beginning of the main Flathead. In about ten miles, the unpredictable flow of the South Fork joins in. At times the South Fork hardly moistens its streambed, but at peak discharges it may more than double the size of the main Flathead.

For its 55-mile journey to Flathead Lake, the big river meanders broadly through an increasingly populated floodplain. With a gradient of less than 4 feet per mile, the sluggish water languishes in sloughs and backwaters and braids around islands. In the marshy country near the outlet, the river and lake become almost indistinguishable; the exact division depends on the season and on releases from Kerr Dam at the south end of the lake.

The last few miles of river not only make a thoroughfare for the migrating fish; they also hold some good numbers of nonmigrating fish year-round. Many

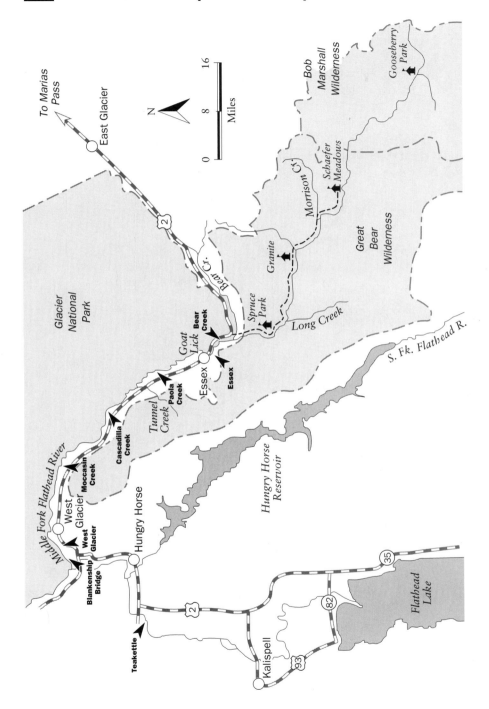

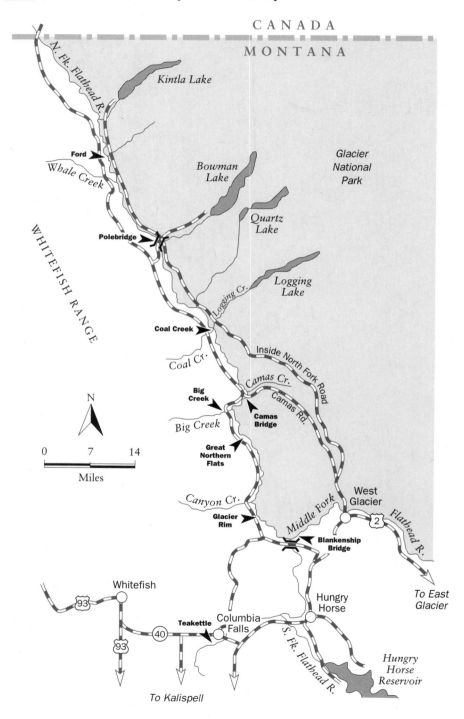

CANADA

MONTANA

N. Fk. Flathead R.

Kintla Lake

Glacier
National
Park

Ford

Whale Creek

Bowman
Lake

Quartz
Lake

WHITEFISH RANGE

Polebridge

Logging Cr.

Logging
Lake

Coal Creek

Inside North Fork Road

Coal Cr.

N

Camas Cr.

Big
Creek

Camas Rd.

Camas
Bridge

0   7   14

Big Creek

Great
Northern
Flats

Miles

Canyon Cr.

West
Glacier

Glacier
Rim

Middle Fork

2

Flathead R.

Blankenship
Bridge

Whitefish

93

To East
Glacier

Teakettle

Columbia
Falls

Hungry
Horse

40

S. Fk. Flathead R.

93

Hungry
Horse
Reservoir

To Kalispell

of the big cutthroats spend the winter in this section of the river. Because of this and the section's proximity to Kalispell, anglers pressure this stretch more than any other.

The main Flathead below the lake continues to hold its picturesque qualities but holds little promise for the trout-seeker. Poor spawning streams may be to blame for the dearth of trout. Most available streams either dry up due to diversions or silt over so badly that they become unsuitable for fishing.

The lower Flathead does have a few cutthroat, rainbow, and brown trout, but in such a large river their small numbers make them few and far between. The northern pike provides most of the piscatorial excitement, especially in the backwaters and below Dixon. Larry Petersen, a fisheries biologist, found he could tag a pike, release it, and return to the exact same place in the river weeks later to find the pike again. The northerns often weigh in at over thirty pounds.

The Northwest Power Planning Council hopes to restore populations of cutthroat and bull trout in the main Flathead to offset losses incurred by the construction and operation of hydroelectric dams. The council's plans call for enhanced habitat, improved fish passage, regulated water temperatures, and stocking with hatchery fish.

Strategies: On most other rivers, anglers can usually approach their favorite holes anytime during the season confident that fish will be there. This, however, is not so on the Flathead.

When those fish aren't migrating past a particular hole, that hole may well be empty of fish. Thus, knowing the fish, and when they do what, is helpful—even critical—to the Flathead angler.

The westslope cutthroat move out of the lake first. Before completion of Hungry Horse Dam, the cutthroat apparently waited until April. Now, fooled by the relatively warm releases from the reservoir, the cutthroat sense spring has sprung as early as February 9. By the time runoff has reached full tilt, cutthroat are spawning in the tributaries, some as far as 136 miles from the lake. Also, a number of cutthroat appear to winter in the lower 30 miles of the river due to the relatively warm 39 degree water coming from Hungry Horse Dam. They can provide some good winter catch-and-release fishing.

While the slow journey upstream takes several months, the trip back may be accomplished overnight. Graham thinks most come back to the lake while the full tide of runoff still swells the river. He has tagged fish to back up his theory.

Yet anglers report catching some big cutthroat even into August. Bill Schneider proudly remembers a beautiful 19-inch cutthroat he caught in a backwater pool late in the summer. Graham notes that the upper Middle and South Forks produce more large fish during the summer than the North Fork.

Fishing season on the Flathead traditionally opens in the latter part of May, when the river runs pell-mell with snowmelt and dirt. Once the water clears,

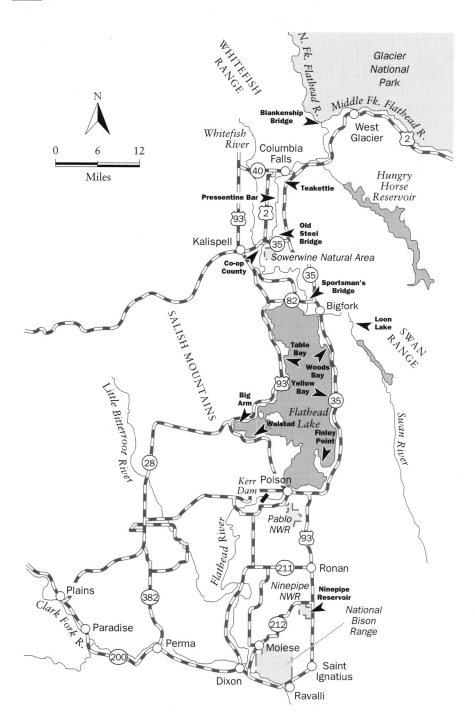

All three forks of the Flathead have sizeable populations of cutthroat trout, a species requiring high water quality.

hungry cutthroat will take most mayfly and stonefly attractor patterns. In addition, fishing a trailing nymph can be quite effective.

Fish biologists rate the cutthroat as the least predacious of the trout family. Oddly enough, the Flathead cutthroat share the river with the highly predacious bull trout and increasingly non-native lake trout. Lake trout appear to be bad for bull trout and bad for cutthroat. Sections of river separated by dams, including the South Fork and the Swan River, appear to be maintaining their bull and cutthroat trout populations, while sections undammed and still linked to Flathead Lake's lake trout population appear to be doing poorly.

An addition to the Flathead fishery is a run of lake whitefish in the fall. Lake whitefish generally do not spawn in rivers, but the Flathead population apparently has not read the textbook. They crowd into the river by the hundreds of thousands from the mouth of the Stillwater to Blankenship Bridge. These fish are the alter egos of their cousins, mountain whitefish. They range from 1.5 to 3 pounds and prove as tasty as they are hard fighting.

Lake whitefish show up in late September and stay into January, but October and early November are the most popular and productive time to fish for them. About 40,000 whitefish are caught each fall. "Sometimes you have to bring your own rock to stand on," says Jim Vashro at FWP. Anglers jostle shoulder to shoulder around the popular holes near Kalispell to vie for a bucketful of whitefish. Contact FWP in Kalispell for a free flier on how to prepare and cook these tasty fish.

The standard set-up is a green or chartreuse jig fished on the bottom in calm eddies. The jig has to be skipped on the bottom, as the fish will hit the instant the jig hits the bottom and will spit it out just as quickly.

Historical Note: *Until recently, the Flathead also produced a spectacular fall run of kokanee. Anglers lining the banks would snag more than 100,000 salmon, and another 100,000 fish would squeeze between the banks of McDonald Creek in Glacier National Park to spawn. Their dying throes attracted hundreds of bald eagles, which in turn attracted thousands of tourists who came to watch the drama. Currently there are no salmon runs and stocking of salmon has been discontinued indefinitely.*

TRIBUTARIES

All three forks of the Flathead derive their water not from one or two major tributaries, but from a myriad of small streams. An angler walking along the banks of these tiny streams would expect to find only pan-size fish. Imagine the surprise of seeing hefty 2-pound cutthroat and bull trout so big they may be mistaken for logs as they swim in water hardly deep enough to cover their backs.

Fish as far along in their spawning cycle as those found in the tributaries rarely feed until after spawning is completed.

Mortality rates for the spawning bulls may run as high as fifty percent. The exhausting run up the river, lack of food, predation, and the stress of spawning in tiny streams takes a heavy toll on the big fish. For this reason, FWP closes certain tributaries to fishing to protect the bulls from harassment. In addition, to protect cutthroat trout, the entire drainage is closed to the taking of any cutthroat trout, although catch-and-release fishing for cutthroat is still allowed. No taking or fishing for bull trout is allowed and is not likely to be allowed until the population recovers totally. Check current regulations closely before fishing.

Glacier Park feeds the North Fork through streams coming out of Kintla, Bowman, Quartz, and Logging Lakes. The fish in these streams are under the jurisdiction of the National Park Service, not FWP, but angling in the park is also closely regulated. Check park regulations before wetting a line.

The Whitefish and Stillwater Rivers combine and flow into the main Flathead not far upstream from Flathead Lake.

The Whitefish River has a lively population of northern pike. 8 or 10 miles down from Whitefish Lake, the gradient picks up and so does the trout fishing. Where streambank alterations haven't disturbed habitat, pools and riffles harbor cutthroat and some dandy 1.5- to 3-pound rainbow. But the last stretch of the river flattens out again, and fishing is often disappointing here unless the angler hankers after trash fish.

Going after a big one—as usual. The Flathead River system has fishing for all anglers.

Belying its name, the upper Stillwater River rolls out of the Whitefish Range on a steep gradient and slows down only after it hits the valley floor. Try the section around Stillwater Lake and down to the mouth of Logan Creek for rainbow, brookies, and cutthroat. Below this, the river becomes much too slow and heavily silted for trout; the challenge here is northern pike, some in the 20-pounds and up range. The last segment from U.S. Highway 93 to the Flathead provides a minor exception, offering a few pools and riffles that furnish acceptable trout habitat.

The **Swan River** empties into Flathead Lake right in the midst of the town of Bigfork, but it begins in some of the most rugged, wild, and strikingly beautiful country in Montana—the Mission Mountains Wilderness. Tumbling out of cold, pristine lakes such as High Park, Grey Wolf, and Crystal, the headwater streams drop rapidly until the Swan nears Montana Highway 83. Thereafter, it meanders with a riffle, pool, riffle pattern to Swan Lake.

Below the lake, the Swan River sprints 4 miles, then flattens out for a very slow 10 miles to the small impoundment near Bigfork. Below the dam, the Swan goes through one last frenzied rush—"the wild mile"—over a boulder-strewn streambed before calmly running into Flathead Lake.

Anglers catch a few rainbow and lake trout below the dam; some rainbow below Swan Lake; and cutthroat, rainbow, and brook trout above Swan Lake and in the tributaries.

The tributaries of the lower Flathead suffer badly from irrigation diversions. Of the possible streams, Larry Petersen, a fisheries biologist, singles out only the **Jocko River** for passable fishing. Petersen reports that a run of rainbow comes up the Jocko during high water. Anglers also find a smattering of cutthroat and browns. However, the Jocko River is almost entirely under the jurisdiction of the Flathead Indian Reservation and governed by the Salish and Kootenai Tribal Council. Fishing by non-tribal members is strictly regulated. A special reservation permit is required that can be purchased at some local sporting goods stores.

ACCESS

North Fork: To fish the North Fork, most anglers utilize the **North Fork Road**, which runs about 55 miles from the Canadian border to Columbia Falls. The Glacier Natural History Association publishes a map, *Three Forks of the Flathead*, which is invaluable for any Flathead River adventure.

The North Fork Road closely parallels the river, giving anglers considerable casual access, especially for the southern third of the river. Major points of access include **Blankenship Bridge, Big Creek Campground, Camas Bridge, Coal Creek, Polebridge,** and the **Ford Station.**

The North Fork can also be reached from Glacier National Park by two roads. One is the paved Camas Creek Road from Apgar to the **Camas Bridge,** where it joins with the North Fork Road. Aside from the Camas Bridge, this road gives no other access to the river.

The second road is a narrow, twisting dirt road that also departs from the Apgar area and forks at Polebridge to either Bowman or Kintla Lakes. From Logging Creek to Kintla Creek, this monster of a road stays close to the North Fork. Anglers who don't mind short hikes through timber can reach many otherwise inaccessible spots via this road but must count on very slow driving.

ACCESS

Middle Fork: Above Bear Creek, the Middle Fork flows through the Great Bear and Bob Marshall Wildernesses. To fish the upper Middle Fork, the angler faces an unusual choice—hike, ride a horse, or go by plane to the Schaefer Meadows airstrip. Those who do make the effort maintain that it is well worth the rewards. Fishing in a beautiful wilderness area is the peak experience of a lifetime for some, but reaching the river obviously requires more effort and planning than just pulling off the highway into a developed access area.

From Bear Creek down to the confluence with the North Fork, river and road stay close together. Several access points exist, including **Bear Creek, Essex, Paola, Cascadilla, Moccasin, West Glacier,** and **Blankenship** fishing access sites. Anglers need only cross the railroad tracks or negotiate some steep hillsides to reach the river.

ACCESS

South Fork: Like the Middle Fork, the South Fork has wilderness beginnings. Anglers hike or pack in from Seeley Lake or Holland Lake to the headwaters in the Bob Marshall Wilderness. Another route is to drive around Hungry Horse Reservoir to **Spotted Bear Ranger Station** or to **Bunker Creek,** and then hike along the river.

ACCESS

The main Flathead is accessible at the **Blankenship Bridge,** along a small park next to U.S. Highway 2, at **Teakettle** FAS and **Pressentine Bar** FAS, from the old **Steel Bridge,** and at **the mouth of the Stillwater.**

The lower Flathead flows through the Flathead Indian Reservation and has no formal, developed access sites. However, it can be reached right in **Polson,** at **Buffalo Bridge, Sloan Bridge,** and from **Highway 200** most of the way from Dixon to the confluence with the Clark Fork. Within the Flathead Indian Reservation, anglers must have a tribal recreational use permit. Inquire at local sporting goods stores.

For information about floating anywhere on the Flathead River system, and especially on the forks, read Hank Fischer's *Floater's Guide to Montana.* The North and Middle Forks contain stretches of highly technical and dangerous whitewater that should be avoided by all but experienced rafters. The Middle Fork boasts several reaches of class IV rapids, notably from Schaefer Meadows to Bear Creek and just above West Glacier. Float maps are available from the Flathead National Forest and the Glacier Natural History Association.

8 Gallatin River

Overview: The Gallatin drainage offers a diversity of trout fishing opportunities unmatched by Montana's other major rivers. The angler working the 40-mile canyon of the Gallatin River can choose among mountain stream riffles, boulder-dotted pocket water, surging runs, and deep pools. Below the canyon mouth, the Gallatin braids and spreads out to provide a selection of readily wadeable channels for the angler. The East Gallatin River represents a totally different fishing experience—a serpentine hay-meadow stream, lined with deeply undercut willow banks. Finally, the main Gallatin River, formed by the junction of the East and Upper Gallatin Rivers, hosts a full complement of steady runs, long pools, and gravelly riffles, along with an opportunity for solitude not often experienced on southwestern Montana's other major rivers.

> **Key species:** Rainbow trout, brown trout, cutthroat trout, and whitefish.
> **Use:** The section from the headwaters to Spanish Creek ranks 24 statewide, the section from Spanish Creek to the East Gallatin ranks 14 statewide, and the lower section to the mouth ranks 73 for fishing pressure. All of the floating pressure concentrates below the East Gallatin, because it is illegal to float it above that point.
> **Key flies and lures:** Flies—Girdle Bug, Sofa Pillow, Elk Hair Caddis, Humpies, Royal Trude, Royal Wulff, bead head Pheasant Tail, Al's Hopper, muddlers, and Woolly Buggers. Lures—Panther Martin, Rapala. Bait—night crawlers.

The fishing: The quality of trout fishing within these sections of the Gallatin drainage depends on the angler's ability to adapt his approach to differences in flows, habitat features, and fish populations. Armed with the proper techniques at the proper time and place, the angler may have the opportunity to see the true colors of the blue-ribbon Gallatin River.

The Gallatin River heads in the remote northwest corner of Yellowstone National Park and, after exiting the park, parallels U.S. Highway 191 for its northward journey through Gallatin Canyon. From the park boundary downstream for about 15 miles to the mouth of the West Fork, the Gallatin hosts a trout fishery of primarily pan-sized rainbow, although occasional browns and cutthroat are taken. Lack of deep holding areas and snowmelt-cold water temperatures are the major factors limiting trout numbers and growth rates, with most fish less than a foot long. Still, some of the biggest fish in the river lurk in this upper section below Yellowstone National Park.

8 Gallatin River

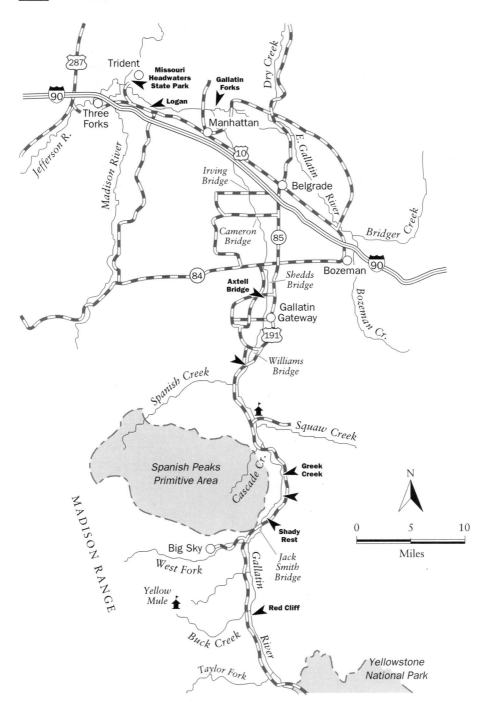

Whitefish thrive in the shallow riffles that characterize this stretch of the Gallatin, and the angler can enjoy good action on "whities" and feisty rainbow. This upper part of the Gallatin is a particularly good place for beginning fly fishers because of the open channel, generally manageable wading conditions, and the agreeable nature of whitefish and rainbow to take a fly.

Near the confluence with the West Fork, the rocky substrate of the Gallatin becomes peppered with numerous large boulders. The trout take advantage of the protection from the current and hold in the pockets behind the midstream rocks. Picking these pockets with either flies or lures is the most successful technique, especially when water temperatures have warmed enough to put fish on the feed. An occasional big rainbow can be taken here, particularly by anglers who work some of the less obvious or difficult-to-reach holding areas.

The waters of the West Fork boost both the flow and the trout population of the main river. For 22 miles below this largest tributary, the Gallatin surges through a series of powerful runs and swirling pools. Submerged boulders and large rapids give rise to some of Montana's best whitewater. The final 8 miles of the canyon below Squaw Creek lose the whitewater but retain a swift flow with good deep holding water.

Trout populations in the canyon section of the Gallatin are estimated at about 1,300 fish over 10 inches in length per mile of river. Most of the trout are rainbow, the majority less than 14 inches long. The shortage of big fish relates to cold water temperatures and relatively slow growth rates; it

The Gallatin River offers good fishing spiced with outstanding scenery and easy access.

Fast-moving water in the upper Gallatin River can make fishing a challenge.

takes about five years for most rainbows to reach a length of 14 inches in the rushing canyon waters. Nevertheless, rainbow and occasional browns in the 3- to 5-pound class are caught in the canyon each year, not to mention the "ones that get away" in the strong current.

The most productive section of the Gallatin runs from the mouth of the canyon to the bridge at Gallatin Gateway. Here the river tames to a series of riffles, runs, and pools; and undercut cottonwood banks replace the rocky, pine-dotted slopes of the canyon. A few fish over 2 pounds inhabit this stretch, with brown trout becoming common. Fish in the 10-pound class are reported almost every year.

Below Gallatin Gateway, the river spreads across the valley floor into a network of channels. Here the waters of the West Gallatin are coveted by more than trout anglers. Agriculture is king in the Gallatin Valley; and pumps, canals, and diversions start claiming their share of the flow for irrigation. Banks altered by bulldozers compound the problem of water withdrawals in some locations. Some sections in the river literally go dry each summer, and most of the remainder is dewatered enough to keep trout populations far below their potential.

The entire Gallatin, from its headwaters in Yellowstone National Park to its junction with the East Gallatin near Manhattan, is closed to float fishing, by order of the Montana Fish and Game Commission. This closure, designed to prevent conflict between floaters and bank anglers, has been generally well accepted because of good public access to the river throughout the canyon and because the stream is relatively narrow and thus can be fished effectively by a wading angler.

The East Gallatin River

The East Gallatin River flows in countless tight meanders over a course of about 20 air miles from Bozeman westward. Its smooth-flowing runs, sinuous channels, and often impenetrable willow banks bring to mind a miniature Beaverhead River—and the potential for lunker browns in the East Gallatin makes the comparison even more valid.

"The East Gallatin used to be kind of a sleeper around here, but it has pretty much been discovered," notes Dave Kumlien of the Montana Troutfitters shop in Bozeman. Don't overlook this river because of its small size. The river can be knee-deep for a long stretch, with seemingly little ability to hold decent fish. As a result, anglers won't take the time to work the river and discover those 10-foot deep undercut bends where the big fish hold.

Although the East produced many large trout (up to a recorded 17-pounder in the mid-1960s), the river went into a precipitous, fifteen-year tailspin with the opening of the Bozeman sewage treatment plant and resultant discharge of ammonia-laden effluent into the river. Since the late 1970s, however, the pollution problem has been substantially alleviated and trout populations have recovered tremendously.

The new problem on the East Gallatin is access; virtually the entire streambank is in private ownership, except at bridge crossings. You can access the river from a bridge on U.S. Highway 10 north of the railroad overpass on the outskirts of Bozeman. This allows anglers access from both banks. Floating the East Gallatin is possible, although the narrow channel; slow, winding flow; and occasional cross-stream barbed-wire fences must all be considered before launching.

The Main Stem of the Gallatin River

The East and Main Gallatin Rivers meet about 2 miles north of Manhattan, and the resulting main stem Gallatin is a marvelous hybrid. On its 10-mile journey to join the Madison and Jefferson, the Gallatin River passes through some of the wildest bottomland habitat remaining in southwestern Montana. Moose, otters, and nesting herons and cormorants join the normal complement of white-tailed deer, beaver, mink, and Canada geese as the river channels its way through cottonwood forests.

The abundance of wildlife is nearly matched by the abundance of trout. Biologists report that the Gallatin holds about 750 browns and rainbow over 11 inches long per mile. Most of the rainbows are less than 13 inches long, while the browns run quite a bit larger. A recent estimate puts the number of browns over 16 inches long at 80 per mile, and many of these fish weigh from 3 to10 pounds.

The main stem Gallatin is a large river, best fished by floating. The deep undercut banks provide holding water for big browns, while the riffles host rainbow. Water conditions are the key to success on this part of the Gallatin. Spring runoff puts the Gallatin out of shape in terms of both color and flow beginning in early May, and the water can remain cloudy for several months due to bank erosion and silty return flows from upstream irrigation. In midsummer, dewatering for irrigation can drastically reduce the flows in the main Gallatin, causing the river to warm and the fishing action to slow down. Fall is the most predictable time to find clear water and active fish on the main stem Gallatin, although the periods just before and just after spring runoff can be very good.

Strategies: The diversity of fishing techniques necessary for the Gallatin mirrors the diversity of the river system. The angler's choice of naturals or artificials, time of day, season, and type of water to fish all change in relation to the section of the river being fished.

The riffly uppermost section of the Gallatin is perhaps least demanding, as it is readily wadeable and shallow enough to ensure that fish will be accessible. One key here is fishing when the water is warm enough to get the trout active. In the well-shaded Gallatin Canyon, fish are most active from midday through early evening during the mid-summer period. The standard high-floating attractor patterns will work well for fly fishers, while any number of small spinning lures will also produce. Before you start casting, take some time to look for the smooth surface slicks or submerged rocks that mark holding water for the bigger fish.

The pocket water sections farther down the canyon call for quick, pinpoint casts, whether the tackle is spin or fly gear. The trout will be holding behind the rocks, watching for a potential meal in the slower current along the edge of their protected lie. Cast repeatedly, as the fish won't be readily spooked from these prime holding areas.

The powerful flows in the canyon from the West Fork of the Gallatin downstream are among the most challenging waters to fish. The runs harboring the best fish should be fished deep unless the fish are working the surface during an insect hatch. The successful fly fisher will generally have to cast a heavily weighted nymph upstream and allow it to bounce on the bottom. You'll need short line to keep control of the fly and to be able to detect a strike. Lure anglers should cast upstream, allowing time for spinner or spoon to drop near the bottom before beginning to retrieve. The retrieve should be just slightly faster than the current, to give the lure some action but not to raise it much off the bottom. Size 2 and 3 lures are recommended, as smaller sizes won't get down quickly enough. Bait fishermen will do best bouncing the bottom of the runs and pools with stonefly nymphs or worms, especially during high water.

Although Gallatin Canyon has a very good salmon fly hatch, it doesn't draw the crowds that descend upon the Madison and Big Hole Rivers during their hatches. This fortunate circumstance is in part due to the ban on float fishing on the Gallatin; despite their enthusiasm for salmon flies, most anglers don't relish the prospect of wading in Gallatin Canyon during high spring flows. A related factor is the frequently coincidental timing of muddy water and the emergence of salmon flies. The Taylor's Fork is an infamous sediment producer, and in most years it will color the Gallatin brown during at least part of the mid-June hatch.

Working the mid-day shadows in the scenic Gallatin Canyon.

Nevertheless, fishing can be good during the hatch, especially during low runoff years. The bushiest, highest-floating salmon fly patterns will work for fly fishers in the swift current. Work the banks, as they provide the best holding water for trout and the most likely spot for natural salmon flies to fall into the water.

Throughout the summer after the high-water period, Gallatin Canyon hosts good evening caddis hatches; along with sporadic may fly activity. Royal Wulffs, Royal Trudes, Elk Hair Caddis, and Humpies are all dependable patterns. Grasshopper patterns—or live grasshoppers for the bait anglers—can be very effective producers in any of the grassy bank areas of the canyon from late August through mid-September. Fall fishing in the canyon is primarily a nymph proposition for the fly fishers, while lures and bait will continue to be successful for the spin angler.

The section of the Gallatin just below the canyon mouth provides excellent nymph and spinner fishing just prior to high water. During the hatch, dry salmon fly patterns will bring up large fish if water conditions provide at least a foot or two of visibility. After high water, concentrate on the deeper runs with large, dark nymphs and on the banks with Muddlers, Woolly Buggers, or other streamers. Lures fished on the bottom of runs and under the cut banks will also produce. Evening caddis hatches, mid-day stoneflies, hoppers, and other terrestrials will provide some good dry fly action throughout the summer.

During the warmest periods of summer, work the riffles carefully. Dave Kumlien notes, "In the fast waters of the Gallatin, the bottom is very uneven. Good fish can hold in the depressions or behind the rocks—the biggest rainbow I've ever caught have come out of these pockets surrounded by water only 6 inches deep."

Sculpins and other small fish, along with caddis, mayflies, and some crane fly larvae, are the major food items for browns of the silty-bottomed East Gallatin. Streamers, rubber-legged nymphs, and spinning lures fished beneath the undercut willow banks will provide the best opportunities to move a big fish. Water clarity is a key on the East Gallatin, as irrigation returns can cloud the river well after runoff has finished. Bait fishermen concentrate on the deep, quiet pools and the back eddies where the river turns.

The main stem Gallatin provides the greatest range of habitats, including deep runs, riffles, undercut banks, and quiet banks. Here again, fishing to the deep, protected lies offers the best chance of success. Dry flies are most effective during late summer evenings when the water is clear but not too warm. Fall streamer or lure fishing can be excellent, offering the chance to catch resident fish and some of the huge browns moving up from the Missouri River. A weighted fly line is a good idea for getting the streamer deep, and the float fishing angler would be advised to stop and carefully work the 3- to 5-foot deep runs.

TRIBUTARIES

Squaw Creek and the **West Fork of the Gallatin** are the largest tributaries in Gallatin Canyon. Both offer good fishing for trout up to 1 foot long. Many other swift canyon streams hold pan-sized rainbow, and brook trout are well established in the small meadow streams.

The best stream fisheries in the Gallatin Valley below the canyon are the spring creeks which run through fertile agricultural lands. These waters, however, are entirely private and not available to the visiting angler.

ACCESS

Access to the Gallatin River is excellent, with numerous pullouts and Forest Service campgrounds throughout **Gallatin Canyon**. Below the canyon, access is provided by a series of seven county bridges, beginning with **Williams Bridge** a few miles below the canyon and ending with the highway bridge east of Manhattan. A good local road map is the best guide for finding these bridges, which provide the only public access to the lower part of the Gallatin.

The East Gallatin is also surrounded by private land, with county bridges providing access. These access sites are located near Bozeman, north of Belgrade, and northeast of Manhattan.

The main stem Gallatin is accessible from bridges at its sources **north of Manhattan** and at **Logan,** 5 miles downstream. **Missouri Headwaters State Park,** just north of Three Forks, provides the final access point. The floating angler can take good advantage of the access set up on the main stem Gallatin River and plan a whole day 10-mile float or a half-day 5-mile float at either the upper or lower end. For more information on floating the Gallatin, pick up a copy of *Montana Afloat #11, the Gallatin River.*

9 Jefferson River

Overview: Much of the Jefferson River remains as wild and remote as the day Lewis and Clark first encountered it in 1804. Cottonwood bottoms, thick shrub fields, and expansive hay meadows isolated the river from civilization along much of its length. The abundant wildlife and waterfowl that use the river and its banks, only add to the Jefferson's appeal.

The Jefferson flows for about 70 miles northeast from its origin near Twin Bridges to its confluence with the Madison and Gallatin rivers at the headwaters of the Missouri River outside of Three Forks. A broad, multichanneled river, the Jefferson has a gentle gradient and deep water.

> **Key species:** Rainbow trout, brown trout, cutthroat trout, and whitefish.
> **Use:** The Jefferson ranks 52 statewide for angling pressure.
> **Key flies and lures:** Flies—bead-head Girdle Bugs, Bitch Creek Nymphs, Marabou Muddlers, Yuk-Bugs, Marabou Streamers, Royal

The Jefferson River has a few lunker browns, especially in the backwaters.

Wullfs, Royal Trudes, and Humpies. (A bushy dry fly pattern often brings trout up for some of the best dry fly fishing on the Jefferson, but a medium-sized nymph size 6 to 10 is apt to be the best producer.) Lures—heavier Panther Martins and Mepps. Bait—worms, hoppers, and cheese balls.

The fishing: The broad, beautiful Jefferson Valley provides the backdrop for the upper half of the river. The Tobacco Root Mountains tower over the river both to the east and to the south, while the gentle Highland Range dominates the western scene.

Autumn colors are particularly spectacular along the Jefferson during the first weeks of October. After flowing through a picturesque rock-walled canyon east of Cardwell, the Jefferson opens into another broad valley north of Three Forks. Ringed by a series of small mountain ranges, this scenic valley typifies the arid southwestern Montana region.

For the angler, the big, lumbering "Jeff" provides a peaceful escape and a change of pace from the fast-paced float-fishing on the Beaverhead, Madison, and other southwestern Montana rivers. However, because the Jefferson is large, and more private than most rivers, it takes more time and patience to master.

Along the Jefferson, the brush banks and deep runs and pools provide good fish habitat and good fishing opportunities. Brown trout are the dominant trout species, though an occasional rainbow is taken, particularly on the upper end of the river. Thanks to catch-and-release regulations and a habitat improvement effort by the Montana Department of Fish, Wildlife and Parks (FWP), the rainbow population is on the upswing and gaining toe holds throughout the river. While the Jefferson is known for its trophy 5- to 9-pound browns, these are not common. More characteristically, the river produces trout in the 10- to 15-inch range, averaging about a pound.

A variety of factors, including high water temperature, low flows, and altered streambanks, keep trout populations well below their potential. Consequently, populations of trout on the Jefferson are substantially lower than on other rivers in the area.

While all of the Jefferson has good fishing potential, the river is naturally divided into three distinct sections, each providing different fishing conditions: the upper river, between Twin Bridges and Cardwell; the canyon section; and the lower river, downstream from Sappington Bridge.

The **upper Jefferson** has the steadiest current, though only in high water would the word "swift" apply. Deep pools and riffles intermixed with some long, sluggish runs characterize this section of river. The river is braided in many places, especially between Waterloo and Whitehall, where there are also a lot of sloughs and backwater areas. Habitat and water conditions on the upper river are the best on the Jefferson—trout in this section average better than 14 inches. Trout populations are also best in the upper river where rainbow comprise about 15 percent of the population. This is the most popular area of the Jefferson for guided float-fishing trips.

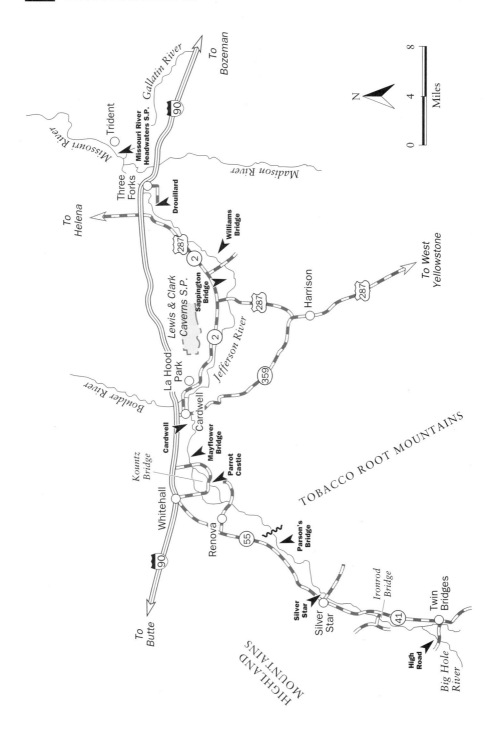

In the canyon east of Cardwell, the Jefferson is mostly a single channel river running deep and slow. Early afternoon shade in the summer helps cool the water and provide some good evening fishing. A paved road and railroad tracks on both sides of the river detract somewhat from the aesthetics and solitude of this area. The canyon has the poorest trout population on the river, but an occasional lunker is still taken from these waters—particularly by bait anglers working some of the deep holes by the railroad tracks.

Downstream from the canyon, the Jefferson is mostly a single channel, pebble-bottom river lined with cottonwoods and hay meadows. Between Three Forks and the Missouri Headwaters State Park, the river braids extensively. This is the wildest reach of the Jefferson, where moose are sometimes seen, and good trout habitat is widespread.

The **lower stretch of the Jefferson** ranks as intermediate in fishing quality. Low water flows and warm water temperatures keep the trout population below its potential, but fishing can be good for 11- to 14-inch browns.

Fishing on the Jefferson fluctuates widely and is notoriously unpredictable. Fish move around depending on season, time of day, weather, and water conditions. Timing is therefore all important. "Wait for a cloudy day and clear water with at least 2 feet of visibility," says Scott Waldie, owner of Four Rivers Fishing Company in Twin Bridges, "and you'll have a long wait for an evening of fishing that will rival it." This combination can result in some 50-fish days for the catch-and-release angler, Waldie adds.

Unfortunately, clear water is often a scarce commodity. High water from spring runoff (mid-May into June) brings the first of the muddy water conditions but lasts only a short time. The lower Beaverhead's murky waters contribute silt to the upper river throughout the summer. Irrigation return flows on the Jefferson compound the problem, and the summer rainstorms can muddy the river overnight by further eroding unstable banks.

Despite these problems, most of the Jefferson does have fairly clear water during the summer and fall. Late June and July generally offer good fishing conditions. During the hot summer weather of August, the Jefferson is great for lazy recreational float trips but is not noted for good fishing. However, the fish do concentrate in riffles on hot, sunny days; and fishing can be quite good, although you may encounter lots of whitefish.

Severe dewatering becomes the major problem on the Jefferson later in the summer. During peak irrigation season, between mid-July and mid-September, the river's flow may drop to less than half of the level that fisheries biologists believe is necessary to support optimal trout populations. The drought of 1987-89 hit the Jefferson particularly hard, reducing some reaches of the river to a trickle between stagnant pools. Juvenile trout are most affected by such dewatering, and the numbers of big fish may not decline until several years after the drought.

As a result of low flows, water temperatures rise dramatically. In one area of the lower river, water temperature has been measured at 74 degrees Fahrenheit;

Typical brown trout water in the Lower Jefferson River.

ideal for swimming but not good for trout. Warm water reduces growth rates and trout activity. As a result, cooler periods of early mornings and evenings are the best bet for fishing.

In the fall the Jefferson regains its character, and the big browns begin their spawning runs. The fish move into shallower runs and riffles, where they are more easily accessible. This provides some of the best fishing the Jefferson has to offer.

Guide Tony Schoonen thinks the Jefferson "is underrated. And I'd like to see it stay that way. Unlike the Big Hole, you can always catch some fish here."

Strategies: Trout on the Jefferson River are not dainty eaters. Crayfish are abundant on the Jeff; sculpins and small fish comprise a majority of the trout's diet. Consequently, the angler must generally use flies and lures that imitate small fish

The Jefferson does not have the variety and abundance of aquatic insects found on other southwestern Montana rivers. Among the aquatic insects, caddisflies are available throughout the summer. Large stoneflies, once abundant on the upper river, have been virtually eliminated from the Jefferson over the past twenty years due to siltation of the river bottom.

Grasshoppers provide a source of food for trout in areas near hay meadows in the fall, and a variety of small terrestrial insects supplement the trout diet during the summer. Imitations of these insects offer anglers opportunities for surface action.

Accurate casting to the best trout habitat is one key to success on the Jefferson. Good trout habitat lies under the undercut or brushy banks and also near the riprapped banks. In the spring and fall, Schoonen also likes to work the mouths of sloughs where trout congregate to eat the abundant food.

"Areas with clean, rocky bottoms where the sediment has been washed away are particularly good," according to Al Troth, nationally recognized fly tier and Dillon area outfitter. "Avoid the slow, muddy bottom waters; they are generally unproductive."

"During the summer, work streamers or Yuk bugs (a large block rubber-legged concoction) along the deep banks and dikes," says Waldie, "but in fall work the shallow water and riffles."

Wading can be difficult on the Jefferson due to steep, brushy banks and deep water. Mid- to late summer provides the best wading during low water. Rarely is the best fishing water found near access points, so be prepared to walk a long way to reach good areas.

Spin-fishing is popular and effective on the Jefferson before warm temperatures clog the bottom with moss. Drawdowns of the river have created warmers water temperatures and a serious moss problem. Lure fishing is almost impossible in late July and August. The broad, deep water allows each cast to cover a lot of water. Cast to the banks and let the lure sink before retrieving it. Heavier Panther Martins and Mepps that will get down quickly are standards on the Jefferson, but most lures and spinners are likely to work if cast to the right spots and presented properly.

Schoonen, who caught a 7.5-pound brown on the "Jeff", observes that a lot of people think the bigger the fly, the bigger the fish. "No way," declares Schoonen. "Those folks just do a lot of hard casting and a lot of cussin'."

Troth backs him up with documentation from the fishing diary he keeps. "In one season, my clients caught and released fifty-eight trout over 4 pounds; fifty-five of these were caught on 10- to 14-sized flies." Troth goes on to point out that smaller flies catch fish more consistently because there are more small life forms in a river than large ones; small flies can be fished more naturally in low water; and "there is less of a fraud to be suspicious of." He also finds fishing a dropper fly to be very effective at times.

The fly fisher will generally do best using weighted streamers or wet flies that imitate the sculpins and small fish on which Jefferson brown trout feed. Girdle bugs, Bitch Creeks, Yuk-bugs, and black or white Marabou Muddlers are commonly and effectively used. A heavy leader facilitates retrieval of flies from the brushy banks. "Large streamers and Marabous tend to catch the larger fish not the smaller fish because small fish numbers are down," notes Tony Schoonen.

In the mornings and evenings, Royal Wulffs, Royal Trudes, and Humpies can be effective throughout the summer. These flies are suggestive of the beetles, bees, flies, and ants that fall into the water along the banks. Late in the summer, grasshopper and caddis patterns bring the trout to the surface.

On hot, sunny days when the fish are concentrated in riffles, the fly fisher can find surprisingly good action. A bushy dry fly pattern often brings trout

Much of the Jefferson is relatively flat water, broken by only a few riffles.

up for some of the best dry fly fishing on the Jefferson, but a medium-sized nymph (size 6 to 10) is apt to be the best producer.

Floating provides the best access to good water, if you have the time and equipment. While it's possible to cover a lot of river floating, the slow Jefferson current generally requires a minimum of four to six hours even for a trip of relatively short mileage. More often, a float trip on the Jefferson is a full day's undertaking, requiring frequent stretches of serious rowing to move through slow, unproductive water. Strong headwinds can slow progress to almost a standstill, so it's wise to plan plenty of extra time for a trip to avoid being caught on the river after dark.

Traditionally, the Jefferson has been a bait angler's river. The long, slow, deep pools are well suited to dangling a line on a peaceful summer evening. Bridges on the Jefferson are conveniently located near the deep holes well suited to the casual bait angler. Bouncing bait off the bottoms of riffles and into the heads of deep pools is also a successful technique for the Jefferson, however.

TRIBUTARIES

The Jefferson River has only a few noteworthy tributaries, although there are numerous lakes and creeks containing fish throughout its mountainous head-waters. In its upper reaches, **Hells Canyon Creek** provides good fishing for an abundance of small rainbow trout. The lower five miles of the creek are in a canyon with rattlesnakes and rugged terrain, but a Forest Service road joins the creek a few miles upstream. Rainbow trout from Hells Canyon Creek move

97

into the Jefferson and contribute to the substantially higher percentage of rainbow on the upper Jefferson as compared to the lower river.

The **Boulder River** north of Cardwell was once a prime fishing stream, but years of abuse have diminished its quality drastically. Past and present mining activities have contributed excessive levels of heavy metals to the lower half of the river. The metals, still found in the riverbed substrate, are blamed for eliminating the willow bank cover in some areas, thus reducing trout habitat. Stream alteration and streambank grazing contribute to siltation problems, while excessive irrigation withdrawals dry up the stream annually. The result is poor fishing in the lower Boulder River. The uppermost 20 miles of the Boulder, however, with more difficult access and less habitat degradation, still produce a good population of small brook trout. The lower end of the Boulder is closed to fishing at the end of September (check current fishing regulations for exact date) to protect a vulnerable population of spawning brown trout.

The **South Boulder River** flows from high in the Tobacco Root Mountains to its confluence with the Jefferson east of Cardwell. The lower end is bordered by private land, but the upper stretches are on public forest land. Access is by a good gravel road that follows the stream. Fishing is good for small rainbow and brook trout, though an occasional 15- to 16-inch brown is taken from the lower reaches.

Willow Creek flows from Harrison Reservoir in the Tobacco Root Mountains to its confluence with the Jefferson near the town of Willow Creek.

Fishing the head end of large pools common on the Jefferson often brings good results.

Despite low flow releases from the Harrison Reservoir during the winter, Willow Creek supports a healthy population of rainbow and brown trout. The upper end is far better than the lower stretch but is surrounded by private land, so ask for access permission. The middle section flows through a canyon reported to be a haven for rattlesnakes—a major deterrent for many anglers—but fishing can be very good for those willing to hike in. Willow Creek has become a popular fly fishing spot over the past several years due to its proximity to Bozeman.

ACCESS

Although surrounded by private land, the Jefferson River nonetheless has good fishing access. Bank anglers may have to walk to reach the best water, but boat anglers have numerous choices for their floating.

The only access to the uppermost reaches of the Jefferson is by way of the **Beaverhead** or **Big Hole** Rivers in Twin Bridges. Either place provides a good starting point for floaters but only difficult access for bank anglers.

Downstream between Twin Bridges and Silver Star, you'll find both boat and bank access on the Hells Canyon road north of the Ironrod Bridge. This is a popular fishing area, especially for whitefish in the winter. Twin Bridges to Ironrod Bridge is a good four-hour float, but many people take out at Hells Canyon to cut a few miles off the downstream end.

County bridges cross the Jefferson at **Silver Star** and about 6 miles up the road near **Waterloo**. At the **Parsons Bridge** on the road to Waterloo, a major water diversion requires portaging. Between these two bridges it's a long, slow float, providing plenty of solitude.

An FWP fishing access site is available downstream at **Parrot Castle**. This spot does not provide boat access, however, unless you are willing to carry your boat across a slough and several hundred yards to the river. Boat anglers interested in access to this section of river can use a small section of Bureau of Land Management (BLM) land abutting the river on the east side near the remains of the Parrot Castle smelter. Check the maps to be sure you're not trespassing.

Southeast of Whitehall, **Kountz Bridge** and **Mayflower Bridge** both provide boat and some foot access. Only 3 river miles separate these bridges.

Another FWP fishing access site is maintained **outside of Cardwell**. Downstream at **LaHood** is the last official access to the Jefferson before the river enters Jefferson Canyon. Throughout the canyon, there is walk-in access across the railroad tracks.

Outside the canyon are several access sites before the Jefferson ends at the Missouri Headwaters State Park. **Sappington Bridge, Williams Bridge, Willow Creek Bridge, Drouillard,** and the **Old Town Bridge** east of Three Forks provide good access; though not all have easy boat access.

Access is limited to float-fishing between Three Forks and the Missouri Headwaters State Park. This stretch of river is braided and excessively brushy, making wading difficult. A river map and additional information for floaters can be found in the pamphlet, *Montana Afloat #10, the Jefferson River.*

10 Kootenai River

Overview: Half of Montana's 99-mile share of the Kootenai River was flooded by Libby Dam. So what remains of interest to anglers? With the recent combination of a new discharging system from Libby Dam, spawning closures, and slot limits, the Kootenai is fast becoming one of the finest tailwaters in the west.

> **Key species:** Kamloops rainbow trout, westslope cutthroat trout, kokanee, and whitefish.
>
> **Use:** The Kootenai below Libby Dam ranks 27th statewide for angling pressure.
>
> **Key flies and lures:** Flies—Royal Wulffs, PMD Sparkle Dun, Parachute Adams, CDC Emergers, Tan and Black X-Caddis, Caddis Pupa, Bead-Head Soft Hackle Hare's Ear, Bead-Head Prince Nymph, Olive Woolly Bugger, and Olive Sculpin Streamer (for the big ones). Lures—Thomas Cyclones, silver Mepps and Panther Martins Bait—worms, grubs, and maggots.

The fishing: Because the river just clips the northwestern corner of the state, most Montanans never see the Kootenai. Kalispell anglers who were accustomed to catching 8-inch cutthroat in the streams around their area, have discovered that they can drive the 100 miles to the Kootenai and be astonished by the big rainbow.

The average creeled rainbow—usually in excellent condition—measure between 12-14 inches. And anglers catch fish from the Kootenai at about the

Although not highly touted, the Kootenai River produces large trout at a rate equal to other famous Montana rivers.

10 Kootenai River

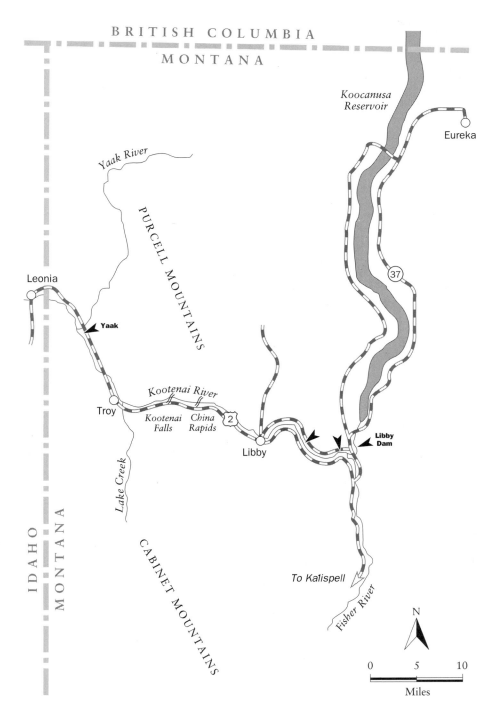

same rate as from other more highly touted blue-ribbon streams of Montana. "In my mind, it's clearly the best big-river trout fishery in northwestern Montana," concludes FWP director Pat Graham.

This is no dainty, intimate trout stream. Anglers do not wade back and forth across the Kootenai as they do the Big Hole. The Kootenai's annual flow exceeds that of even the Flathead or the Yellowstone. A visit to the rim of Kootenai Falls provides dramatic proof of the river's immense power.

The river rises in a long, broad Canadian valley, fills Koocanusa Reservoir behind Libby Dam, then flows past the communities of Libby and Troy to join with the Yaak River before exiting the state bound for the Columbia.

In the 49 miles of river from the dam to the state line, four distinct segments of water stand out. Most reminiscent of the lost, inundated river beneath Koocanusa Reservoir, the first segment, from Libby Dam to the town of Libby, features some big bends, islands, gravel bars, and a clear progression of riffles and pools.

Just downstream from Libby begins the section known locally as "the rocks." Many boulders imbedded in the cobble streambed resist the powerful current of the river's westwardly flow. Near the lower end of this section, the turbulent water pours through China Rapids, a challenging hazard to floaters.

At Kootenai Falls, the river cuts through the bedrock of the Purcell Range. Fault lines in the bedrock make a spectacular stair-step series of falls. Below, the river races through a tortuous, confined canyon, then subsides into a deep gorge.

The Kootenai yields a lot of rainbows, big and small. RUSS SCHNEIDER PHOTO

A walk across the suspension bridge near Kootenai Falls gives a full impression of this river's size and strength.

The last Montana segment of the river flows placidly through a heavily timbered valley to the state line. After the Yaak River adds its volume to the already ponderous river, the Kootenai meanders more in its last five miles; riffles, gravel bars, and islands become few and far between. Long, deep runs merge into pools. At the Idaho border, the Kootenai flows just 1,820 feet above sea level, Montana's lowest elevation.

Tim Linehan, a celebrated guide for the Kootenai River Guide Service, points out that the "Libby Dam has had a profound effect on the river." He and others lobbied hard to lessen the effect on the river. Libby Dam is now operated based on a computer model called the Integrated Rule Curves. This change has benefited the Kootenai River fishery tremendously. Linehan said, "Gone are the days of severe fluctuations. Discharges and flows are kept steady for weeks at a time. Any reductions in flow are gradual throughout the summer and into the fall and are designed to give insects a chance to move to the new wetted edge." Average July flows range around 15,000 cubic feet per second (cfs). This number drops to 12,000 cfs in August, and to 10,000 by fall.

Always noted for its large rainbow, the Kootenai has, in recent years, rewarded anglers with many 2- to 5-pound trout. Lunkers up to 18 pounds have shocked an occasional lucky angler, and even bigger fish have found their way into the record books. The Kootenai garnered statewide attention by producing rainbows weighing 26 and 29 pounds, shattering the previous state record of 21 pounds, but then in 1997

Kootenai River rainbows run consistently larger than those from other northwestern Montana streams.

below the dam, Jack Housel caught a Kamloops rainbow trout weighing 33 pounds 1 ounce for the both world record and state record. The previous world record was 31.5 pounds out of Lake Michigan.

These record-breaking fish were the end result of good water temperatures and a "chum line" of dead and dying kokanee churned out by the turbines at Libby Dam. Although an impressive number of big rainbow have shown up in the Kootenai, FWP biologists recommend catch-and-release on everything except trophies and pan-sized trout.

Although rainbow reign supreme, Tim Linehan's clients often catch cutthroats in the 15-20 inch range. While the rainbow and cutthroat have fared fairly well, Montana's only known white sturgeon population seems to have had greater trouble adapting to the new conditions imposed by the dam. This giant, prehistoric fish once swam in sizeable numbers up the Kootenai to the deep gorge below Kootenai Falls. Biologists assume the sturgeon spawned there, but efforts to learn more about the mysterious fish have so far turned up little information except that very few sturgeon still return. Graham surmises that the new flow fluctuations may confound the sturgeon.

Although rainbow reign supreme as the most desired game fish, others deserve mention. A few Kokanee make it through the turbines alive. Cutthroat trout occasionally drop from the reservoir and move downriver in search of other impoundments. The cutthroats comprise an increasing percentage of the catch. Much more numerous, whitefish have rebounded in great numbers since 1975, to the concern of local trout fanciers who fear the whitefish may be competing heavily with the rainbow. Before the dam, local anglers caught many whitefish through the winter ice, but the river no longer ices over, leaving the whitefish population unchecked.

Already chopped in half by the Libby Dam, the free-flowing Kootenai might be affected by future decisions involving the National Marine Fisheries Service's salmon recovery plan which could lead to drawdowns.

Strategies: This is rainbow country with few brown trout. Don't waste time looking for undercut banks. The rocks and the riffle pools harbor the rainbow.

The river from the Libby Dam to Libby and from below Kootenai Falls to the old Troy Bridge has some very fine fishing holes. Distinguish the productive holes from the unproductive by looking at the stream bottom, according to Pat Graham. The big rainbow avoid sandy bottoms or flat bedrock. They seek broken backgrounds like cobble and gravel or, especially in the Kootenai, the cover of macrophytes (or, as it's called locally, "moss").

Guide Tim Linehan recommends fishing with a dropper. He said, "Most anglers forget that before a hatch actually starts, the nymphs are very active in the water column. A size 14 or 12 Royal Wulff or Trude with a more imitative dropper chosen specifically for the immediate hatch is hard to beat on the Kootenai." In July, he also recommends a PMD Emerger or a Pheasant Tail Nymph, as dropper flies are extremely effective. In general, Bead-Head nymphs are terrific on the Kootenai. The extra weight helps get the nymphs down, especially with the fast current of the Kootenai.

Later in the summer, Hoppers work well, contrary to some rumor. Linehan reports that hopper fishing in 1997 was spectacular and giving the fly action with short one-inch "hops" was often the key to a strike. But remember, he cautions, "to let it ride drag-free for several feet after giving it action."

Anglers who prefer bait generally gravitate to the pools. Nightcrawlers are the most popular enticement. Graham believes lures work well in the upper reaches of the river, where less turbulence favors hardware. Besides, the new world record trout came on a cheap silver lure. Thomas Cyclone tops the list of favorites.

"Fly fishermen do well," explains Graham, "especially during hatches of small mayflies in spring and caddis flies in the late summer." The most successful fly anglers float the "rocks" section and cast toward the banks, because hatches usually begin there.

Whatever the angler chooses to fool the fish, the most favorable conditions for fishing come when the dam releases lower flows. Graham found that fishing success was fully 50 percent higher when the flow ran less than 10,000 cfs. Tim Linehan recommends fishing from a drift boat even during high flows. He has had some of his best days on the river with flows in the 20,000 cfs range. Local anglers know simply by watching rocks in the river when the water is down, but for the inexperienced, the Army Corps of Engineers has a phone number listed under "U.S. Government" for flow information, or you can easily access current flows for western Montana on the internet. During the summer, the Corps has an informal policy of reducing the flow of the water for weekend fishing when feasible.

Special regulations designed to protect spawning rainbow may prohibit spring fishing in the Kootenai just below the dam until the opening of the general season. Check with a local sporting goods dealer or FWP to be sure.

By mid-May, turbidity from the Fisher River may slow fishing down until early June. From then on the water has excellent clarity, and fishing can be good at any time the river is low. Graham notes that the few anglers who are still on the river in the fall have very high catch rates.

TRIBUTARIES

Anglers looking for a change of pace from the big river may wish to try some of the feeder creeks or the **Yaak River**. Of the streams flowing onto the Kootenai River, Pat Graham picks a trio of especially appealing creeks to investigate.

O'Brien, Callahan, and Lake Creeks all join the river near Troy. **O'Brien Creek** has good numbers of brookies and some spawning rainbow in the spring, but may have special regulations and closures around the mouth. Steep **Callahan Creek** proves difficult to fish, but it supports some good-sized natives and rainbow plus occasional bull trout. **Lake Creek** proves popular due to its nice rainbow, cutthroat, and pan-sized brookies.

The **Yaak River** and its forks harbor multitudes of rainbow and cutthroat. Above the Yaak Falls, anglers can easily see their quarry in the clear, slow water. A parallel road for most of the length of the upper river provides good access.

The steep, confined canyon below the falls propels the water far faster than the lazy stretches above. "You have to be a mountain goat to fish it," say some locals. The only heavy fishing pressure on the Yaak comes at its mouth by the campground.

Anglers should also give the **Fisher River** a try. Although not as good of fishing as it once was, it still offers a pleasant break from the big and popular Kootenai. Access is good from its mouth below Libby dam south to U.S. Highway 2.

The larger tributary streams of Lake Koocanusa have been planted with fish by FWP in hopes of establishing spawning runs up these streams. The success of these ventures swings on the ability and willingness of the trout to cross mud flats and steep banks created by the huge drawdowns of the reservoir.

ACCESS

With a few hazardous exceptions, the Kootenai presents little difficulty to the floating angler. China Rapids should not be attempted by anyone without prior experience in whitewater and the foresight to study the water first before attempting it. This holds true especially during high flows.

Kootenai Falls stands as an absolute barrier to floaters. A dummy raft used in the movie *The River Wild* recirculated in the falls for almost two days. If the first fall didn't kill, the tumble into the maelstrom below would have.

The standing waves where the Yaak pushes into the Kootenai might pose an upsetting problem to those with little freeboard or navigational skills. Otherwise, the river runs nearly flat and hazard free.

However, you can easily gain casual access to the section from Libby Dam to Kootenai Falls from the parallel highways. Below the falls, access is through private land, except near Troy and at the Yaak River Bridge. The road access at the state line has been chained on occasion, so check locally before anticipating access here.

11 Madison River

Overview: The Madison is, in many people's opinion, Montana's river of superlatives, with a list including highest trout density, most consistent action, best dry fly fishing, and the most spectacular scenery. Not surprisingly, this southwestern Montana jewel is also the second most heavily used river fishery in the state, growing more popular annually.

> **Key species:** Rainbow trout, brown trout, Yellowstone cutthroat trout, whitefish, and Arctic grayling.
>
> **Use:** The section from Hebgen Dam to Ennis Lake ranks 4th statewide and only the Missouri River below Holter Dam receives more river fishing pressure. From Ennis Lake down to the mouth it ranks 18th statewide for angling pressure. The Upper section gets the least pressure but is still heavily used by Montana standards, ranking 35th statewide.
>
> **Key flies and lures:** Flies—Bitch Creek Nymphs, Girdle Bugs, Yuk Bugs, Parachute Adams, bead-head Pheasant Tail, Sofa Pillow, Bird's Stonefly, Elk Hair Caddis, Royal Wulffs, hoppers, Woolly Buggers, and Marabou Streamers. Lures—Rooster Tail Spinners; gold, silver and black lures; and black Daredevles. Bait—hoppers and worms. Be sure to check current regulations on bait restrictions.

The fishing: The Madison River heads at the junction of the Firehole and Gibbon Rivers in Yellowstone National Park. (This book covers the park section of the river in the Yellowstone Park chapter.) From here, it flows for over 100 miles to its confluence with the Jefferson and Gallatin Rivers at Missouri Headwaters State Park near Three Forks. The Montana section of the Madison begins just inside the park boundary. After a few meandering miles, the river collects in Hebgen Lake, a sprawling reservoir created by a Montana Power Company dam built in 1916. Only 2 miles downstream from the Hebgen spillway, the Madison is again confined. Quake Lake, a striking testimony to the continued geologic unrest of the Yellowstone Plateau, was formed on an August night in 1959, when a major earthquake shook loose a mountainside of rock across the river. This natural dam has since been civilized, courtesy of the Corps of Engineers, and is now operated for flood control.

Just below Quake Lake, the Madison turns from its westward course and begins a 50-mile run due north to Ennis Lake. The upper Madison, as this section is termed, flows between willow-lined banks, bordered on either side

11 Madison River

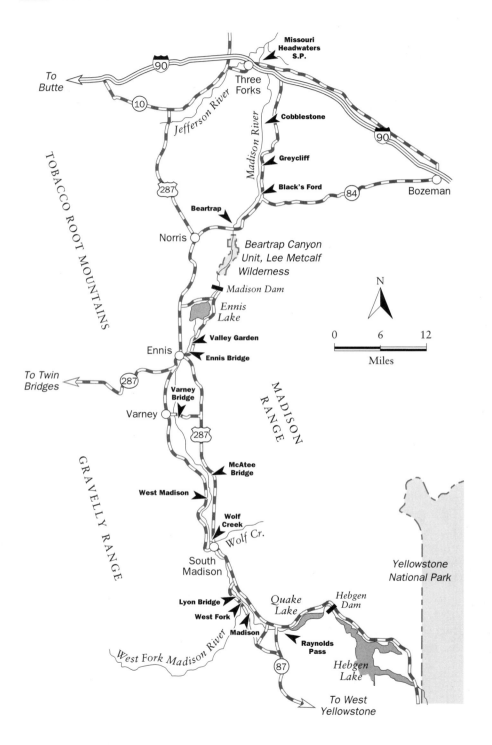

by miles-wide grassy "benches" so flat that many tourists think they were leveled by man. Above the benches to the west rise the jagged 10,000-foot peaks of the Madison Range; to the east are the timbered slopes of the Gravelly Range. In *The Living River,* angler supreme Charles Brooks aptly describes the upper Madison as "one of the loveliest river valleys anywhere."

The flow characteristics of the upper Madison are almost as distinctive as the scenery. Through nearly its entire course, the river is broad, rapid, and shallow, a veritable "fifty-mile riffle," as it has so often been described. Gravel and cobbles compose the substrate, and occasional boulders rise above the water surface. The upper Madison is primarily a single channel from Quake Lake down to Varney Bridge, but between the bridge and Ennis Lake, the river braids freely, undercutting banks and separating scores of cottonwood-dotted islands. Riffles still dominate the flow in this "channels" section of the river.

Three miles north of the town of Ennis, the upper Madison empties into Ennis Lake, the product of another Montana Power Company dam. Ennis Dam is the dividing line between the upper and lower Madison.

From the outlet of Ennis Lake, the lower Madison roars through the rugged Beartrap Canyon Wilderness Area. The 7-mile canyon is one of the most challenging whitewater stretches in Montana, with powerful runs and rapids over 6 feet high. At the mouth of the canyon, the river broadens and slows for its final 30-mile journey. The river continues northward, lined by dense willow thickets and productive pastureland. The 105-foot-high Grey Cliffs form a distinctive border to the middle reaches of the lower Madison.

The Madison's fame and exceptional fishery stem to a large degree from the river's role as a living laboratory for wild trout management. In 1968, the Montana Department of Fish, Wildlife, and Parks (FWP) initiated a two-year project to assess the effects of its artificial stocking program on trout populations in the upper Madison. The results of this pioneering research led to the revolutionary but inescapable conclusion: The addition of thousands of hatchery-reared trout each spring was actually reducing the number of fish in the river. Fisheries researcher Dick Vincent reasoned that the influx of hatchery fish was displacing the resident population from the limited number of holding areas in the Madison, but the hatchery fish were unable to survive more than a short time in the demanding river environment.

The fallout from this study raided on rivers throughout Montana; in less than a decade, most rivers and streams in the state had been converted to wild trout management (natural reproduction only) with spectacular improvements in the quality of trout fishery.

For the Madison, elimination of stocking was only the first of a series of steps designed to bring the river to its fishery potential. The second item to be addressed was harvest. Creel surveys and population censuses indicated that anglers were keeping so many of the larger trout that, despite good reproduction, only small fish remained. The average fish size had dropped to about 10 inches, a sorry state of affairs for a river with the exceptional water quality, habitat, and food supply of the Madison.

Float fishing is very popular on the Madison, especially during the salmon fly hatch.
AL TROTH PHOTO

Backed by mountains of Dick Vincent's data and scores of sportsmen demanding the restoration of quality fishing, the Montana Fish and Game Commission designated the 30 miles of the upper Madison from Quake Lake to Varney Bridge as a "catch-and-release" section for artificial flies and lures only. The results have been remarkable. Total trout populations have more than doubled since the advent of the special regulations in 1977. Numbers of 13- to 18-inch fish have risen even more sharply, and are now estimated at more than 800 per mile.

The success of the catch-and-release regulations has created a new problem on the Madison, namely, "handling mortality." Vincent documented this occurrence by comparing trout populations in the catch-and-release section to those in a research area of the Madison, which had been closed to fishing for five years. Populations in the closed section were about 20 percent higher than in the catch-and-release area, indicating that many of the trout handled by anglers were not surviving after release. Biologists now recommend that fish be brought to net or hand quickly, not played to exhaustion. A tired fish will have extreme difficulty regaining its equilibrium in the swift Madison current, especially when the water is at summer temperatures. If a fish has been played out, it should be held upright in calm water and moved back and forth gently until it has recovered its strength. The cavalier "fish drop" release so commonly seen may prove a deathblow to trout in the rushing waters of the Madison River.

After dealing with wild trout management, catch-and-release regulations, and handling mortality, you might think Dick Vincent and his crew would rest on their research laurels. Hardly. "Species management" is the next phase on the Madison, as biologists attempt to adjust harvest regulations in the river below Varney Bridge to increase the number of rainbow trout. Whirling disease was discovered in Madison rainbow trout and it is feared that it will enter other major fisheries connected to the Missouri River drainage. Because of the particular vulnerability of rainbow trout to whirling disease, special regulations may be in effect. Check current regulations.

Surprisingly, the years of protective regulations have not resulted in great numbers of trophy trout in the upper Madison. Even in the section which had been closed to fishing, biologists report relatively few trout longer than 18 inches. The shortage of fish over 3 pounds, particularly rainbow, probably results from the cold water temperatures, short growing season, and, for rainbow, lack of a major food source. Browns, which readily become fish-eaters, will continue to grow even after reaching 16 inches, while rainbow tend to maintain this size once it's attained. Another factor may be that the large population of trout and even greater number of whitefish are simply dividing the food resource between too many mouths. Below Varney Bridge, where brushy banks and slower channels provide better brown trout habitat, trout up to 4 pounds are not uncommon.

The special regulations have brought the upper Madison close to its potential for producing trout. It hosts an exceptional number of 1- to 2-pound fish,

The Madison is heavily spiced with boulders, creating a somewhat unusual but very productive habitat.

offering the knowledgeable angler the opportunity to experience a forty- or fifty-fish day. As Dick Vincent wrote, "At times, catch rates on the upper Madison can average about three fish an hour. That's fantastic fishing, especially when you consider how many novices are included in that figure." The lower Madison, on the other hand, is far from its potential as a fishery. Trout fishing here suffers from "thermal pollution," a fancy way of saying the river just gets too darn warm.

During the summer, daily maximum water temperatures over 70 degrees Fahrenheit are the rule in the lower river. At these temperatures, trout feeding and angling success can come to a screeching halt. Temperatures over 80 degrees have caused local fish kills in the lower Madison. Trout growth rates are well below normal levels, and veteran anglers report that numbers of fish over 3 pounds are only a fraction of what they used to be.

The thermal problem stems from Ennis Dam and its reservoir, Ennis Lake. Since dam construction in 1900, the lake has silted into an average depth of 9 feet, about half its original depth. During summer, the shallow reservoir acts like a 6-square-mile solar collector. Upon discharge at Ennis Dam, Madison waters have warmed by about 8 degrees. Montana officials are now evaluating the feasibility of various engineering options to channel the flow quickly through the reservoir and thus alleviate the summer warming problem. A successful resolution of the lower Madison temperature problem could readily transform the lower Madison into one of the best trout fisheries in the nation.

Despite temperature problems, the lower Madison still holds a very respectable trout population—in fact, trout numbers can equal those in the Varney Bridge section of the upper river. The key for the angler is to fish when the temperature conditions are conducive to trout activity. In general, this means the months of April to June and again in late September to November.

Most early season fishing on both the upper and lower Madison is done from rubber rafts or drift boats, as high-water conditions make wading difficult. Float fishing is restricted in some sections of the river, so check current regulations before starting a trip. The Madison is floatable year-round, although the late summer flows can occasionally cause some bottom bouncing.

After the water drops, wading becomes feasible, and the best spots can be found between Varney Bridge and Ennis Lake. The exceptional number of channels at the Valley Garden fishing access site near Ennis, for example, provides a great opportunity for the walking angler to find a private place to fish.

Ennis Lake also harbors a rebounding population of grayling. A recent FWP study determined that these grayling may be a native, fluvial strain, one of two remaining populations in the state. To protect this unique resource, fishing for grayling is catch-and-release only for the entire length of the Madison.

Strategies: For most anglers, the annual fishing agenda on the upper Madison begins in May prior to spring runoff. At this time, the fish are concentrating on the black, 2-inch-long nymphs of *Pteronarcys californica*. This large stonefly, known as the salmon fly for the orange color of the winged adult, is abundant in the riverbottom cobbles. Large Bitch Creek nymphs, Yuk bugs, Girdle bugs, and similar heavily weighted, rubber-legged concoctions in sizes 2 to 6 are the most reliable patterns. These flies should be worked right against the banks—just where the trout are waiting for the clumsy crawling naturals that stack up along the shoreline before emerging.

The float angler should cast slightly downstream to allow the fly to sink before it begins to drag behind the boat. An upstream mend of the belly of the fly line will extend the dragfree drift, and the quick movement of the fly will often entice a strike. As soon as the fly does drag, pick it up carefully and cast again. If this technique brings a few results, test your patience and drift a big nymph along the bottom about 10 to 20 feet from the shore.

The wade angler should quarter his cast upstream, allowing the fly to sink in the swift current and dead drift along the bank. As the water warms through the spring, the fish will also chase gold, silver, and black spinners; again, cast right against the bank in the pre-hatch period.

Runoff flows typically last from late May through June. Fishing can remain good during the high-water period if the river retains at least 1 or 2 feet of visibility. Forget the days when the river has risen more than about 6 inches in a twenty-four-hour period. The West Fork of the Madison is a major sediment producer, and at times the angler can find fishable water upstream from the confluence.

Adult salmon flies begin to emerge around July 1 in the channels just above Ennis, and the hatch works its way upstream for the next three weeks. Fly fishers from across the nation converge on the Madison in the hopes of catching many and large fish on the big dry salmon fly patterns. Sometimes this scenario plays out; at other times, fishing is only fair or poor in the face of high, turbid water or trout already gorged on naturals. Persistence is the key during the hatch. An angler who puts in long days of floating has the best chance to have those magical few hours when virtually all the 2- and 3-pounders go on a feeding frenzy.

A number of salmon fly patterns are effective, and it's a good idea to have both tight-silhouetted patterns (like the Sofa Pillow or Bird's stonefly) and bushy patterns (like the fluttering stone or other well-hackled elk hair ties). Alter your tactics frequently during the day, and don't be timid about switching to nymphs or wet patterns if the dries won't produce.

Dry fly action on the upper Madison is remarkably good from the end of the high water through the summer. The clear, shallow, fast water probably accounts for the willingness of trout to work the surface. Even inexperienced fly fishers can find some action on most afternoons. The consistent success of a variety of attractor patterns—especially the gaudy Royal Wulff—belies the purist's match-the-hatch credo on the upper Madison.

Despite the relative ease of dry fly fishing on the upper Madison, the ability to cast to the right spots will make a tremendous difference in the number of fish taken. Reading the water is the key—even though at first glance the famed 50-mile riffle may seem indecipherable.

The Madison not only offers world-famous fishing, but easy access.

"Look for a change in speed or a change in depth," advises Bud Lilly, founder of the famous Trout Shop in West Yellowstone. "If you can identify a feeding station where the trout don't have to work so hard, that's where they'll be." These stations can be along the banks, on the edges of the faster runs, behind visible or submerged boulders, or in small gravel depressions. A good pair of polarized sunglasses is a necessity for reading the streambottom subtleties of the upper Madison.

The famed Madison caddis hatch is the bread and butter of summer fishing.

Light brown caddis in sizes 10 to 14 hatch throughout July and August; clouds of the moth-like adults can be seen along the shore line willows, particularly on warm evenings. Elk hair caddis, Humpies, Royal Trudes, and Royal Wulffs are the top dry fly producers, while hare's ears and other soft hackle patterns will take trout feeding on the emerging caddis pupae just under the water surface.

By late August, terrestrials dominate the trout diet. A trout creeled on the upper Madison (below the catch-and-release boundary at Varney Bridge, of course) is likely to have ants, grasshoppers, bees, spiders, and half a dozen different species of beetles in its stomach. The message here is opportunism both on the part of the trout, which will take nearly anything, and on the part of the angler, who should select a visible, high-floating attractor pattern in size 12 or smaller. Royal Wulffs are the favored pattern; their white, upright wings provide excellent visibility in the surface glare and chop. For the sharp-eyed angler, a size 12-14 parachute Adams can also turn the trick when the attractors don't.

By early September, the grassy edges of the upper Madison are jumping with grasshoppers, many of which are deposited in the river channel by the afternoon winds. Trout take greedy advantage of this "wind fall," and anglers do likewise. Any of the standard hopper patterns will bring enthusiastic strikes; many of the fish that strike will also be in the 14-to 18-inch class. A Muddler fished just under the surface can also be very effective.

The grasshopper period coincides with the highest floating pressure and the lowest water levels. These are prime conditions for boats or wading anglers to spook fish from their bank holding areas. Anglers might do well to try some of the mid-river holding areas behind boulders in addition to the typical bank spots.

Fall in the upper Madison Valley brings subfreezing nights and a sharp decline in surface insect activity. Trout begin keying in on aquatic nymphs and sculpins. Black or olive Wooly Buggers, dark Marabou streamers, and brown sculpin imitations all can be effective stream patterns, while nymphs will also produce well. Fall is a good time for the lure angler as well, because fish are no longer looking to the surface for food.

Anglers interested in working hard for big autumn browns might consider the section of the Madison above Hebgen Lake and on into Yellowstone Park. A good spawning run leaves Hebgen in October, and deeply laced streamers and nymphs will take fish.

Even winter can provide some good fishing on the upper Madison for the angler willing to brave the cold temperatures and work weighted black nymphs along the streambottom. The trout might be a bit sluggish in the near-freezing water, but they will feed, as will scores of the more cold-adapted whitefish.

With the many attractions of the upper Madison now firmly in mind, an angler should also consider a few cautions. The strong summer afternoon winds in the valley can make casting—and even floating—extremely difficult. Use a heavier rod to counter the wind. The heavy current and slippery cobbles will limit the range of the angler on foot, especially during high water or where the river flows into a single channel. To avoid slipping, try felt-bottomed waders. Finally, the summer angler needs a tolerance for crowds. During a typical summer day, as many as forty guided drift boats from Ennis and West Yellowstone, along with a good number of private trips, will float the catch-and-release section. The bank angler may see a flotilla pass before him, while the floating angler will be sandwiched between "dudes" flailing the water. Most of the guide boats put in between 10 and 11 a.m.

On the lower Madison, the basic tactic for early season (March through June) success is to cast large, dark, rubber-legged nymphs tight to the banks. As in the upper river, trout are looking for the natural salmon fly nymphs getting ready to emerge during high water. Spinners, along with streamers giving the impression of a darting sculpin or crayfish, are also effective. Bait anglers focus on the deep runs and occasional holes along the cliff faces or beneath the cut banks. Dead-drifted salmon fly nymphs are the most effective bait throughout the year on the lower Madison.

Anglers often do well working the slower water in front of the many big boulders in the Madison.

The dry fly fisher on the lower Madison has his heyday in April and early May, when a thick mid-day caddis hatch blankets the smooth-flowing portion of the river just below the mouth of Beartrap Canyon. Typically, water temperatures are ideal, and trout rise freely to the naturals and to size 12 elk hair caddis imitations.

The salmon fly hatch on the lower Madison is sporadic, as nymph populations have been decimated by the warm summer water temperatures. Some dry fly action is possible, but most anglers continue to work the weighted nymphs along the banks. Again, high roily water can interfere with salmon fly fishing.

The hatch in Beartrap Canyon is more consistent and can provide good dry fly fishing. The turbulent waters of the canyon, however, are a radical change from the rest of the river, and the angler must adjust his tactics. Floating is restricted to the expert oarsman, and during highest flows, the canyon can be impassable. The angler on foot should ignore the midstream torrent and work the back eddies, bank edges, and spots behind or in front of boulders instead. A well-hackled elk-hair pattern is best suited to imitate the dry salmon fly in the rushing canyon waters.

The lower Madison has generally warmed by late June, and at this point, trout activity tapers off. Thick mats of green algae carpet the streambottom and wave in the current, making it almost impossible to fish with bait, spinners, or weighted nymphs. Dry caddis patterns can still provide some morning and evening action if the weather remains cool. During July and August, however, the knowledgeable anglers head for the upper river, conceding the lower Madison to the inner tube set.

Wading out and then working back toward the banks also works well on the Madison.

Cool temperatures can put the trout on the feed again by the end of September, and fishing can remain good into November. Dark streamers and spinners are the best producers in the fall.

TRIBUTARIES

The area between Hebgen Lake and Yellowstone Park contains three of the most important tributary fisheries to the upper Madison. The South Fork of the Madison is a clear narrow stream meandering through brush fields and meadows just outside of West Yellowstone. The undercut banks and deep holes of this stream do hold some very large brown trout, but getting in a good cast without spooking the fish is a tremendous challenge.

Grayling Creek and **Duck Creek** are shallow, willow-lined streams holding good numbers of brookies, cutthroat, and rainbow, a few grayling, and occasional large spawning browns moving up from Hebgen Lake in the fall.

From Quake Lake to Ennis, the **West Fork of the Madison** is the most productive tributary fishery to the upper Madison. The West Fork's lower section is the classic free-stone mountain stream, with good fishing for rainbow averaging about 12 inches. Further upstream, the West Fork becomes a meandering, silt-bottomed stream with many beaver ponds and pan-sized trout. The West Fork is paralleled by a Forest Service gravel road and is readily accessible.

The Madison has been called "a 50-mile riffle." AL TROTH PHOTO

The dedicated dry fly fisher on the lower Madison might want to try **Darlington Spring Creek** (also called Darlington Ditch), a crystal clear stream flowing within an irrigation levee through Cobblestone fishing access site. Darlington has been improved greatly through a stream rehabilitation program by the Bozeman-area chapter of Trout Unlimited; the stream now offers good dry fly fishing for wary browns under a catch-and-release regulation.

ACCESS

Public access to the upper Madison is generally excellent, as **U.S. Highway 287** parallels the river from Hebgen Lake to Ennis. Where the road borders the river, you can simply park at a pulloff and start fishing. At other places, the river can be as much as 3 miles from the highway, so the angler should use one of the many public access points along the way. **Lyon Bridge** just below the West Fork; BLM's **Palisades** and **Ruby Creek campgrounds; McAtee Bridge;** and FWP's fishing access sites at **Varney Bridge, Eight Mile Hole, Burnt Tree Ford, Ennis Bridge,** and **Valley Garden** near Ennis provide an excellent south-to-north chain of access sites for floaters and waders.

Access to the lower Madison is very good from the mouth of **Beartrap Canyon** for the next 5 miles downstream. The canyon itself can be reached by trail, starting from the mouth or from the powerhouse below Ennis Lake. The final 18 miles of the lower Madison are surrounded by private land, with public access provided about 6-miles by the **Grey Cliff** and **Cobblestone** fishing access sites and by the **U.S. Highway 10 bridge** near the river's mouth. Floating anglers should be forewarned that taking a boat out at Cobblestone requires a trek of about 100 yards over two levees and across a shallow canal. A map of the entire river and details for floaters are found in the pamphlet, *Montana Afloat #15, the Madison River.*

12 Missouri River

Overview: Anglers from Helena to Great Falls and elsewhere have learned the Missouri's secret: There are big fish in that big water! The river has garnered some publicity in the big sporting magazines, and news of lunker trout has a way of spreading.

>**Key species:** Rainbow trout, brown trout, whitefish, northern pike, walley/saugey, paddlefish, sturgeon, carp, sucker, perch, lake trout, smallmouth bass, salmon, catfish, goldeye, cutthroat trout, brook trout, and almost any other fish found in Montana, considering the Missouri runs from Three Forks near Bozeman through major reservoirs and warmwater sections all the way to North Dakota.
>
>**Use:** The section from Holter Dam to Cascade receives the most fishing pressure of any river in the state. Only Canyon Ferry Lake receives more fishing pressure, although the sections below both Canyon Ferry and down from Cascade also get quite a bit of pressure. Most of the lower sections of the river get overlooked by anglers headed for reservoirs.
>
>**Key flies and lures:** Flies—bead-head Pheasant Tail, Elk Hair Caddis, Royal Wulffs, hoppers, Goofus Bug, Red Quill, Olive Dun, Polywing Spinner, parachute Adams, Buzz Ball, Griffiths Gnat, Woolly Buggers, Road Kills, Happy Hookers, Spruce flies, sculpin imitations, and Marabou Muddlers. Lures—non-lead head bucktail and Marabou jigs, hammered brass lures and Rapalas. Bait—hoppers, worms, maggots, grubs, and marshmallows.

The fishing: Ask an angler what he thinks of dams and he will probably respond, "It depends on which river." Anglers bitterly oppose some potential dams, but in other cases, anglers must admit that some blue-ribbon trout streams owe their excellence to dams. The Yellowtail Dam, for example, transformed a muddy, troutless Bighorn River into one of the nation's fine tailwater fisheries. Trout fanciers also benefitted with the advent of several dams on the Missouri.

For a hint of what the Missouri looked like before dams, regard the upper Missouri today. No dams impede the river from the confluence of the Gallatin, Madison, and Jefferson near the town of Three Forks down to the Toston Dam Reservoir. As with the other sections of the river, the upper Missouri is flat and very big, a football field or two across. But unlike the rest of the river, this stretch has a horrendous runoff. Even when the high waters have run their course, the water remains somewhat turbid through the irrigation season.

12 Missouri River (Upper)

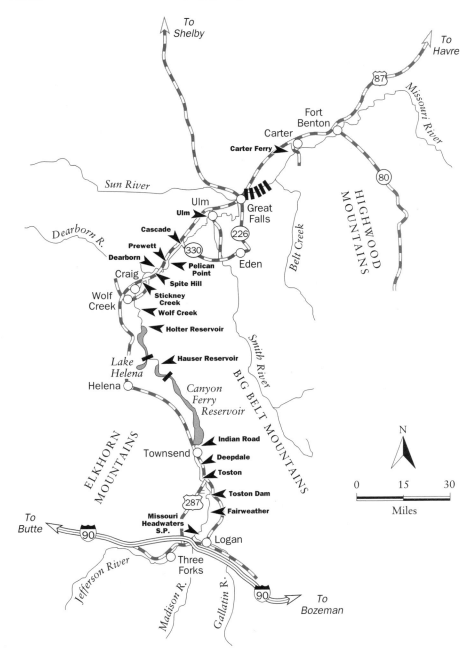

12 Missouri River (Wild and Scenic)

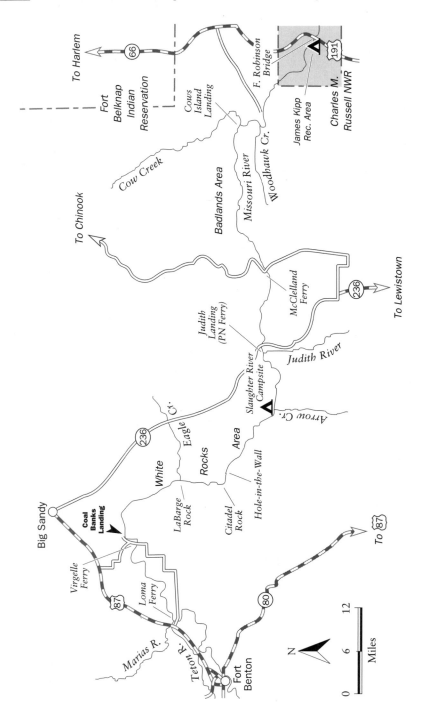

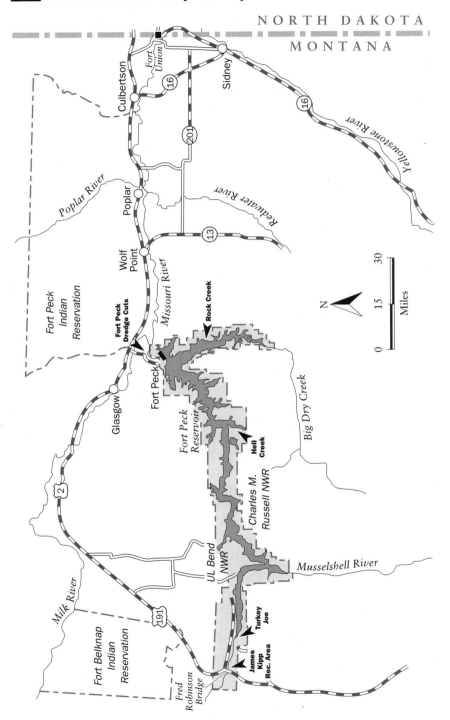

NORTH DAKOTA

MONTANA

Make no mistake about it, this upper section holds thousands of trout averaging a very respectable size, with a few in the lunker and trophy classes. But if biologists had a ratio of number of trout to volume of river water, the trout density in this section of the Missouri probably would rank rather low. This part of the river is simply not as loaded with trout as other sections. Those trout that do live here don't, with minor exceptions, concentrate on any one area of the river. Anglers find that they need to cover a lot of river to do well here.

Because of its reputation as a good, but rarely spectacular, fishery in desolate-looking country quite distant from Montana's major population centers, the upper river does not see as many anglers. A few anglers poke in around Clarkston, gamble on the back roads and rattlesnakes around Lombard, or run their power boats up from Toston Dam, but these people certainly don't return with complaints of elbow-to-elbow fishing. For those who value solitude, the upper Missouri waits.

At Toston Dam, the picture changes radically. While it's only a low diversion type of impoundment, the dam stops migratory trout from proceeding up river any further. Because of the migratory rainbow and browns coming from Canyon Ferry Reservoir, FWP biologists find it difficult, if not impossible, to come up with solid population estimates of just what fish lurk in this section of river. But from their studies, several key facts do come clear.

First, some rainbow and browns stay in the river most, if not all, of the year. The number of resident fish drops when especially big influxes of migratory fish come up the river, much like what used to happen to the wild trout of the Madison when hatchery fish were stocked alongside them.

Second, brown trout from Canyon Ferry and the Missouri make spawning runs in the late fall. These browns concentrate in the upper section of the Missouri, mainly between the Deepdale access and Toston Dam. Based on the records, a few brown trout in the 8- to 14-pound class will be in the river below the dam each November.

Third, the spectacular fall rainbow runs witnessed in the 1970s no longer happen in comparable numbers. FWP biologists suspect that two factors account for this drastic decline: a mysterious change of some sort in Canyon Ferry Reservoir and the unique characteristics of the Arlee strain of rainbow. Traditionally, FWP stocked the fall spawning Arlee rainbow in Canyon Ferry because the strain has some good characteristics. They are very catchable and fast-growing. A 5-incher planted in July will grow to 10 inches by November and 13 or 14 inches by the following summer. This amazing pace matches the growth rate of fish that are hand fed in a hatchery.

Biologists think this fast growth carries a price. At 2.5 years of age, 18 inches long, and weighing about 2 pounds, Arlee rainbow not caught by anglers may soon die of old age. Moreover, biologists think that few Arlee rainbow spawn successfully in the Missouri River. Thus there is little, if any, recruitment of future generations, and FWP had to keep up the never-ending cycle of stocking new fish.

The Missouri is known for its large trout, such as this 4-pound brown that fell for a five-inch bucktail. AL TROTH PHOTO

Consequently, FWP is experimenting with plants of De Smet and Eagle Lake rainbow in Canyon Ferry. Spring spawners which grow more slowly, but live much longer, the De Smets may prove a valuable addition to the reservoir and the river above, especially if they spawn successfully.

The upper Missouri receives more than half its water from the Madison, water that has been heated by Ennis Lake. Peak temperatures in the mid-70s make trout lethargic. One biologist suggests the cooler seasons for more lively action.

The cooler season of spring brings anglers out to muck through the mud and fish for the rainbow moving in and out of the river just above Canyon Ferry. Most of these fish measure 12 to 18 inches, but a very few reach into the 3- to 4-pound class.

The next section downstream on the Missouri is a 1-mile stretch between Canyon Ferry and Hauser Lake. Though short in length, the river here supports kokanee and tremendous numbers of trout, both resident and migratory, and survives equally tremendous fishing pressure. Ten- to 20-inch rainbow comprise most of the catch year-round, but most of the anglers who fish here have hopes of a trophy brown. Every year sees a few browns in the 10- to 12-pound size brought to bay, though catch rates have dropped off from those of the early 1980s. Some optimists even suspect the presence of a 40-pounder below either Canyon Ferry or Hauser.

Anglers find the monster browns mostly during their fall spawning runs which peak in late November. Fishing for these browns tests the dedication of any angler. Catch rates are very low. November winds and temperatures can make fishing miserable. But for those who persist, fishing fantasies can come true.

A similar situation exists below Hauser Dam. Here anglers have several miles of free-flowing river to work. Though most anglers congregate around the mouth of Beaver Creek, FWP's Jim Vashro suggests hiking to other excellent spots up or down the river. This stretch is more broken than the mile below Canyon Ferry. Anglers can wade the shallows to reach more of the river. And a notable run of rainbow up to 6 pounds can make this section an early season hot spot in addition to the autumn action.

Right below Holter Dam, anglers and fish again congregate in large numbers. Good under ordinary circumstances, fishing is red hot when the dam spills over the top, dropping lake fish on top of the river trout already at the bottom. When the word gets out, angling here becomes a shoulder-to-shoulder affair.

Below Holter Dam, the river runs free of dams for 90 miles until it reaches the city of Great Falls. FWP rates the river down to Cascade as class 1, blue-ribbon class. Rainbow outnumber browns six to one from Holter to the mouth of the Dearborn River. From electrofishing surveys, FWP estimates 2,674 catchable trout per mile, including 100 fish 18 inches or larger. The number of big trout drop off below the Dearborn. Around Cascade, the river starts changing

Perhaps more than other rivers, the Missouri attracts anglers in search of a relaxing fishing experience.

to deeper water and fewer riffles. When the Smith dumps its heavy load of sediment into the river near Ulm, the trout become few and far between.

As a sidelight for anglers who know how to fish for them, some walleyes up to 10 pounds swim in these waters. Walleye fans think their fish taste better than any other caught in the state. Some boating anglers with sonar find and work 20-foot-deep holes below Cascade for the walleyes and even some ling. Below Great Falls, anglers still have a few hot spots to try out. There are reports of some trout fishing below each of Great Falls's five dams, especially Morony Dam, although access is difficult. Sauger also swim below Morony Dam, but catch rates have declined since a peak in the 1980's. FWP's Steve Leathe reports that you can catch almost any game fish found in Montana in the stretch from Morony Dam to Carter Ferry.

Strategies: Successful Missouri River anglers use a wide variety of baits, lures, and flies. Success does not hinge on what an angler ties onto the line so much as where the bait, lure, or fly is fished. And the advice of everyone, except dry fly fishers, is to fish the hooks down near the bottom of the river. Rarely does advice from so many anglers come so unanimously.

Local bait anglers like the Missouri. The river is not littered with dead tree limbs or boulder fields to snag their hooks. It has lots of deep holes. And bait anglers do very well along the banks during the spring. Worms do work here. Unfortunately, they work not only for trout, but also for suckers, carp, and other trash fish. Unless the angler wants to catch these trash fish, worms are not the best bait.

Unfortunately, fish parts used as bait can spread whirling disease. FWP urges anglers to avoid using anything other than worms and insects for bait. Harmless to humans, whirling disease is devastating to trout: it is a parasite that deforms their spinal cords, forcing them to swim in circles. Eventually, of course, they starve. FWP is currently working to solve the problem. Until they do, please observe the recommendations at the front of this book, and do your part to prevent the spread of this disease.

Throughout the Missouri's length, sculpin imitations do well for anglers. This holds true especially below the dams, where the trout are looking for injured sculpins and minnows which have come through the turbines. In the latter half of the summer, grasshoppers fished near the banks also fool many a fish, especially on windy days.

Bait and fly anglers face a problem with getting their baits or flies down near the bottom without fouling up too often. Father Charlie Gorman, who had a winning way with fish as well as with congregations, finds the solution is to add sinkers near the hook and then a bobber adjusted to keep the hook off the bottom. Just how well the angler adjusts the distance between hook and bobber does much to determine how successful the angler's day will be.

Jim Vashro recommends that anglers stock up with the larger sizes of spinning gear for the Missouri. Popular choices include different patterns of hammered brass lures and Rapalas. But on the Missouri, perhaps more than on any other Montana river, anglers use non-lead head jigs. Vashro prefers the white or black Marabou over the Bucktail type. Retrieve with lots of little twitches to simulate an injured minnow.

The Missouri below Holter Dam is noted for its dry fly fishing and produces some large caddis hatches in the summertime. Anglers keyed into these hatches report excellent action in the magic hour just before dark. These July and August hatches are usually matched with the familiar caddis imitations such as Humpies, Goofus, and Elk Hair Caddis. Hopper patterns also fool their fair share of fish.

Bring along some leech imitations, some caddis emerger patterns, some pheasant tail nymphs, and perhaps some big Royal Coachmans to fish wet. Use the Coachmans as an indicator fly and trail a small nymph pattern.

When the mayflies hatch in August and September, fish below Holter with a size 18 fly, such as Red Quill, Olive Dun, Polywing Spinner, or Adams. To catch fish consistently on flies, you have to learn the river, learn the places where the rainbow hang out, and the places that just hold hundreds of whitefish. One way to learn these places is to observe carefully how the fish rises. "The rainbow makes a white flash, tends to make a swirl, and may show the dorsal fin; with a whitefish rise, the forked tip of the tail comes out," says Fred Tedesco, of Western Rivers Guide Service.

In the spring and fall, most fly fishers use large nymphs and streamers in combination with basic steelhead tactics. When light levels are low, the trout will be out on the shallower gravel beds and at the riffle-tails; when the light is bright, the fish stay in the deeper pools and runs. With large rods and sink tip or high density sinking line, the casts should go quartering upstream to allow the weighted flies a chance to sink. Once the river takes the slack out of the line, the angler strips the line back in. After a couple steps downstream, the process is repeated.

Many anglers make the mistake of not letting the fly get down to the bottom. Tedesco finds a lot of people disappointed with how hard it is to fish this way. "The average person would be better off somewhere else. This dredging the bottom is not casual; it's trophy fishing, and you pay the price of hours on end with nothing."

In three years of very hard fishing in this manner, Tedesco has caught two rainbow over 4 pounds and a number of lunker browns, including an 11-pounder. He notes that success in the fall depends on the flow—the lower the flow, the better the fishing. Other than that, he has not found any reliable indication of how the fishing will be from one day to the next. "You just keep plugging and hoping," he says.

In addition to traditional patterns, such as dark and white Spruce flies, Marabou Muddlers, and Wooly Buggers, several local favorites also reportedly catch the fishes' fancies: Road Kills (tied with rabbit), Happy Hookers, and perch imitations tied with yellow and orange color. These are generally tied on with beefy leaders. Tedesco remarks that the need for flimsy, light leaders "is a great big myth perpetuated by outdoor writers."

When fishing for big browns, whether by fly, lure, or bait, anglers should keep in mind the nocturnal habits of these fish. Take a flashlight to watch for hazards. Night anglers may not have great suntans, but they do have plenty of excitement.

TRIBUTARIES

Anglers who know **Sixteenmile Creek** regard it as a mixed blessing. As a fishery, it is exceptionally productive. A relatively small stream, it harbors large numbers of brookies 9 to 13 inches, rainbow 10 to 17 inches, and resident browns up to 22 inches. These fish hang out in the boulder pockets, under the heavy streamside brush, and in the riffle-pools. The stream provides consistently good action just about any time of day and throughout the fishing season.

However, the stream runs almost entirely through private lands. There are no Public Access Exits for Sixteenmile Creek, so you must get landowner permission to fish, which may be difficult. Fee fishing may be possible by contacting Dan Bailey's in Livingston to arrange an outfitter for Sixteenmile Creek.

Little Prickly Pear Creek, despite all the alterations to its streambed, still grants very good fishing for its lively population of 10- to 14-inch rainbow and occasional browns. The creek joins the Missouri a couple miles below Holter Reservoir. Anglers will find easy access along old U.S. Highway 191, now officially a "recreation road."

With its canyon, limestone cliffs, and deep holes, the **Dearborn River** looks like a smaller version of the Smith River. The lower section from the Highway 287 bridge down to the Missouri has much of the best fishing and the only floatable water, according to Former FWP employee Al Wippermen. Again, the predominate rainbow run 8 to 12 inches, and the holes house some browns up to 5 pounds.

Unfortunately, the floating season does not coincide well with the summer fishing season. By July, just when the fishing is picking up, the water drops to such a degree that anglers must drag their canoes or rafts across the shallow riffles.

Downstream, the **Sun River** joins the Missouri at Great Falls. A sluggish, muddy river at the end, the Sun has pristine beginnings in the Bob Marshall Wilderness. Anglers willing to hike to the headwaters find good fishing for unsophisticated trout in the usually crystal-clear water. Wipperman terms the river below Gibson Reservoir a sleeper because it gets little fishing pressure. Rainbow provide the bulk of the catch along with a smattering of browns. Wipperman rates the section between Simms and the town of Sun River as the best. Here, the access is only through private lands except for the FWP access at Fort Shaw. Anglers can float the Sun, but they should watch for some mean diversion dams and cottonwood snags. Wipperman notes that some of the slower sections above Muddy Creek yield some exciting fishing for northern pike from 5 to 15 pounds, as well as winter ice-fishing—when the wind is taking a day off.

Releasing a big one for another angler's future enjoyment. AL TROTH PHOTO

In a very attractive park right in Great Falls, FWP stocks catchable rainbow in the river at **Giant Springs**. As the springs are right next to the hatchery, this fishery is something of a pet project of FWP's. Many families enjoy the fishing in this beautiful spot.

The first 10 miles of the **Marias River** below Tiber Dam yield some good fishing for rainbows, browns, sauger, walleye, and northern pike. Local anglers try for some lunkers up to 6 pounds.

Trout fanciers need not pay much attention to the **Judith River**, but one of its tributaries, **Big Spring Creek**, deserves a lot more attention. Although the 1975 flood tore up Big Spring Creek, the fishery has made a tremendous comeback. FWP found more than 1,800 catchable trout in less than 1 mile, astounding for a medium-sized stream. For a comparison, note that the best sections of the mighty Missouri have about the same number of atchables per mile. In 1968, an angler caught a 19-pounder just below the big springs—proof of what this phenomenal fishery can grow.

Big Spring is gaining in popularity among anglers. FWP has accesses: Upper Spring Creek and Brewery Flats above Lewistown; and Carroll Trail and Hruska below Lewistown. Fishing this fast-moving water buffaloes some anglers. Try fishing along the edges or down in the 6-foot-deep holes.

The last trout-inhabited tributary of the Missouri is the unheralded **Musselshell River**. The lower river runs too silty and warm for trout, but FWP planted smallmouth bass as late as 1982. A fair smallmouth fishery has developed downstream of Lavina. Trout anglers head upstream of Harlowton where some big browns lurk in the cleaner water, especially in the 20 miles upstream of the town of Twodot. Trout populations have responded to recent wet years and are at least holding their own. The Selkirk Fishing Access Site (FAS) helps anglers reach the river in an area otherwise privately owned. Or anglers can go further upstream into the headwaters in the Castle and Little

Belt mountains where the Forest Service owns some riverbanks. Here, anglers encounter a mix of pan-sized brookies and some rainbow that wouldn't fit into most pans.

Like the Shields River to the south, the Musselshell grows fish quickly but runs out of the way of major highways and the travel routes of most anglers. Thus, anglers along the Musselshell do not bump into each other often. Miles of excellent river fishing await the more adventuresome anglers.

ACCESS

Anglers can first reach the Missouri right where it starts, at **Missouri Headwaters State Park**. This informative facility is reached from a well-marked exit off Interstate 90 just east of Three Forks.

The **Fairweather FAS** is more elusive. FWP's Recreation Map describes the usual route starting at Logan, going west a mile on U.S. Highway 10, then 3.5 miles north on the Logan-Trident Road, then 10 miles northeast on the Clarkston Road. As with all FWP's fishing accesses above Canyon Ferry, Fairweather has a good boat ramp.

Near the town of Toston on U.S. Highway 287, anglers are directed to the **Toston Dam FAS** by an obvious sign. Or anglers can reach the east side of the river by a county road running southeast from Toston. This road, if passable, will eventually bring the angler to **Lombard**, where Sixteenmile Creek joins the river.

Below Toston, anglers reach the river when it bends over to US 287, at **Deepdale FAS** 4 miles south of Townsend; and at **Indian Road FAS** a mile northwest of Townsend, also just off US 287.

About 6 miles east of East Helena, on US 287, Montana Highway 284 leads to **Canyon Ferry Dam**. A campground just downstream gives both bank and boat anglers access to this short, but intensely fished, section. Entry fees are now charged at these sites.

To reach the river just below **Hauser Dam**, drive from Helena past the Lakeside Resort and across the river to York, then turn northwest to Beaver Creek, then west on County Road 138 down to the river. Or drive 8 miles north of Helena on Interstate 15 to the Lincoln Road exit, then 4 miles east on County Road 453, then 3 miles north to **Black Sandy** and **White Sandy** State Recreation Areas.

Anglers wishing to fish between **Holter Dam** and **Ulm** get off I 15 and onto a recreation road which intertwines with the river and the interstate. A short spur road leads to the base of the dam from the Wolf Creek exit. Below, some nine fishing access sites and state recreation areas, plus considerable casual access where the river and road come together, give the angler lots of choices.

Anglers interested in the river below Great Falls can launch their boats at Fort Benton, the Loma Ferry, Coal Banks Landing near the mouth of the Judith River, at the PN Ferry due north of Winifred, and at the Fred Robinson Bridge where U.S. Highway 191 crosses the river. Anglers can also launch rafts and canoes below Morony Dam and enjoy a 12 mile float to carter ferry, but beware of heavy whitewater the first 3–4 miles. The section just above Fort Peck Reservoir offers good fishing for sauger in early spring and catfish in late spring. Last of all, for fishing just below Fort Peck Dam, anglers should check out the **Fort Peck Dredge Cuts** FAS.

13 Rock Creek

Overview: For many residents of Missoula, the road to paradise begins only 20 miles east of town at Interstate 90, Exit 126—Rock Creek Road. A drive along Rock Creek offers an escape from the sprawling metropolis of 50,000 inhabitants into a wild and beautiful mountain valley. It also provides access to one of the most delightful and challenging fishing experiences in Montana.

Throughout its 50-mile length, Rock Creek is a classic fast-water trout stream. The riffles, runs, and occasional pools host five species of trout, all of which have the agreeable disposition of being where they're supposed to be. Literally any place that offers hiding cover and some relief from the current will harbor trout.

The close proximity to Missoula brings large numbers of anglers to Rock Creek.

Key species: Rainbow trout, brown trout, cutthroat trout, whitefish, brook trout, and bull trout.

Use: The section from Hogback Creek to the mouth at the Clark Fork ranks 21st statewide for fishing pressure, while the upper section receives about half as much pressure. Don't expect to be alone.

Key flies and lures: Flies—Sofa Pillow, Bird's Stone, Orange Stimulators, Elk Hair Caddis, golden stonefly nymph, gold ribbed Hares Ear, Parachute Adams, Parachute Olive, Marabou Muddlers and Woolly Buggers.

The fishing: Rock Creek is one of the most studied streams in Montana. The Montana Department of Fish, Wildlife, and Parks (FWP) has monitored fishing pressure, harvest, and fish populations during the past thirty years.

During the 1970s, intensive fish population sampling through electro-shocking confirmed what Rock Creek anglers had long suspected—the good-sized fish were disappearing. By 1978, few rainbows beyond 16 inches were being caught; and the biggest brown taken was 20 inches, down from the 23- to 24-inch fish of earlier years. Cutthroat, typically the easiest trout to catch and thus the most susceptible to overfishing, were all but eliminated from the population.

In 1979, the Montana Fish and Game Commission followed the recommendations of fisheries biologists—and the desires of local sports enthusiasts—and instituted new regulations designed to let Rock Creek again reach its potential as a quality trout fishery.

The new regulations restrict the use of bait to children under fourteen years of age to minimize fish mortality. All other anglers may use only artificial lures.

Although Rock Creek provides excellent angling throughout the season, the annual salmon fly hatch provides its single biggest drawing card. The cobble bottom of Rock Creek supports an amazing density of the 2-inch-long *Pteronarcys californica* nymphs. The flights of thousands of these bright orange, winged adults make for a fascinating natural spectacle.

Adult salmon flies begin emerging at the mouth of Rock Creek around June 1. During the month of June, the hatch gradually works its way up the 50-mile stream course. A mid-day drive along the Rock Creek Road is the best way to locate the hatch, as the ungainly, helicopter-like adults are impossible to miss when they hover over the stream or land on the roadside bushes.

The proximity of Rock Creek to Missoula means intense fishing pressure throughout the summer, a situation compounded by the numerous Forest Service campgrounds along the stream's upper and middle reaches. "Opening day, holidays, and weekends are good days to avoid if you are looking for solitude," cautions Don Peters, FWP fisheries biologist in Missoula.

Be sure to check the special regulations before fishing. Whirling disease recently detected in the upper reaches of Rock Creek has impacted the rainbow population but luckily less than the Madison River decline in rainbow. In the Hogback area, Don Peters reports some 40 percent of rainbow, but significant increases in brown trout populations has offset some of the rainbow losses.

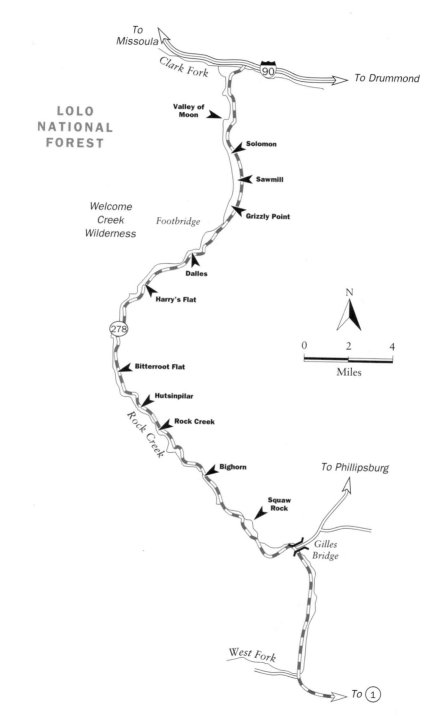

To
Missoula

Clark Fork

90

To Drummond

**LOLO
NATIONAL
FOREST**

**Valley of
Moon**

Solomon

Sawmill

*Welcome
Creek
Wilderness*

Footbridge

Grizzly Point

Dalles

Harry's Flat

278

N

0   2   4

Miles

Bitterroot Flat

Hutsinpilar

Rock Creek

Rock Creek

Bighorn

**Squaw
Rock**

To Phillipsburg

*Gilles
Bridge*

West Fork

To **1**

Whirling disease appears to affect each creek differently and so far it has left the Rock Creek fishery largely intact.

Strategies: The sparkling, clear water and a wide variety of aquatic insects contribute to Rock Creek's proven ability to produce trout. These same factors also force the angler to refine his techniques to achieve consistent success. In general, overdressed fly patterns or large, gaudy lures will not do the trick, especially on Rock Creek's sophisticated browns and larger rainbow. For the fly fisher, this means reasonable imitations of whatever adult insects are hatching or of the nymphs crawling along the streambottom. The hardware angler must give his lure realistic action and careful placement in order to attract a strike rather than spook the fish.

The angler will find a good, diverse insect population on Rock Creek every day during the season. Aside from the major salmon fly hatch, there are caddis, mayfly, and small stonefly hatches throughout the summer. A size 14 to 16 chartreuse-bodied stonefly is ideal during the summer evening hatch. The spruce moth adult emerges in August when the water is low and clear. An elk hair caddis is effective during this mid-day hatch. With such an abundance of aquatic insects for trout to feed on, the spin angler will often do best by fishing a bubble and fly set-up.

During the salmon fly hatch, conventional wisdom says to go to the head (upstream end) of the hatch for best fishing. However, trout often continue to look for salmon flies where the hatch has passed over, sometimes for weeks.

Floating has become increasingly popular as a way to combat the difficult high-water conditions in the early season, especially during the salmon fly hatch. However, conflicts between floating anglers and bank anglers have arisen due to Rock Creek's small size and narrow channels. After monitoring the situation, FWP set restrictions prohibiting fishing from boats after June 30 until November 30. Anyone wishing to float Rock Creek should consult the pamphlet, *Montana Afloat #3, Rock Creek,* for a map and detailed information on the stream.

In the early season, wading Rock Creek provides both a challenge and an opportunity to the angler. The challenge is to make your way safely amid the swift currents and slick cobble bottoms. The opportunity is that hard-chargers can reach water—and fish—that most anglers only give a passing glance.

By mid-summer, anglers can wade most sections of the stream without too much difficulty. The best crossing points, where runs become shallow at the head of a riffle, are usually not more than a couple hundred yards apart. Rocks grow slicker with algae throughout the course of the summer, so felt-soled waders are recommended.

Subtle changes in topography and stream habitat divide Rock Creek into three sections, each from 10 to 15 miles in length. At its upper end, immediately below the confluence of the east and west forks, Rock Creek hosts gentle pocket water, which twists its way through a 0.5-mile-wide valley. Relatively small and unsophisticated cutthroat dominate the trout population here. Both flies and lures will produce reasonable catches of 8- to 12-inch fish if casted into the likely spots behind midstream rocks and at the heads of the few deeper pools.

The middle section of Rock Creek begins where the canyon walls constrict just above the mouth of Big Hogback Creek. From this point downstream for the next 15 miles, Rock Creek's swift flow becomes that much swifter, and holding water becomes a thing to be cherished. Although the continuous, swift riffles look somewhat unpromising, by all means stop the car, put on your waders, and start fishing. The trout are here—in excellent numbers. And don't forget your polarized sunglasses. They're a must for reading the rushing water and allowing you to distinguish between the 1- to 2-foot-deep runs where fish can be found and the less-than-1-foot-deep stretches where they can not.

Rainbow trout constitute about 60 percent of the fish population in the middle section of Rock Creek, but cutthroat numbers are still not what they should be. FWP may propose catch-and-release for all cutthroats to protect their numbers. These scrappy, but vulnerable, natives now make up about 20 percent of the population, after having dwindled to negligible numbers when the former liberal limits were in force. Most rainbows will go 12 to 14 inches, with cutts averaging a little smaller. The slot limit regulations requiring catch-and-release of trout between 12 and 20 inches have helped increase the number of rainbow larger than 14 inches.

FWP cautions that fishing for bull trout is prohibited and all bull trout must be released unharmed. The best way to identify a bull trout is to look for black on the dorsal fin. If there are no visible black spots, throw it back.

The lower section of Rock Creek offers the greatest variety of trout habitat, with logjams, undercut banks, deep runs, and deeper pools. Brown trout and rainbow predominate here, with good numbers of 14- to 18-inch browns and 10- to 14-inch rainbows. Typically, the browns hold in the most protected lies; consequently, they prove hard to catch, making up only half the reported catch. Big spawners from the lower Clark Fork River show up in late fall, including some over 5 pounds. The deep pools and swift runs hold a few rainbows up to 2.5 pounds.

Successful fishing on Rock Creek requires diligent wading and careful reading of the swift water. "This is hard fishing for the novice fisherman, who often believes the fish aren't there," Peters claims. A ten-year creel census found that nearly half the anglers on Rock Creek don't catch any fish, while a small minority of anglers get most of the catch. Rock Creek is one stream where experience really pays.

TRIBUTARIES

Rock Creek has two major tributaries that provide fishing. The **East Fork of Rock Creek** flows through pasture and haylands with natural brushy banks. A small creek, the East Fork has good fishing for nice cutthroat and brookies. Permission must be gained from private landowners for access, however.

The **West Fork of Rock Creek** has easy access through National Forest land, but due to a sediment problem, it has a low fish population. There are some nice cutthroat, though, and the creek receives only light fishing pressure. The West Fork is small, running through low meadowlands with brushy banks.

ACCESS

The **Rock Creek Road** follows Rock Creek closely along much of its length, providing good stream access. This is a narrow gravel road requiring slow travel. Area residents like it this way, because it helps minimize the road traffic. Anglers get too impatient with the slow, bumpy pace and pull off early to hit the river.

The lower 15 miles of Rock Creek are bounded by National Forest land, with private lands along the road. There are several access sites where you can walk in to the river as well as various points where the road meets the river. Once on the streambank, the angler has unlimited access to the river.

The middle stretch of river offers the easiest access, as it is bordered by the road for almost 15 miles.

The upper river has the toughest access. Private lands between the road and stream limit access. Permission may be sought from any of several landowners, whose large ranches can provide access to long stretches of river. The road from Philipsburg is the best way to reach the upper river.

The Lolo National Forest maintains eight small campgrounds along the length of Rock Creek. They are open from late May through September, with a maximum fourteen-day limit on use. Needless to say, these are popular recreation spots on weekends.

14 Smith River

Overview: In the long list of reasons why people fish, one of the most frequently mentioned is "getting away from the rat race." Even an hour or two of fishing refreshes the spirit and puts the world in the right perspective. Imagine the tonic of a fishing trip lasting several days through the spectacular Smith River Canyon. As a getaway experience, floating and fishing the Smith certainly ranks among the best.

In recent years, however, the word about the Smith has gotten out. Due to heavy floating use, currently only 9 parties may launch daily. Launches are given out by lottery drawing. Information on applying for a float permit is included later in this chapter.

> **Key species:** Rainbow trout, brown trout, brook trout, and warm water species below Truly Bridge
> **Use:** Regulated floating by permit system, but the section from Camp

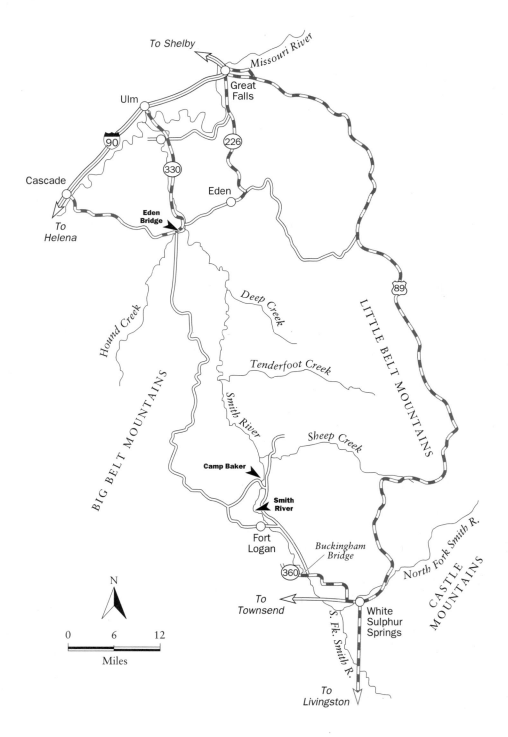

Baker to Eden Bridge ranks 50th statewide for fishing pressure despite restricted access.

Key flies and lures: Flies—Muddler Minnow, Olive Sculpin, Yellow Humpies and Goofus Bugs, Royal Wulffs, stonefly nymph, Hares Ear Nymph, Yellow Stimulators, Joe's Hopper and Parachute Adams. Lures—Hammered Brass, Red and White Daredevle, Mepps, and Krocodile Patterns. Baitfrom Rock Creek to Eden Bridge, the Smith is closed to bait fishing to all but children under twelve years of age, but below Eden Bridge bait anglers enjoy good success in warmer waters.

The fishing: Like the forks of the Flathead and the wild Missouri, the Smith float appeals even to those who don't own a fishing rod. The usual float trip starts at the Camp Baker Fishing Access and ends nearly 60 miles downstream at the Eden Bridge. In between, the river bounces from one canyon wall to the other. Rarely does the river head in any one direction for long. The fairly swift current and thousands of boulders combine to make innumerable minor rapids. Other than a few clusters of cabins and an occasional fence, floaters see few signs of man.

Former fishing guide Frank Johnson once described the canyon float as a progressive learning experience for the beginning angler. In the upper section, large numbers of rainbow (few of them big) provide fairly easy fishing. Rainbow numbers are down in recent years with higher brown trout populations, but you'll still find a few healthy rainbows around the rocks.

The whole canyon section of the river conforms to the classic riffle-pool-run pattern. As the Smith gains volume with additional water from tributaries such as Rock Creek and Tenderfoot Creek, the riffles and pools become deeper, favoring larger fish. The water flows in more complicated patterns with more eddies and undercut banks. And brown trout make up an increasing percentage of the population. The middle and lower reaches of the canyon call for more skill and sophistication from the angler.

Once the Smith leaves the canyon, the runs lengthen and the gradient begins to flatten. Past the Eden Bridge, the angler begins to run into what former FWP employee Al Wipperman describes as "catfish water, with lots of slack water and mud streambed." The Truly Bridge marks the end of significant numbers of trout.

The upper Smith down to Camp Baker once provided lively fishing for the few anglers who tried it. John Bailey, son of the late great angler, Dan Bailey, liked to drive the short distance from Livingston to the expansive hay meadows along this meandering stream. The section from Fort Logan to Sheep Creek was almost devoid of other anglers, but full of cut banks, deep pools, and plenty of trout. But Bailey reports that several dry years coupled with a couple severe winters, devastated the upper Smith. Indeed, many of Montana's smaller shallow streams froze out during the winter of 1989–90, but fishing appears to be picking up again as fish recruits re-enter these waters. Bailey has high hopes that the upper Smith will soon offer terrific dry fly fishing once again.

When talking with people who have floated the Smith, worries about the future of the river frequently surface. Hank Fischer, author of *Floater's*

Guide to Montana, hopes that new cabin subdivisions won't spring up along the banks, ruining the wilderness feeling of the canyon. The current float fees contribute toward a fund for conservation easements and other strategies for preserving the experience. FWP's efforts and the efforts of non-profit conservation groups may help ensure future preservation of the wild Smith River Corridor.

Bailey and Wipperman both mention that unhealthy water temperatures due to extensive flood irrigation in the upper basin can be a problem.

In recent years the main concern on the Smith has been use. After instituting a lottery-based floating permit system, FWP is concerned about several maximum use targets that were exceeded in the early 1990s. The number of days with more than 300 floaters in the corridor was at a record high of 21 in 1997. This prompted the adoption of higher user fees and reexamination of the management plan. For current regulations and to apply for a permit write:

Department of Fish, Wildlife & Parks
P.O. Box 6610
Great Falls, MT 59401

There are some dangers and difficulties in floating the Smith. It's unusual not to see a rattler on the trip, for example. And there are so many rocks that the Smith can beat the bottom out of any craft.

The permit system does limit the number of floaters. And so far, FWP research shows a fishery that is holding its own. The river's protectors would like to keep it that way.

A trip down the Smith River is an unforgettable fishing experience.

All successful lottery permit winners floating the Smith must pay a user fee at the put-in, and the number of outfitters working the river is now limited. In addition, all parties must declare which campsites they will use during their journey down the Smith. A seasonal river ranger ensures compliance with these regulations and offers aid and information to those requesting it. A good river map and detailed information can be found in *Montana Afloat #9, the Smith River.*

When can anglers float and fish the canyon section? Each year's weather pattern differs, but the average peak runoff comes the last week of May. The record high runoff peaked at around 3,000 cfcs, but most year's peak runoff stays below 500 cfcs. In a year of at least average precipitation, the river is both dangerous and very muddy at the height of runoff. Hank Fischer has had a good trip in April, when he saw black bears and elk on the riverbanks, but some Aprils in Montana can be miserably cold and wet for floaters.

Somewhat more predictably, the period of June 10 to July 10 should have mostly clear water at levels that are neither too high nor too low. Later in the summer the heavy demands of irrigation mean too little water for most crafts to clear the rocks. In some autumns after the irrigation gates close, the Smith has enough water to float it again. The secret here, in John Bailey's experience, is "a slippery bottomed boat."

A heavy thunderstorm in the watershed translates into a rapid rise in the river's level almost immediately, but unlike some rivers, the Smith will usually drop and clear with equal rapidity.

Between the stable banks of the Smith lives a nice range of trout food: mayflies, caddis, a few stoneflies, a good numbers of sculpin, and schools of minnows. Combine this food and excellent cover with good water quality, and the result is a fine fishery. Mixing in a spectacular and unspoiled canyon makes a recipe for a float-fishing getaway trip among the best in the west.

Strategies: Whatever an angler chooses to tie on the end of the fishing line, whether it be a lure or a fly, the Smith has the right kinds of water for that choice. Spin anglers will find plenty of deeper riffles and runs as well as the holes to their liking. Cut banks, boulder pockets, and riffles await the fly fisher. From Rock Creek to Eden Bridge, the Smith is closed to bait fishing to all but children under twelve years of age, but elsewhere on the river bait anglers enjoy good success.

In the upper river basin from above White Sulphur Springs down to Camp Baker, the Smith meanders through hay meadows and pastureland. A modest-sized stream at this point, the river still provides lots of deep water at the bends. The rainbow and brookies stay in the pools or right up against the bank most of the time, except during the twilight feeding frenzy. Fling your flies and lures at the banks.

Below Camp Baker, in the bigger river, boulders change the picture somewhat. Holes and banks still hold plenty of promise but rocks provide good cover, too, harboring many a trout. A skillful angler can really operate a well-rigged nymph with plenty of weight. In any river, trout spend the vast majority of their time hugging the bottom out of the current's heavy flow. As food tumbles or swims toward the trout, they may move a short distance to seize it. The closer a weighted nymph gets to the bottom where the trout waits, the more likely it will be taken. In the Smith, holes can be very deep and anglers should load up with plenty of split shot.

Spin anglers happily find the Smith relatively free of serious moss problems. Standard wares such as hammered brass and red-and-whites work well; but if you're floating the canyon, bring a good stock—it's a long way to the nearest tackle shop.

Fly fishers will not encounter massive hatches of any one bug. Both Bailey and Johnson think it relatively unimportant to match the hatches perfectly. Bailey uses attractor patterns such as Wulffs and Goofus. Hoppers work very well during the grasshopper season and should be fished up against the banks.

Bailey and Johnson also recommend trying any of the standard larger stonefly nymphs, weighted in the pools. Keeping in mind the good population of sculpins, try Muddler Minnows as proven performers, although Johnson confesses he is not convinced trout eat sculpin imitations because they think they are sculpins. In the autumn, stick a few small streamers in the vest.

Early and late in the fishing season any time of the day might be good, but when the hot days of mid-summer bear down on the river with their glaring sunlight, fishing is generally best in the mornings or evenings.

Bailey finds that most anglers are not aggressive enough in fishing the Smith. By this he means that anglers will frequently stand in just one spot,

A young angler fishing one of the many deep riffles in the Smith River.

fruitlessly whipping the water into froth without any luck. These anglers assume that if they can't catch fish in the spot they are in, they can't catch them anywhere in the river. Bailey often finds that, while the first riffle-pool may be dead, the next one might be alive with feeding fish. Keep moving!

TRIBUTARIES

Most of the tributaries to the Smith River run through private land so follow stream access laws accordingly. "Some people swear by the North Fork," Bailey reports. Much of the **North Fork of the Smith** runs through one ranch. Above the fork's reservoir, anglers find a smattering of rainbow mixed in with crowds of brookies. Below the reservoir they find mostly brown trout, which thrive in the warmer waters.

The **South Fork of the Smith** produces pan-sized brookies by the carload. A small, meandering stream, the South Fork makes a good place to teach youngsters the joys of fishing.

Wipperman singles out three other tributaries of the Smith as good fisheries. The first is **Sheep Creek**, one of the largest feeder streams and an excellent fishery for rainbow, which is followed by roads much of its length. Second, 10 or 12 miles from the Smith, a natural falls interrupts the flow of **Tenderfoot Creek**. Above the falls hybrid rainbow and cutthroat swim ; below, browns and rainbow rule the stream. The third tributary is **Rock Creek**, which is strong for rainbow and browns.

ACCESS

Floating the Smith is by lottery drawing and restricted only to private floaters. The Smith has just three developed fishing access sites. The first is at the end of a county road downstream a couple of miles from Fort Logan, above Whitetail Deer Creek. FWP does not recommend this spot for putting in to float, but anglers can fish a considerable length of the river up and down from the camp-ground and picnic area and still be within this block of public land.

About 6 miles downstream from the first access site is **Camp Baker**, where floaters traditionally put in to run the canyon. While there are no facilities at Camp Baker, FWP has posted a considerable amount of information including an extremely helpful map of the Smith. Floaters must register here. Also, anglers can fish 0.5-mile or so of the west bank on this smaller parcel of public land.

The next access site for the floater is **Eden Bridge**, but it does not offer much access to the non-floating angler. Below the canyon, **the Eden Bridge Road** provides some casual access, but for most of this section, anglers need to knock on doors for permission.

Other than at a few bridges, no other public access exists. In the upper basin, anglers need to inquire at ranches to reach the river. In the canyon section, several rough roads do reach the cabin communities along the river, but these roads are private and the gates are often padlocked.

15 Stillwater River

Overview: "Stillwater" is a misnomer. One suspects that the early explorer who named this river either looked only at a short section or had a wry sense of humor. The Stillwater has less quiet water proportionally than any river in the state.

Intrepid kayakers love this roly-poly stream. Boulders, many the size of large chest freezers, stud almost the entire length of the river. The melt water from Montana's loftiest mountains courses its way through these boulder fields with plenty of foam and froth. Long after it enters the prairie land of eastern Montana, the Stillwater still looks like a mountain stream.

Surrounded by fabled trout waters such as the Bighorn, Yellowstone, and Madison Rivers, the Stillwater receives little national or state attention. Instead, it makes a popular destination for local anglers who know its beauty and excellent fishing. Trout fanciers in any state would love to have the Stillwater nearby.

> **Key species:** Yellowstone cutthroat, rainbow trout, brown trout, brook trout, and whitefish.
>
> **Use:** The lower section from Nye to the Yellowstone ranks 29th statewide for fishing pressure, but the upper section is less fished.
>
> **Key flies and lures:** Flies—Muddler Minnow, Black Matuka Sculpin, Yellow Humpies, Royal Wulffs, stonefly nymphs, Sofa Pillow, Bird's Stone, Elk Hair Caddis, Light Cahill, Joe's Hopper, and Parachute Adams. Lures—gold-colored selections of Mepps, Thomas Cyclones, and Panther Martins. Bait—worms, grubs, and hoppers.

The fishing: A high glacial cirque including Daisy Pass marks the source of the Stillwater. On the edge of this basin stands the remains of mining activity, some of it recent. Water seeping from the mine tailings has a sickening orange color, the telltale of the acid mine drainage which pollutes the first 5 miles of the river. Below the confluence of Goose Creek the pollution has been almost entirely settled out or diluted.

Despite the tainted beginning, a hallmark of the Stillwater is its clear water, exceptional for rivers east of the Continental Divide. Fisheries biologist and author of *Fishing the Beartooths*, Pat Marcuson, who spent several years surveying the Beartooth lakes for the Montana Department of Fish, Wildlife, and Parks (FWP), thinks the enduring granite rock of the headwaters is responsible for the low dissolved solids of the water. So few electrolytes exist that FWP has trouble during its fish-shocking surveys in the upper reaches and Marcuson once resorted to swimming with a snorkel in the river to count trout.

Below Lake Abundance, the Stillwater cascades out of the high basin and charges through a narrow canyon, pausing only a couple of times in mountain meadows. Wounded Man and Flood Creeks add appreciably to the water volume.

Along the popular Woodbine-Stillwater hiking trail, the cascading water slows in pocket pools of deeper water where throngs of pan-sized brookies

Fishing the boulder pockets on the Stillwater.

15 Stillwater River

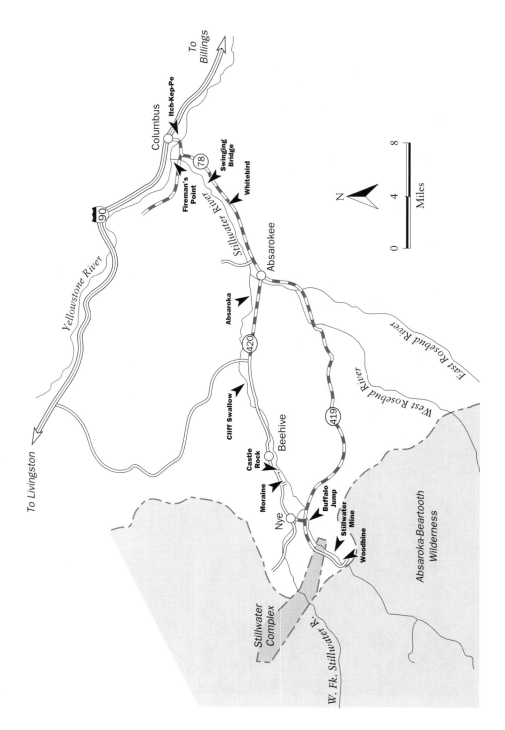

compete with occasional rainbow and cutthroat. The river widens briefly at Sioux Charley Lake and then plunges by Woodbine Campground and into the prairie.

In the short section between Woodbine and the Stillwater Mine, the numbers of brookies and cutthroat sharply diminish while rainbow, and increasingly, browns predominate. Near the community of Nye, the West Fork of the Stillwater adds some more water volume. The river warms up and picks up more minerals.

Below Nye, the river no longer stair-steps its way in cascades but continues to act like a mountain stream. The gradient is still steep enough to make a very swift current and, with the constrictions in a riverbed of boulders, the river has rapids, and whitewater as well. Boating in an open canoe between Beehive and Absarokee has been termed suicidal; for the angler wading waist deep, this means continual apprehension about footing and many furtive glances downstream.

Below Cliff Swallow Fishing Access, the velocity slows another notch; the riverbed broadens and braids around islands. Irrigation diversions subtract a considerable portion of the river's water volume, especially in August and September.

At Absarokee, the two Rosebud rivers add their water, but also some silt. The boulders so common to the upper river give way increasingly to smaller cobble. Although more easy-going, the Stillwater continues to feature an occasional swift section, especially a sharp drop-off over a ledge below the White Bird Fishing Access Site (just above the Beartooth Hereford Ranch bridge)

The lower river supports more large fish, due in part to a substantial interchange with the Yellowstone. Anglers could tie in to brown trout up to 6 pounds and more between Absarokee and the Yellowstone, while 2- to 4-pounders make up the vast majority of the top weight class in the river between the Mouat Mine and Beehive.

Marcuson found "pretty good numbers of 1- to 2-pound resident rainbow" throughout the river from the Stillwater Mine downstream to the Yellowstone. But from March 20 to May 20 during the years he studied these waters, he also found migrant rainbow surging up the Stillwater from as far away as Big Timber. Why would these fish, some weighing 6 pounds and more, travel up to 120 river miles to spawn? Marcuson thinks "the spawning rainbow have a critical need for small gravel, and they can't find enough of these kinds of gravel beds in the Boulder and middle Yellowstone." Fortunately, the riverbed between Beehive and the Stillwater Mine is much more to their liking. Sometimes in just 6 inches of water, often in the side channels, these wild rainbow start stocking future generations for both the Yellowstone and Stillwater—maybe even some for the Boulder.

In contrast, Marcuson thinks the browns may not move very far to spawn in October and November. "They tend to pick the area behind boulders in 2 to 4 feet of water." Such places are widely available in the Stillwater. The browns may move only a few yards or a few miles—the spawning run is plainly not as dramatic as the rainbow.

Some anglers love whitefish, some hate them, and some just find them a bit of a nuisance. Regardless, the Stillwater has its share. Marcuson notes on the positive side that the river has "some of the best whitefish fishing in the state, in terms of size, around Absarokee." The community of Nye has an annual and popular gathering to catch and smoke whitefish. Yet guide Curt Collins and a chorus of other anglers find the whitefish frustrating and fear they are taking over the river. Collins suggests that trout would be much better off if the whitefish population could be sharply reduced.

But the Stillwater has more serious problems than too many whitefish. Above Nye, the Benbow and Mouat Mines stand as evidence to past mining for chrome in a band of mineralized rock known as the Stillwater Complex. Today the Stillwater Mine has revived the threat to the Stillwater's health. Such undertakings involve large-scale blastings of tunnels and removal of enormous quantities of ore.

Extra roads, erosion, and potential pollution concern anglers and the FWP. What happens, for example, if an adit hits a column of underground water which gushes down the watershed loaded with nitrates? An extreme case, perhaps, but John Manville already has shut down one adit that flooded. Fortunately, state laws restrict the miners in terms of pollution. FWP has good base-line information on water quality and fish populations; any substantial change could be spotted.

Mike, Steve, and Dewey Mouat, former fishing instructors and guides on the Stillwater, point out the larger concern. "The mines bring in lots of people and make them locals. The result is much more fishing pressure." In response, FWP set a two-trout limit, of which only one can measure over 13 inches.

Strategies: Wherever found on the Stillwater, the traditional hot spots—logjams, deep banks, the inside of riffle-corners, fast water dumping into slow—will produce fish as they will in any trout stream. But the special feature which the Stillwater displays even more than the Gallatin or Boulder is the boulder-pocket. Like the fellow who orders a hamburger in a restaurant famous for its prime rib, many an angler misses the most exciting part of the Stillwater by dismissing its boulder-pockets.

To the inexperienced eye, whitewater breaking around and over the boulders looks much too fast and shallow to hold trout. Yet, as a wade into the midst of one of these boulder fields will prove, there are many quiet, deep holes, or pockets, behind the current-braking boulders. Trout feel secure beneath the fractured water surface. The aeration of whitewater makes these areas veritable food factories. Once an angler discovers the concentration of trout around these boulders, that person begins to seek this kind of water which so many anglers shun.

The hydrology of these boulder-pockets creates problems for spin and bait anglers. The washing machine action of the water behind the boulders wraps the hardware around unseen tree branches or wedges the hooks between rocks. Even though skillful anglers could catch lots of trout in these

Deep-water pockets near the Stillwater shoreline are great places for trout.

Fast water alternating with deep pools—one reason the Stillwater has good fishing.

spots, the bait and spin anglers usually gravitate to the pools where they feel more comfortable.

As a rough generalization, Pat Marcuson points out that the lower river is more suited to bait, the middle section to spinning, and the upper to flies. The bait usually used is worms. May and June mark the best months for bait fishing—on all parts of the river.

As the water drops and clears enough for trout to see at least a couple of feet, lures come into their own. Try Mepps, Thomas Cyclones, and Panther Martins. Red and white lures do not work well. Gold metal brings more fish to the net than silver or brass. Using a 6.5 to 7.5 foot rod with fourth-ounce lures, cast upstream and reel back fast or cast downstream with a slow retrieval.

Above Nye during high water, some anglers believe gaudy streamers are the only flies that work. Anglers should stick to the backwaters, sloughs, and shallows.

In mid-June around Absarokee and ten days later near Nye, a medium size stonefly known in Latin as *doroneuria* emerges and provides some surface action if the water has cleared sufficiently. Several other smaller stonefly hatches come off the water in the next month, occasionally bringing on the spectacle of 2-pound brown trout rolling on the river's surface like tarpon.

Small versions (#8) of popular stonefly imitations like the Sofa Pillow and Bird's Stone fished dry or slightly submerged will hook feeding fish.

Marcuson calls the Stillwater "a pretty good stream for caddis hatches in May and on." The rainbow he catches are full of caddis and caddis cases. Mouat likes a light green caddis with an orange head. Or try an elk hair caddis. And if no hatch is on, Mouat advises using searcher patterns such as #12 Royal Wulffs, Humpies, Adams, and light Cahills.

Floating such a turbulent, dangerous stream, especially with waders on, is an invitation to an early grave. Know the troublesome spots in advance, buy good equipment, and know how to use it. But anglers who don't like the sound of these cautionary notes should relax. The Stillwater provides terrific wade fishing from early July throughout the summer. And perhaps the best part, as mentioned before, is wading through the boulder fields.

But where does one cast in the midst of the chaotic currents and boulders? The eddies behind the boulders almost always hold fish. A few fish, including some of the larger ones, will station themselves just in front of the boulders, which bump the flowing water and create an easy place for trout to hover. Watch for the spots where fast, narrow channels deepen and slow—trout wait under the tell-tale choppy haystacks, gulping down the food brought by the conveyor-belt current.

Anglers do best casting just slightly to one side or the other or straight upstream. "Don't cross your pockets," one outfitter advises. Casting into a pocket from the side results in immediate drag on the fly, which does not look natural to trout. Using short casts helps minimize drag as well.

Caddis fly hatches such as this can drive trout crazy. AL TROTH PHOTO

Curt Collins thinks the most common problem fly fishers exhibit is feeling that they must fish with a dry fly. "If they worked with nymphs and streamers they would catch more and larger trout." Gold-ribbed Hares Ear, fished near the surface in a free drift, are recommended. For weighted nymphs fished to bounce along the bottom, try a green latex caddis or golden, brown, and black stonefly nymph imitation. Occasionally, a Bitch Creek nymph fished like a streamer also works well. For real streamers, try a black Matuka. Anglers familiar with Muddler Minnows will find they work well on the Stillwater.

Streamers come in handy both early and late in the fishing season. For anglers willing to brave the windy and cold early fishing for the spawning rainbow, cast up and a little across, then retrieve with a little tension. One fishing guide thinks this aggravates the trout, which will strike at the streamer sometimes without intending to eat it. The net result of this is many missed strikes, especially for the inexperienced angler. Practice helps.

Streamers will also catch fish in August and September, especially in the lower half of the river. But this is also the time to use terrestrials. Pat Marcuson calls the Stillwater "a great grasshopper stream." Former FWP employee Clint Bishop recalls seeing numerous black and orange caterpillars as well. Since terrestrials usually fall in along the banks, anglers do best when they concentrate their efforts along the edge. Grasshoppers and their imitations will bring fish to the surface, but on bright, sunny days fish will go after the slightly submerged, "drowned" hoppers more often. Black and orange Wooly Worms make excellent representations of the caterpillars.

TRIBUTARIES

Of the many streams that combine to make the Stillwater, the three largest deserve mention here. All three drain watersheds in the lofty Beartooth Mountains not far from the main river's drainage.

The **West Fork of the Stillwater** cascades and pools past Initial Creek Campground at the edge of the Beartooth-Absaroka Wilderness. Skirting Horseman Flats, this medium-sized stream flows through private lands almost all the way to Nye and the main river. Above Initial Creek, the West Fork supports mostly pan-sized brookies; below, some chunky rainbow and browns populate the stream.

Born in the meltwater of Beartooth glaciers, **West Rosebud Creek** runs through Silver, Island, and Mystic Lakes. It furnishes hydroelectric power below Mystic Lake, then provides good fishing through a narrow canyon before running out into the irrigated prairie land for its last 25 miles.

Pat Marcuson terms the stream "a good, small fishery," especially between Emerald Lake and the flatlands.

Marcuson rates the **East Rosebud** as something of a disappointment. The wilderness sections between the lakes furnish some good fishing, but from East Rosebud Lake down to the confluence with the West Rosebud, fish numbers and sizes are small. FWP has experimented with plantings of different trout, but without marked success. Still, some weekend anglers report fun fishing for pan-sized trout both in the meadows near Black Mountain and below Roscoe along the cottonwoods.

ACCESS

Because of the Stillwater's close proximity to Billings and Yellowstone County, FWP has wisely tried to spread out the angling pressure. Seven FWP accesses, combined with two Forest Service strips of riverbank land plus some casual access, all help anglers reach some of the river, but the large majority of river frontage remains in private hands.

Fireman's Point Fishing Access Site (FAS) provides the first public fishing spot on the drive upstream from Columbus.

The next developed access is FWP's **White Bird** FAS, which, combined with an unmarked access just below White Bird, gives anglers a considerable distance of good riffle water.

Just 1 mile below Absarokee, Thompson's Bridge crosses the Stillwater. A dirt road to the left runs along the river for quite some distance. Even though the river is so close in places that it could be fished from the car, ask permission.

West of Absarokee, four more FWP accesses allow the angler to reach the middle river. **Cliff Swallow** FAS features practically every kind of trout water found in Montana. **Castle Rock** has some shallow riffles and pockets. **Moraine** has outstanding pocket water. And **Buffalo Jump**, known locally as Nye Bridge, has some pool, boulder-pocket, and riffle water.

Upstream several miles from Nye lies an unnamed Forest Service access. This strip of land gives a taste of the upper, smaller river with a spectacular mountainous backdrop.

Lastly, the Forest Service's **Woodbine Campground and Trailhead** stand as the gateway to the upper wilderness section of the Stillwater.

During weekends from mid-April to mid-July, anglers wishing to fish the Stillwater have three choices. The first alternative is to wedge oneself in at one of the established accesses. Watch your backcast, please.

Other anglers may prefer to attempt float-fishing. While opening many miles of otherwise inaccessible river, this alternative nevertheless has several drawbacks. Some sections of the river are too hazardous. On the safer sections, the runoff waters still push downstream at a swift clip, which test the proficiency of even expert casters on occasion. Floating anglers should stay in their boats—easier said than done when a lure-eating log has hold of the hardware.

The third alternative is to seek permission from private landowners, who often grant it to anglers who will respect their property. Be aware that one bad experience with an angler, whether it is a gate left open, litter, fire, or the like, can close that section of the river to the public for years.

16 Yellowstone River

Overview: Annually, anglers from all over the country and abroad come to the banks of the Yellowstone to pay homage to this revered river. The Yellowstone commands respect and inspires devotion, with a veritable Who's Who of Fishing in its roll call of admirers. Some have even called the Yellowstone "the Yankee Stadium of trout fishing."

> **Key species:** Yellowstone cutthroat, rainbow trout, brown trout, brook trout, whitefish, walleye, northern pike, bass, sturgeon, paddlefish, catfish, and other warm water species.
>
> **Use:** The section from Pine Creek down to the Shields River ranks 13th statewide for fishing pressure and is the most fished section of the river, although most sections rank in the top fifty for statewide fishing pressure.
>
> **Key flies and lures:** Flies—Yellow Marabou Muddler, Woolly Buggers and Worms, Royal Trudes, Bead-Head Stonefly Nymphs, Sofa Pillows, Elk Hair Caddis, Yellow Stimulators, Light Cahill, Joe's Hopper and Parachute Adams. Lures—gold and red-striped lures, Thomas Cyclones, Gold Panther Martins, and gold Krocidiles. Bait—worms, stoneflies, and hoppers.

A cutthroat coming up for a big salmon fly.

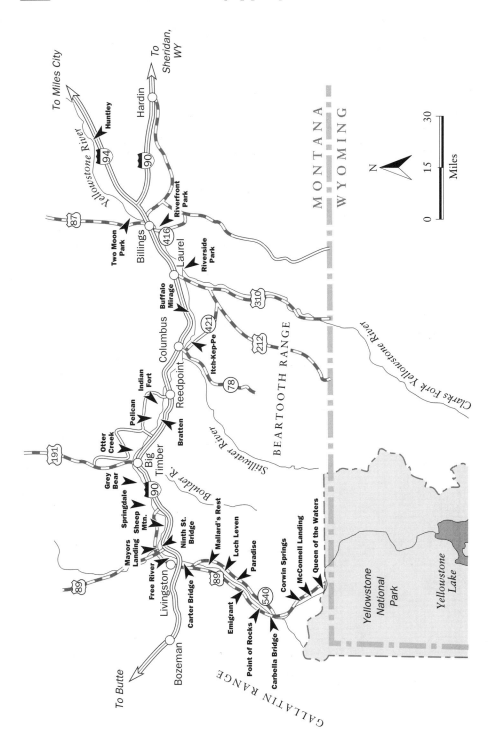

16 Yellowstone River (Lower)

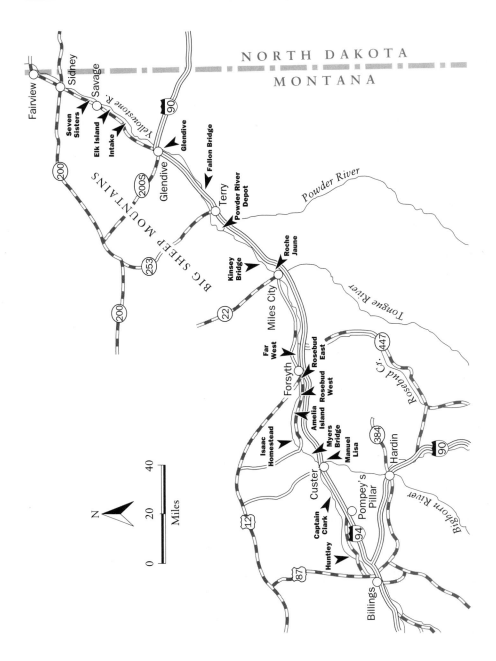

The fishing: What makes the Yellowstone so special? For starters, it drains an extraordinary watershed, including some of America's wildest scenery. The river rises just south of incomparable Yellowstone National Park in the Shoshone National Forest of Wyoming. From its beginnings until the river leaves the park at Gardiner, the Yellowstone has a pristine background rivaled by few rivers. Even after it forges its way past Gardiner, the Yellowstone draws added water from the congressionally mandated Absaroka-Beartooth Wilderness. Most trout waters can only wish for such impeccable sources.

Unlike other major rivers, the Yellowstone runs its entire 678-mile course without a major dam. Running free of impounding concrete slabs, the Yellowstone evokes awe in all river lovers who honor things wild. The faithful are attached to the free and wild spirit of the Yellowstone. In keeping with this wild spirit, the trout that swim in the Yellowstone are the progeny of their wild ancestors. The Yellowstone cutthroat is a true native; the browns, rainbow, and occasional brookies are many generations removed from any hatchery.

Another special attraction of the Yellowstone is the presence of trophy-sized trout. As with most major trout streams in Montana, trout over 18 inches comprise a small minority of the Yellowstone's population. Former guide and FWP biologist Rich Stevenson found that such fish were from less than 1 to 5 percent of the trout he sampled, depending on which section he was electrofishing. He also found the growth rate to be unspectacular, even low when compared with tailwater fisheries such as the Beaverhead and Bighorn.

Nevertheless, the Yellowstone does harbor some lunkers. John Bailey, of Dan Bailey's Fly Shop in Livingston, cites the example of a female brown caught on a streamer years back, which weighed 14 pounds, 14 ounces. Stevenson once shocked a brown 28 inches long with an incredible 21-inch girth; the fish was too heavy for the scale, but it weighed somewhere between 15 and 20 pounds.

Why does this river grow big trout when so many others don't? Several actors come into play here. With only minimal irrigation withdrawals, mining, and timber cutting, the Yellowstone's water quality is superior to most. High water quality results in an abundance of food for trout. In the Yellowstone, this means prodigious numbers of caddis and sculpin. As sculpin are less tolerant of poor water than trout are, the sculpin serves as the canary in the coal mine.

And, as the famous angler Dan Bailey once pointed out, the trout in the Yellowstone have deep pools in which to hide and rest. In the Madison River from Hebgen Dam most of the way to Ennis, trout do not have many of these hideouts and thus remain vulnerable to anglers. Hurley thinks that, in the Yellowstone, fish may die of old age without ever seeing a hook. They simply have a better chance to get big.

It is also possible that wild trout are more intelligent than hatchery fish, and that certain genetically superior trout continue to grow when they become 16 or 18 inches by switching their diets increasingly to other fish and not wasting much energy on insect larva. Stevenson once shocked a 5-pound brown

Sculpins make up a major part of the diet of big trout in western Montana rivers, including the Yellowstone. AL TROTH PHOTO

which had a 13-inch whitefish in its stomach. Obviously this fish was well on its way to becoming a trophy.

The Yellowstone has a long fishing season so there's no need to put the fishing equipment in cold storage. The late Joe Halterman, a superb angler and powerful friend of the Yellowstone, described the Yellowstone as an "all-season river." Even in January and February, when most western Montana streams are locked up in ice, anglers ply the banks of the Yellowstone on warmer days. Often these hardy anglers find success, even with dry flies.

While to the experienced eye the river looks much the same throughout its length from Gardiner on down, differences between stretches make for some variety. The river comes out of Yellowstone Park at a moderate rush. From Gardiner to the head of the Yankee Jim, the current is mostly strong, the streambed is studded with boulders, and the riffles and pools are very obvious. Anglers find this upper section does not seem as big, even though the river has about the same volume of water here as it does at Livingston. Thanks to appreciable numbers of cutthroat, this upper section has the strongest mix of species.

Despite Yankee Jim Canyon's reputation for wild water, the river actually slows as it narrows. Most of the truly deep water in the Yellowstone occurs in the canyon. Richard Parks, owner of Park's Fly Shop in Gardiner and author of *Fishing Yellowstone National Park*, recalls reports of a diver who dove to 60 feet. Three or four large rapids break up this otherwise placid stretch of river. Parks rates the canyon as generally tough fishing, but with outstanding holding water for some big fish.

Below the canyon, the river spreads out and slows further. A few islands begin to appear as the river moves around the foot of impressive Emigrant Peak. Very stable riverbanks make this a good section for bank-fishing. On the other hand, riffles here are poorly defined and weak for the most part. Few boulders break the smooth water surface of the long pools. Brown trout dominate here, with rainbow and cutthroat in the minority. The scenery alone can keep an angler coming back for years.

Near Mallard's Rest Fishing Access, the streambed tilts downward and the river speeds up. The difference is hardly perceptible from the highway above, but in the river, the change is profound. The floating angler encounters more riffles per mile; these riffles run faster and deeper. The river eats away at the banks much more voraciously. Rainbow now outnumber browns, and by a wide margin. The trout from Mallard's Rest down to below Livingston are larger and more numerous than in the river above.

Many of the best riffle-pools in this section have reputations and colorful names to match—Weeping Wall, Joe Brooks, Big Armstrong, Warm Springs, Whorehouse, Super, and Pumphouse.

Several miles below Livingston, the river turns its flow from northerly to eastward. In this "Big Bend" section, the river shifts channels from year to year and braids around many islands. The multiple channels create challenging, complex flow patterns and excellent fishing.

Below Springdale, the riffles become farther apart. The angling pressure here drops off slightly.

From Columbus to Billings, the Yellowstone enters a transitional phase to a warm-water fishery. Increasing sediment, turbidity, and water temperatures cut down on the number of trout, especially after the Clarks Fork dumps in near Laurel. On an encouraging note, anglers recently have caught more trout in the Billings area than in previous years. But below Billings, the angler's quarries are walleye, sauger, catfish, and even paddlefish.

FWP's Phil Stewart reports that sauger and walleye are in major decline on the lower Yellowstone, as are channel catfish. Paddlefish and shovelnose sturgeon are found as far upstream as Forsyth, though the majority are caught at Intake just below Glendive. The smallmouth bass fishery is doing well and attracting a growing number of anglers who enjoy the good fight these fish provide. Some burbot and northern pike round out the list of favored quarry.

Walleye are the prime target here, averaging 1 to 4 pounds. Bigger fish are not uncommon, and a walleye weighing over 15 pounds have been caught here. Sauger in the 6-pound range are occasionally caught. In 1991, a sauger—tipping the scales at just over 7.5 pounds—was pulled from the Yellowstone just above the mouth of the Bighorn. The most popular set-up for these two species is a bait combination.

Channel catfish run from Huntley downstream, with an abundance of 1- to 6-pound fish. Ten-pounders are common, and anglers take an occasional 15- to 20-pound catfish. These bottom-feeders go for stink baits and worms.

Angling for paddlefish brings a flurry of activity to the river in late spring. Below Intake, the season opens May 1 and runs through June. At and above Intake the fishing begins May 15. Stewart says that "paddlefish are found throughout the lower Yellowstone, but 90 percent of the season's catch occurs at Intake." The fish range from 15 to 70 pounds, the large spread due in part to a dramatic difference in size between the genders. Says Stewart, "You can usually guess a paddlefish's sex based on its weight. Males run smaller, from 15 to 35 pounds, and females go from 40 to 70 pounds." As of 1992, anglers are limited to one paddlefish per season and the fish must be tagged.

Shovelnose sturgeon are also common on the lower Yellowstone, even abundant in the lower Tongue and Powder rivers. Though most anglers don't hit the water in search of sturgeon, quite a number are incidentally snagged at Intake during the paddlefish season. All sturgeon must be handled carefully and immediately released.

Smallmouth bass are most common from Forsyth to the mouth of the Powder River. Anglers rely on the tried-and-true bass lures and bait. Fish range from 0.5 to 3 pounds.

Burbot and northern pike also attract anglers on the Lower Yellowstone. Stewart finds northerns from the mouth of the Bighorn River to Intake and recommends fishing at the mouths of tributaries. "Look in the backwater that usually forms where a stream or river spills into the Yellowstone. If the northerns are running, there'll be a crowd in that quiet water." The best time for northerns comes just after the winter's ice leaves the main stem.

Anglers scheduling their fishing trips should be mindful that the Yellowstone's water clears relatively late. Early fishing, such as in March, is often very good. In May, the river muddies and rises. On the average, runoff peaks around June 18. Individual years vary widely in their snowpack and flow patterns, but the river generally clears by mid-July, barring heavy rains in the wrong places. The Yellowstone often runs dirty even in July and August following major rains in the upper basin. Sometimes these murky flows last for one to two weeks, depending on the severity of the storm. FWP says the culprit is sediment-laden runoff from the sections of Yellowstone National Park that burned during the fires of 1988. As grasses and other plants re-establish themselves in the burns, the clarity of the runoff should improve. But John Bailey contends that these occasional dirty flows pre-date the 1988 fires. He attributes the problem to long-term overgrazing and top soil erosion in the basin below Yellowstone Park. Despite these concerns, the Yellowstone is usually coming into its prime just when many streams are going into hot weather slumps.

For anglers hoping to catch the salmon fly hatch, how the runoff progresses is of paramount importance. Parks has watched the hatch for thirty years. During the hatch he finds the river unfishable below Emigrant except with wet flies. One year in four will be really good from Emigrant up, and one in four will be "rather useless" below Gardiner. The other two years will see a week or two of fishing the salmon fly hatch above Yankee Jim Canyon about the second week of July. It's best to check the river first hand or call someone who knows the hatch and turbidity conditions.

Few rivers have better fishing today than they did fifty years ago—but the Yellowstone does. In those days, the Yellowstone ran heavy with sediment from mining operations around Emigrant and Jardine. Few sculpins and stoneflies lived in the river then, but now they prosper. In fact, the river seems in very good shape now, and most anglers just hope nothing comes along to muck up the river again. As long as the gold dredgers, dam builders, and coal miners keep their fingers off the Yellowstone, anglers will continue to honor this giant of a trout stream.

Anglers tired of the big water fishing of the main river can try the Yellowstone's spring creek tributaries, but must have reservations and pay a fee.

Strategies: Invariably, the angler's first impression of the Yellowstone is one of bigness. This is no intimate trout stream where the angler can cast or wade from one bank to the other. Small-stream anglers quickly get psyched out looking at this vast expanse of water. And compounding this intimidation is the unmarked, hard-to-read nature of the river. Anglers can't see the familiar nooks and crannies they knew on their streams back in Pennsylvania or New York.

Guides hear these complaints plenty. Their solution is to quickly cut the river down to size. Where is the most productive part of the river? It's in the first part of the strip of water up against either bank, provided the water is 18 inches or deeper. Richard Parks describes this strip as roughly 5 feet wide. If the bank is shaded by trees or brush, its potential ranks especially high.

Because of the Yellowstone's wandering ways, ranchers with river frontage have often resorted to riprapping to protect their river banks. Usually, riprapped banks make for deep water. And the big chunks of rock used for riprap provide excellent hangouts for trout, some of them big. Anglers should consider these spots as class I water.

Guides call the other most productive parts of the river "riffle-corners," "horns of plenty," or "golden triangles." Whatever the name, these places occur every time the river bends. When the river sweeps around these bends, it always leaves some quieter water on the inside of the curve. Between the slack water and the heavy, fast water is a zone, an area in the shape of a horn or a triangle, wherein the trout feed. Here the trout can hold their positions against the slower current while still taking advantage of the conveyer belt of food coming toward them. Where the angler finds those familiar nooks and crannies—such as undercut banks, downed trees, boulders, and the lower ends of islands—by all means, they should be fished. And during a spawning season, the tail end of pools and some side channels can provide lively action. Still, probably 90 percent of the river can be skipped. This goes especially for the middle of the river in the slower straight runs. Also, river trout shun slack, dead water.

As Mark Henckel of *The Billings Gazette* puts it, "The truth is that on few other rivers in Montana does the old rule of thumb about 10 percent of the fishermen catching 90 percent of the fish hold so true." The number one way that anglers can improve their results is to fish the more productive water. This takes time; the Yellowstone takes a lot of knowing. Those who fish the Yellowstone just once haven't given the river a fair chance.

Anglers who want to know the Yellowstone better would be wise to spend a day with a qualified guide. Arrange a lengthy float trip with the aim of learning some of the best fishing stretches. A good guide will provide boat transportation, lunch, and a wealth of knowledge—including instructions on how the angler can later return to especially likeable riffles and pools. Most tackle shops, such as Parks', Bailey's, and Anderson's, are happy to help arrange such trips.

Big western rivers like the Yellowstone demand beefier equipment than Pennsylvania's chalk streams. Generally speaking, the successful 10 percent of anglers cover far more water than average anglers do. Big water and frequently windy conditions require bigger, stiffer rods and more weight on the end of the line. The Yellowstone is no place for an ultra-light spinning rod or a wishy-washy 7-foot fly rod.

It is wise to carry two fly rods—an 8.5-foot rod with 7-weight line for fishing dry flies and a 9.5-footer with 9- or 10-weight line for going deep. With these rods, Hurley has mastered long distance casting, sometimes casting as far as 140 feet, which enables him to present his fly to more fish.

Most expert anglers do not agree that long-distance casting is necessary. The late Dan Bailey once countered that sometimes long-distance casting is "an experience in self-gratification. Some of the most productive fishermen I know," he said, "never cast more than 35 feet." But he agreed that many anglers need stronger rods because, in the wind, even short casts must be made with authority.

When the river runs high and muddy in May and June, only bait will catch fish. The smart angler who soaks worms almost anywhere out of the fast main current can catch plenty of whitefish, suckers, and trout with a can of worms. Other useful bait includes stonefly nymphs, known as "scratchers," and later in summer, grasshoppers.

Once the muddy waters start to settle out and turn greenish blue, the flashy spinning gear becomes effective. Many people with spinning outfits think their only task is to cast as far as possible. However this is not true, especially during this period of clearing water. The main goal should be getting the lure in front of and close to the fish.

When an angler stands on the bank desperately trying to reach the middle of the river with each cast, then retrieves the lure quickly and perhaps 1 foot or 2 below the surface, that angler is bound to be disappointed. Few fish will see the lure. Even if the fish could see it, they probably wouldn't make the effort to come from the bottom into the main force of the current and chase after the fast-moving lure. Lake fish will chase lures long distances, but river fish rarely do.

Instead, the spin angler must spot the quieter water and get the lure down to where the fish are holding. And the only way to get a lure down is to allow it to sink before starting the retrieve. A sure prescription for losing lures? Yes, but also the best prescription for catching trout.

The single most popular lure on the Yellowstone, in Parks' estimation, is the Thomas Cyclone. Parks usually recommends brass for ordinary days, but if the water or the weather is dirty, silver seems to work better. John Bailey suggests a lure with a red stripe. If anglers are after whitefish, they should stock up on Panther Martin Golds.

Spin and bait anglers naturally despise moss. Unfortunately, the green stuff starts showing up on their hooks several weeks after the water clears. August and September usually mark the most bothersome times for moss. The typical hard freeze in early October eliminates most of the problem. Before then, anglers beset by moss will find much less of it above Emigrant, where irrigation returns have not added fertilizer to the water.

A considerable amount of literature in sports magazines and books suggests that anglers must be very particular at choosing their flies, at least on certain trout streams such as the Henry's Fork, Firehole, and the spring creeks. But are the trout in the Yellowstone all that choosey?

"The Yellowstone is not so mysterious," Parks observes. "You don't have to know the Latin names of forty-five bugs. There's so many bugs on the Yellowstone that the fish are looking for everything." The only hatch Parks matches is the salmon fly.

The late Dan Bailey made much of his living tying, selling, even inventing flies. The front counter of his store includes perhaps 40 or 50 square feet of tiny boxes with a multitude of different patterns. But, like Parks, he didn't believe in the exact imitation theory. "Human eyes and fish eyes are different." Bailey laughed. "Even on spring creeks, I can do very well with a size 18 Royal Coachman. Tell me what bug a Royal Coachman imitates."

For dry flies, Bailey suggested picking proven patterns that float well and stand up under use. These patterns include the Royal Wulff, the Goofus, the Trude patterns, the Adams, and one of the grasshopper imitations. He added one more to the list: the wet or dry Muddler, "designed to imitate a sculpin but also imitates a hopper...or maybe it just looks good to the fish."

Richard Parks frequently uses a Coachman Trude, a fly which includes some wraps of peacock fuzz. "Peacock does something to fishes' psyche," he theorizes, "it gets into their brains and twists them around until the fish make it what they want it to be." Parks adds that the Coachman Trude works well for beginners who don't quite have the handle on drag. When the fly gets pulled underwater, it acts like a mini-streamer.

If an angler decides to go after the larger trout, then nymphs, wet flies, or streamers are generally the choices. Big trout eat the lion's share of their meals along the bottom, only rarely rising to the surface for dessert. And sometimes, of course, even the smaller trout don't work on surface insects.

Dan Bailey once called nymphs "the 'in' thing—they've almost completely taken over from the old wet flies. But flies like the wooly worm are probably imitating nymphs more than drowned insects, anyway." Parks likes a long-shanked, olive Wooly Worm as the best imitation of a stonefly nymph. With, most likely, a sink tip fly line, nymphing anglers try to achieve a dead drift, then perhaps impart a twitching retrieve toward the bank at the end of the drift. Feeling or seeing the strike is tricky, but the angler who masters nymph fishing is deadly.

Fishing streamers is perhaps the easiest fly fishing technique to master, once the angler has the right equipment. Guide Ray Hurley, who is the most vocal advocate of streamer fishing on the Yellowstone in the fall, uses a super sink, high density shooting head. At the business end of that line he ties a short stout leader. Behind the shooting head, he uses monofilament shooting line such as Amnesia followed by his backing. Whatever streamers he employs, whether it is a Muddler, Spuddler, dark or light Spruce Fly, the streamer has an extra heavy salt water hook on it. This follows his whole aim of getting the streamer down near the bottom quickly.

From September 15 until winter sets in, Hurley takes his streamer outfit to the inside tops of riffles. He is thinking about the big brown trout which at this time of year are establishing their redds. Once in a while, he will pick up a fat rainbow as a bonus. Whether the fish strike at his streamer out of annoyance, hunger, or defensive protection is subject to debate, but Hurley wants those strikes, whatever the reason.

The first cast is across and slightly upstream. The current immediately grabs the middle section of his line, but Hurley quickly rolls his rod to mend his line back upstream, which gives his streamer a little more time to sink. The current sweeps line and streamer downstream. As the streamer arcs through the heavy water, Hurley jigs it a few times, then starts stripping in his line in sharp, 2-foot jerks. When he has the streamer within 30 feet of his rod tip, he takes a couple of steps downstream and begins to cast again.

In this manner, Hurley works his way through the riffle and the top of the pool. During the middle of a bright fall day, he doesn't bother with the tail of the pool. Instead, he moves on to the next riffle, perhaps tying on another streamer pattern.

But later, as the shadows lengthen across the river, Hurley tries the tail of a pool he especially likes. Here, as the streamer starts its arc cross-river and 100 feet out, he gets a slashing, jarring strike. Hurley strikes back hard. Secure in the knowledge of his strong leader and hook, he applies heavy pressure and soon nets a beautifully colored, 3-pound brown. With a few words of admiration to the fish, he unhooks, revives, and releases the brown into quiet water. "Just because the Legislature says you can kill five or ten trout doesn't mean you have to do it," he notes. Then he's casting again, hoping the pool holds another fine fish.

On most trout streams, the fishing season dies with the falling of the leaves and the forming of ice along the banks. But locals near the Yellowstone take advantage of warmer periods of weather and sometimes find good fishing. With its stock of 20,000 whitefish per mile, the Yellowstone provides the winter angler with an excellent chance to cache a smoked delicacy. Bait and spin anglers can fare well as long as their lines and fingers don't freeze up. Fly fishers sometime encounter mid-winter hatches of tiny snow midges. And once the spring equinox arrives, the big rainbow are moving into the side channels and over the gravel beds, tempting any sort of angler.

"It's a fascinating river," Hurley muses. "You can catch a whole string of 10-inch fish, then the next one to come up is 5 pounds." Or maybe, just possibly, one bigger than any trout ever caught.

The Boulder River, a major tributary of the Yellowstone, resembles the Stillwater in scenery and fishing potential.

TRIBUTARIES

Most rivers offering great trout fishing also have excellent fishing in their tributaries. This self-evident rule has a shining example in the Yellowstone. When the big river is running muddy or when an angler wants a change of pace—a chance to fish smaller, more intimate water—the tributaries of the Yellowstone offer superb alternatives.

This book covers the **Gardner River,** a fine trout stream which empties into the Yellowstone at the town of Gardiner, in the Yellowstone Park chapter. The same goes for the Lamar River. The Stillwater and Bighorn Rivers, major fishing resources in their own right, are described in their own sections. This section describes the Yellowstone's other major tributaries.

Between Gardiner and Livingston, a number of small streams drain the mountain canyons of the Absaroka and Gallatin Ranges. These streams, including **Mol Heron, Mill, Tom Miner,** and **Big** and **Pine Creeks,** provide the river's cutthroat with spawning water. They also provide fun fishing for mostly pan-sized brookies, rainbow, and cutthroat. Gravel roads make them all accessible. These lightly fished streams are best in July and August.

About 8 miles south of Livingston, two short spring creeks flow into the Yellowstone—**Nelson's Spring Creek** from the east side, and **Armstrong** and **DePuy's Spring Creek** from the west. Both are on private land, but anglers can fish them if they make reservations and pay a fee. Local tackle shops such as George Anderson's Yellowstone Angler and Dan Bailey's Fly Shop happily help with the arrangements. The owners allow only fly fishing.

Although the two creeks differ in some respects, especially in the DePuy section, where anglers can fish some dammed-up ponds as well as the main creek, in general the spring creeks are notably similar. Both have some browns and cutthroat, but in each case the star inhabitants are rainbow. Because of the terrific insect life and excellent water conditions, both streams support incredible concentrations of trout, with an impressive number of 2- to 5- pounders. And both, as George Anderson puts it, "demand the utmost in delicate presentation, fine tippets, and small flies."

By "small flies," Anderson means sizes 16 to 22. Anglers who are not accustomed to working with such microscopic tackle would do well to step into Anderson's shop or to consult another expert before stepping into the spring creeks. Matching the hatches of baetis, mayfly, and midges can make or break the day's experience. Likewise, nymph anglers may want to seek advice on the various mayfly nymphs, midge larva and pupa, scuds, and sowbugs.

Many anglers become a touch uneasy with the special techniques used on spring creeks—"Latinspeak and three weight line," Hurley calls it. And paying for fishing rankles more than a few anglers as well. But the beautiful scenery, water, and trout of these spring creeks do offer a different and exciting experience to the open-minded angler who gives it a try.

The **Shields River** rises in the Crazy Mountains, flows by the towns of Wilsall and Clyde Park, and dumps into the Yellowstone just east of Livingston.

Notorious for its silt problems, the Shields nevertheless deserves a good reputation as a trout stream. Along its cottonwood-lined banks, this small river harbors "more 2-pound-and-up brown trout than you might expect," testifies Stevenson, who has run electrofishing surveys in the Shields. The browns hang out in the tree roots, logjams, and deep pools of the lower half of the river. Further up toward the headwaters, anglers catch a mixed bag of rainbow, cutthroat, and brookies. Access is relatively easy.

The Shields suffers from serious dewatering problems and the attendant problem of overheating. Many years ago, Halterman found that the fish in the Shields had one of the fastest growth rates in the state, but increased irrigation has slowed that some. Try this river before the dog days of summer or after the leaves turn color. The river receives only light fishing pressure.

The superlative **Boulder River** bears striking resemblance to its sister stream, just to the east, the Stillwater River. Both feature boulder-pocket fishing in addition to the more familiar riffle-pool type. Both support predominately rainbow and browns, a few of lunker proportions. Both receive an influx of spawning trout from the Yellowstone. And in each case, future mining of the mineral complexes in the Beartooth Mountains may jeopardize the fisheries.

Under the new regulations, anglers on the Boulder and its main tributaries are limited to two trout, only one of which can measure over 13 inches. From Two-mile Bridge to Natural Bridge, fishing for rainbow and cutthroat is catch-and-release and only artificial flies and lures are allowed. The state will also monitor mining activities and water quality in an effort to protect the fishery.

The Boulder River divides the Beartooths from the Absarokas. Along with its west and east forks, it drains three long, narrow canyons that reach far back into the mountains. The main Boulder runs for many miles through National Forest lands with ample access before emerging from the mountains and dropping as a major waterfall. Thereafter, the river swells substantially with the addition of its forks and continues to rush along its boulder-studded streambed until it joins the Yellowstone near Big Timber.

Above the falls, the river has fine fishing, mostly for rainbow in the 10- to 15-inch class. But below the falls, where the water has more nutrients, the river harbors both rainbow and browns in the larger weight classes.

Sadly, there is very little public access to this lower, trophy section of the river. FWP maintains three accesses, two of them quite extensive, but still, 99 percent of the river fronts on private, often heavily posted land.

The Boulder has remarkably little cobble and gravel in its streambed. Anglers must therefore wade on what may be the slipperiest boulders in the state. Floating is not a sensible option for most of the river.

Most of the fishing pressure happens in July and August. Bait and spin anglers have trouble hanging up on the boulders but have some success in the pools. Worms and grasshoppers top the list of bait favorites. Fishing guide Curt Collins advises small lures such as Panther Martins, Roostertails, and gold Kastmasters.

The Boulder has a spotty hatch of smaller stoneflies. For fishing nymphs, Collins selects small golden, early black, and brown stone nymphs. For streamers, he likes olive and black Matukas and small sculpin imitations such as Marabou Muddlers. The four dry flies Collins is sure to have with him include small Adams, Light Cahill, Elk Hair Caddis, and the Joe's Hopper. Anderson would add to the list a couple of attractor patterns such as Goofus or one of the Wulff patterns.

When the **Clarks Fork of the Yellowstone** joins the Yellowstone near Laurel, it doesn't look much like a trout stream. The water runs turbid until October, partly from natural causes and partly due to irrigation returns and overgrazing. Former FWP biologist Pat Marcuson terms the Clarks Fork "a sleeping giant," because it would be one of the most productive trout streams in the state if only sediment loads could be cleaned up.

As things now stand, the segment of the river from the state line to Clark has the best trout water and the most diverse fishery. From Clark to Belfry, Marcuson found mostly whitefish interspersed with a few big browns. From Edgar to the mouth, sauger and some huge ling make the river their domain. In 1981, Marcuson weighed one ling, caught by an angler a week before, which scaled just one-tenth of a pound under the state record.

The Clarks Fork has a tributary that has long delighted local anglers from Red Lodge to Billings: Rock Creek comes out of the Beartooths in three forks and a big rush. Below Red Lodge, the combined stream slows and winds its way through wonderful thickets of willow, aspen, and cottonwood. Above Red Lodge a 10-incher would be an extraordinary catch, but from Red Lodge

Pocket water habitat—trout hang out just above and below such submerged boulders. AL TROTH PHOTO

downstream lurk some very respectable trout. The thickets can make casting difficult, but that is where the fish hold out. Avoid the places where bulldozers have moved the streambed; the trout moved out when the cats moved in.

ACCESS

Note: For information on access to the river within Yellowstone National Park, refer to the chapter on fishing in the park.

Anglers wishing either to wade or float from the park down to Livingston have a long list of potential access sites. In view of the size of the river and the distance between riffles, floating makes especially good sense on the Yellowstone. Float trips can take an hour or a day depending on which access sites are chosen, how often the angler stops, and what craft is used. Anyone wishing to float the Yellowstone should pick up a copy of the pamphlet *Montana Afloat #12, the Yellowstone River.*

Anglers can first reach the river outside the park at the town of Gardiner, where the river splits the town in half. The steep riverbanks prevent launching heavy boats there.

By using the gravel road going northwest from the Roosevelt Arch at the park's entrance, anglers can walk to the river across park land for 2 or 3 miles below Gardiner.

Off Highway 89, FWP has an access known as **"Queen of the Waters"** at the upstream end of the Gardiner airport. A better launch site with more river frontage can be had on Forest Service land just downstream. Reach this spot by taking the dirt road right next to mile-marker three from the highway. As with many of these launch sites, anglers with boats on trailers should be very careful how far they back down here, or they may need a tow truck to get back up the bank.

Another 2 or 3 miles north on the highway, the roadway comes close to the river by Forest Service's **LaDuke Springs Picnic Area**. Several turnouts near here provide views of the spectacular Devil's Slide; they also provide parking for foot access to perhaps a mile of Forest Service riverbank and several beautiful riffles. Closely connected to LaDuke is **Corwin Springs** FAS with an unimproved access where boat launching is possible until the lower water levels in late summer. Anglers would do better by crossing the Corwin Springs bridge and driving about 0.25 mile upstream to an all-seasons boat ramp on Forest Service and railroad land.

At the head of Yankee Jim Canyon, perhaps 200 yards west of the Joe Brown trailhead, the Forest Service provides a boat launch and take-out spot. The 2.5 miles of canyon downstream is within Forest Service land and is easily accessible from the highway.

A mile or two north of the canyon's mouth, a sign marked "Tom Miner Basin" directs anglers to a substantial BLM access stretching downstream from the **Carbella Bridge** on the east side of the river. A landowner has allowed boat launching on the west side of the bridge; please respect this kindness.

A nymph, a partially emerged adult, and an adult stonefly (salmon fly). These big insects trigger the appetites of big trout on rivers like the Madison, Big Hole, and Yellowstone. AL TROTH PHOTO

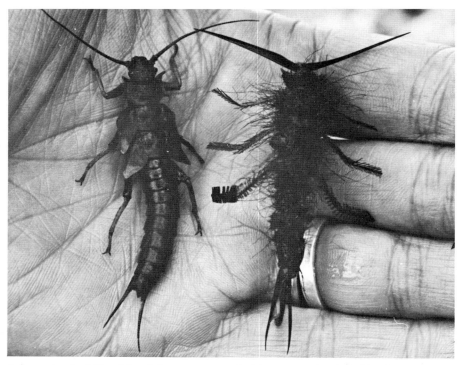

A long-shanked No. 1 hook is necessary to fashion an artificial fly like the Terrible Troth, at right, imitating the stonefly (salmon fly) nymph. AL TROTH PHOTO

About 4 miles north of the Carbella site on Highway 89, you'll find a fork in the highway. To the right, the East River Road closely parallels the river for roughly 30 miles and gives anglers access to the riverbank in several places. Some of these access sites have been developed into campgrounds. If you choose instead to go straight ahead on Highway 89, the roadway will soon cross the Point of Rocks Bridge and parallel the river on the west side.

On this west side, not far downstream from the bridge, anglers can find the FWP **Point of Rocks** access. This site has a good boat ramp into a fast side channel. Downstream a little further, anglers can use the highway rest area access, although boat launchings involve a 50-yard carry. Or go a couple of miles farther to an informal boat access by a big bend in the river just opposite Emigrant Peak.

Downstream on the east side, anglers can take advantage of highway right-of-way access above and below **Wan-i-gan**. McKenzie boat owners will find launching or taking out almost impossible here.

The **Emigrant Bridge** has a popular FWP access for wading and floating anglers alike. Just north of the town of Emigrant on U.S. Highway 89, another FWP access, known as **Emigrant North**, gives walk-in access over a stile.

At the Pray Bridge, which travelers use to reach the Mill Creek road, a private landowner kindly allows access off the east end of the bridge. Downstream on the east side, FWP maintains the **Paradise campground**, which includes bank access but no boat ramp. A little farther downstream and still on the east side, FWP's **Loch Leven** access has a campground and an excellent and substantial bank access.

Downstream on the west side, FWP's frequently photographed **Mallard's Rest** access has another excellent boat ramp and lots of bank frontage. Perhaps 3 miles north the **Pine Creek Bridge** ther is now a good boat ramp at the west end.

Five miles north, US 89 runs right next to a heavily riprapped bank of the river in a place known locally as **Bell Crossing**. Anglers navigate into the east channel; the west (left) channel has a very dangerous diversion dam for the Livingston ditch.

North of here 0.25 miles, the East River Road rejoins US 89. Driving only a short distance east on the East River Road takes anglers to **Carters Bridge**, which has a fair boat ramp, although the water is swift here early in the summer. Just downstream of Carters Bridge, FWP's **Free River** access offers walk-in access by Allenspur.

In Livingston, anglers have a choice of at least four accesses. The **9th Street Island Bridge** has a boat launch area on the west, upriver side, but be prepared for some tricky navigating to avoid wrapping around the bridge pillar. **Sacajawea Park** has foot access for perhaps 0.75 mile. Mayor's Landing at the **old Harvats Bridge** has a fair boat ramp. Anglers can also reach the river at the northeast end of town at the pair of bridges by the radio station.

Northeast of Livingston on Interstate 90, US 89 branches off to the north and shortly crosses the river. A popular, but difficult, launch area is on the

The Yellowstone may be challenging to the angler, but it also can be, like other rivers and fishing in general, a source of family entertainment.

south side of the river near the bridge. Or you can continue north over the bridge to a signed gravel road running 3 bumpy miles downstream to **Sheep Mountain Campground**, which is equipped with a fair boat ramp. Much easier to reach from Interstate 90, the **Springdale Bridge** also has a fairly good boat ramp. **Grey Bear** FAS, reached by turning off at the DeHart exit 5 miles west of Big Timber, affords anglers a campground, facilities, and another boat ramp.

Between Big Timber and Billings, the access points are farther apart. These four all have boat ramps usable by two-wheeled vehicles—**Pelican** FAS, 1 mile northeast of Greycliff; **Bratton** FAS, 16 miles east of Big Timber near Milepost 381; **Indian Fort**, 1 mile north of Reedpoint; and **Itch-Kep-Pe**, just south of Columbus on the road to Absarokee. **Buffalo Mirage** FAS also offers access southeast of Park City.

Riverside Park in Laurel has a boat ramp and a park at the south end of the Highway 212 bridge. Billings has several bridges and, more notably, **Riverfront** and **Coulson Parks**. Also, **East Bridge** FAS has a new concrete ramp.

The remaining 361 miles of warm-water fishery is near-wilderness for long stretches. In recent years, FWP has encouraged use of this resource and is actively adding access sites to the lower river. With 35 species of fish in the lower Yellowstone, fishing pressure is on the rise, hitting 50,000 angler days per year in 1989.

FWP expects to add more access sites as the lower Yellowstone's popularity grows. For now, most of the access is clustered between the Bighorn and Rosebud Creek and from Glendive to Sidney. The city of Glendive provides an unofficial access with a good boat ramp located between the interstate and city bridges.

Major Montana Lake Fisheries

17 Ackley Lake

Ackley Lake is a small, 250-acre reservoir on the open plains of central Montana. Located in Judith Basin County, approximately 4.5 miles southwest of Hobson, the reservoir is accessible via a well-traveled county road. A water canal from the Judith River feeds the reservoir; therefore, the bottom is generally quite muddy. Because it is used for irrigation storage, the water level fluctuates somewhat mid- to late summer, depending on the year.

Because Ackley Lake is a multiple-use reservoir, fishing success depends on how severe irrigation drawdown is and when it occurs. FWP has defined the minimum depth to be 10 feet, so there should always be some water left in the reservoir.

Angling at Ackley is divided between trolling and shore-fishing. If you're trolling, 10 to 15 feet is the best depth for rainbow. FWP currently plants two strains of rainbow, Arlee and Eagle Lake. An occasional brown trout takes a lure too, but kokanee are no longer stocked here. Most anglers stick with standard trolling fare: spoons, spinners, and an occasional bottom bouncer. If you're fishing from shore, the biggest problem you'll have is disposing of all the suckers you catch.

Winter ice-fishing brings lots of anglers out for rainbow. Corn or maggots should do the trick. This is fairly open country, and the wind blowing through Judith Gap can get pretty ferocious, so dress accordingly.

Since this reservoir is in open prairie, it is a favorite stopover for waterfowl of the Central Flyway in the fall. Canada geese and many varieties of ducks can be seen in the fall, and some shorebirds inhabit the area during the summer. The surrounding coulees and plains host mule deer, pronghorn antelope, and many upland game birds, including sharp-tailed grouse and ring-necked pheasant. Many western Montana bird hunters travel to this part of the state every fall to bag their limit of pheasant. In addition, Ackley Lake provides an opportunity to hunt pheasant in the morning and lazily pick up a nice trout or two in the late afternoon—not bad for a day's work!

18 Ashley Lake

Ashley Lake, a large, 3,200-acre lake, achieved notoriety in the early 1980s by yielding the state and world record hybrid rainbow-cutthroat trout. In May 1982, Pat Kelly threw a small lure and a night crawler on an 8-pound test line into the lake. After a 45-minute fight he landed the 30-pound, 4-ounce record rainbow-cutthroat hybrid trout. The fish was 35.75 inches long and 27.5 inches around. The lake also produced the state record pygmy whitefish, a whopping 0.16 pound bruiser landed in 1982 by Orlin Iverson. In 1988, Vernon Schmidt caught the state record Yellow perch at 2.37 pounds out of the lake.

The cutthroat/rainbow hybrid strain was brought up from Georgetown Lake thirty to forty years ago, and though the fish aren't plentiful, conditions are ideal for prolonged life and growth. They do spawn in a few local streams, so anglers can continue to search the lake for these lunkers and hope for another record breaker.

Although big fish have brought Ashley Lake to prominence, there are other unique features that make this lake a popular recreation spot. Located on a rough county road 13 miles north of milepost 105 on U.S. Highway 2 west of Kalispell, Ashley Lake State Park offers visitors adequate campgrounds with toilets and a boat ramp. This popular summer resort has well-maintained public toilets, campground, picnic area, and swimming areas.

For the visiting angler, there is good summer troll fishing for cutthroat trout and kokanee salmon. The cutthroat should not be fished too deep (around 8 feet is usually sufficient), but if you're after the wily kokanee, be prepared to try several depths—usually 20 to 40 feet deep.

Ashley Lake also has approximately 40 acres of shallow areas that are full of water lilies, rushes, and other aquatic plants that can foul a motor or snag your line, but a good place to look for perch and cruise for trout in twilight hours.

Winter ice-fishing is also very popular at Ashley Lake. Cutthroat, perch, and kokanee all are easily fished through the ice. Standard ice-fishing bait and outfits will work very well.

Watching the fly float—a favorite pastime of those who prefer lake fishing. It's very relaxing.

A good day's catch at Ashley Lake should yield a limit of 9- to 11-inch kokanee or four to five 12-inch cutthroat. Winter fishing should yield slightly larger cutthroat than summer fishing, and some nice ten-inch perch. FWP is trying to increase the cutthroat trout population through artificial propagation. The department is also encouraging natural spawning through restriction of fishing on spawning streams and removing beaver dams which block many of the spawning streams. For the latest updates on fishing success, stop in at the Kalispell FWP office or the Snappy Sports in Kalispell.

When you're in the area you might observe mule and white-tailed deer, moose, black bears, and the sorrowful loon.

19 Bighorn Lake

Located southeast of Hardin on Montana Highway 313, Bighorn Lake was created by the construction of Yellowtail Dam near Fort Smith in 1965. The 71-mile lake is in a peaceful setting of steep-sided canyons on the Bighorn River. The dam provides electric power, water for irrigation, flood control, and recreation.

Fishing, boating, water-skiing, swimming, hiking, and camping are highly popular at this isolated southeastern Montana recreation site. The entire lake is surrounded by the Bighorn Canyon National Recreation Area, which extends into Wyoming.

Bighorn Lake is a long, narrow reservoir, with only two public access sites on the Montana end: the Ok-A-Beh boat launch area located near the Yellowtail Dam and Visitor Center; and Barry's Landing, which includes a public campground. Even though Barry's Landing is located in Montana, it is reached by road only from Wyoming. Due to the steepness of the canyon walls, there are very few places where you can pull a boat up to the bank and fish. However, the scenery in the canyons is spectacular.

According to FWP fisheries biologist Steve Swedberg, Bighorn Lake is primarily a walleye fishery, with some limited rainbow and brown trout, and black crappie fishing. Largemouth bass and channel catfish inhabit the Wyoming end of the lake. Smallmouth bass have now become established in the lake and it could develop into a great fishery.

In the spring anglers stick to the "rubble" areas on the points around the lake, mostly still-fishing anchored offshore. Swedberg suggests trying jigs with nightcrawlers attached in about 15 to 20 feet of water.

For fall fishing, Swedberg suggests trying the brushier areas around the lake edges but cautions that anglers should be prepared to lose a lot of gear. Trolling activity picks up in the fall, and some trollers switch to lures, although the jig-crawler combination is also very popular. The mouths of streams such as Black Canyon, Bull Elk, and Porcupine on the south side of the reservoir are excellent places to try in the fall. Dry Head Creek, on the north side, also is popular in the fall.

A good day's catch at Bighorn Lake should yield your limit of 2-pound walleye, with the possibility of hauling in one up to 14 pounds. In addition, a few rainbow and lake trout might turn up, along with some black crappie.

Maps and information about Bighorn Lake and the Bighorn Canyon National Recreation Area may be picked up at the Yellowtail Dam and Visitor Center near Fort Smith, Montana, and at the National Park Service Visitor Center in Lovell, Wyoming. The Crow Indian Reservation borders the recreation area along most of the east side and surrounds much of the rest of it. Trespassing without permission is forbidden.

20 Browns Lake

Browns Lake is located in Powell County 9 miles from Ovando and about 60 miles northeast of Missoula on Montana Highway 200. This is a shallow lake in an open sagebrush area and therefore unique among western Montana's lakes.

Public camping facilities, including toilets and a boat ramp, are available at the south end of the lake. There is also a small boat launch area on the northwest side of the lake.

In the summer, fishing at the lake is evenly split between trolling and shore-fishing. Trolling is best done using weighted flies such as Wooly Worms and standard spoons and spinners. Shore anglers generally prefer bait such as worms, maggots, marshmallows, and cheese, although some anglers use artificial spinning lures and small spoons. Local anglers report a good summertime catch averaging three rainbow trout weighing between 1 and 3 pounds. Late spring usually produces some nice 3- to 5-pound rainbow in the 20-inch range.

Browns Lake really comes alive once the ice forms in winter. It seems to have a special attraction for Missoula anglers. Ice-fishing usually is very good for 1- to 3-pound rainbows and even an occasional brook or brown trout. Corn, maggots, meal worms, and marshmallows are the most popular bait. Ice jigs, in light fluorescent colors, also are widely used. More than a few anglers go home at the end of a day with their limit of trout. Because different temperatures and times seem to have a great effect on fishing success, it's important to have a large variety of tricks in your tackle box. Experimentation is the key to success at Browns Lake. Once you find a successful combination, stick with it.

According to local anglers, the south end of the lake is the traditional area for ice-fishing. They recommend fishing close to the bottom. Two to 3 feet off the bottom is suggested.

FWP, which plans to continue its program of planting rainbow trout in Browns Lake, reports that the lake should continue to provide good fishing.

If you're in Missoula, stop in at Bob Ward's Sporting Goods or Sportsmen's Surplus for the latest conditions and fishing methods. There's always someone around who knows what's happening at Browns Lake.

21 Canyon Ferry Reservoir

Fifteen miles east of the copper dome of the Montana capitol in Helena lies one of Montana's most popular fishing holes, 25-mile Canyon Ferry Reservoir. Covering 35,300 acres, this Missouri River reservoir has become one of Montana's foremost recreation areas because of its proximity to many of the state's largest urban areas—Helena, Great Falls, Butte, and Bozeman. Residents of both eastern and western Montana often drive over to fish and relax here at one of the many recreation areas scattered around the shoreline. In fact, it currently ranks as the most fished water in the entire state of Montana.

Attracted by its excellent fishing, sailing and power boating, water-skiing and swimming, clean air and water, and spectacular mountain scenery, recreationists come here to shed the worries and cares of hectic twentieth century America. There's plenty of room to do so at Canyon Ferry, because there are twenty-four FWP-maintained recreation sites around the reservoir. Access to the area is easy from U.S. Highway 12 east of Helena or just north of Townsend.

In the Gold Rush years of the 1860s and 1870s, about 10,000 people mined the gulches around present-day Canyon Ferry. In fact, Confederate Gulch produced the richest gold mine on record in the United States. Names for many of the recreation sites around the reservoir are based on the old mines: Confederate, Whites, Cave, Avalanche, Hellgate, and Magpie all were active mines at one time. Visitors still come to Canyon Ferry seeking buried treasure, but today the treasure is speckled brown and rainbow-colored, and it's not buried in the hills but beneath the surface of the reservoir's clear water.

Rainbow trout, brown trout, whitefish, yellow perch, largemouth bass, kokanee salmon, and recent illegal introductions of pike and walleye make up the sport fishing population at Canyon Ferry. The reservoir also has a sizeable nongame fish population which includes carp and suckers.

Fishing activity begins in the spring as soon as the ice goes out of the reservoir. By anyone's standard, the fishing is excellent for rainbow, occasional browns, and even perch. Try using spinning gear with a Thomas Cyclone or Crocodile Mepps lure if you want to fill your creel. In early spring, Confederate Gulch and other nearby bays offer excellent fishing.

Trolling activity begins in earnest in May and continues through June. Try keeping boat speed relatively low with no wake by trolling a spinning rod with monofilament and a sinking Rapala lure. Bob Martinka, a Canyon Ferry regular, prefers using a fat-bodied Rapala with spinning gear. He fishes the area around Cemetery Island during May and June for 1.5-pound rainbow and an occasional 2-pounder (when he's lucky). Cemetery Island and the nearby west shore are favorite nesting sites for ospreys. These big white raptors (called fish hawks by some) build their nests, a bulky mass of sticks, at the top of dead trees, on rock pinnacles, or on the ground.

Almost all local anglers agree that as the water warms up in Canyon Ferry, around June or early July, fishing drops off. Try fishing only in the early mornings, late evenings, and after dark. There is another hazard associated with warm weather fishing: fish spoilage. Keep a cooler with ice or a bucket with wet rags in your boat or next to your fishing spot on shore to preserve the fish you catch from June on. The bright summer sun and the wide expanse of reflecting water combine to produce sure-fire damage to caught fish.

Fishing in the dark with a lantern in about 10 to 15 feet of water can provide a lot of fun and a creel of trout. Bait fishing is the rule after dark; worms and marshmallows work well.

Autumn fishing at Canyon Ferry is also excellent. Martinka likes to troll near the inlet of the Missouri River on the south end of the reservoir. He uses a 15-foot boat with a four-horse motor and trolls slowly, creating no wake. He recommends varying the speed and even stopping and casting a bit. Such techniques usually yield ten to fifteen fish in an hour or two. Brown trout begin their spawning runs up the river in the fall.

According to Martinka, the real challenge at Canyon Ferry is hooking one of those lunker browns. Fall is also a good time for shore-fishing, using marshmallows and worms. Fall is also a good time to fish for perch while anchored offshore in 10 to 15 feet of water.

Winter and cold weather really heat up the fishing action at Canyon Ferry. Ice begins to form in the bays around the reservoir from Thanksgiving on, but the water near the dam usually doesn't freeze until February. The west shore near Beaver Creek Bay is a popular ice-fishing area. Perch and trout are the primary species caught through the ice. Many local anglers agree that perch is the best eating there is—all you have to do is fillet them. Maggots as bait is often successful. It is not uncommon to catch one hundred perch in a day. Trout fishing in the winter is similar to fishing for perch, except that deep fishing is not the rule. Bob Martinka uses either a rubber-legged jig or maggots through the ice and fishes for trout in about 6 to 10 feet of water. Rainbow trout are the most common in the winter, but Martinka says that browns up to 5 pounds have been pulled through the ice at Canyon Ferry.

Night ice-fishing with a lantern can be very productive. However, anglers should make sure the ice is thick enough before they venture out. The FWP office at Canyon Ferry or in Helena can provide information on ice thickness, so don't hesitate to check with them. It can get a little chilly at the reservoir in the winter.

Public camping facilities maintained by FWP are located all around the reservoir. Near the dam area, camping areas include Jo Bonner, Chinamans, Ponderosa, Court Sheriff, Riverside, and Overlook. On the east shore, campsites are located at Hellgate and Goosebay Marina. On the west shore, campsites are located at White Earth, Silos, and Indian Road. Boat access is available at all of the campsites. A number of additional public boat launch areas are located near the dam on the north end and near Townsend on the south end.

Fishing, hunting, boating, water-skiing, swimming, picnicking, and camping all make Canyon Ferry Reservoir what FWP finds to be Montana's most heavily used recreation area. Be sure to stop in at the FWP office at

Canyon Ferry Village, near the dam, to pick up maps and information about the public facilities and recreational opportunities available.

22 Castle Rock Lake

On the north end of the town of Colstrip, Castle Rock Lake offers the perfect family diversion for a summer's evening. This 165-acre lake is owned by the Montana Power Company, but is open to the public for day use year-round. Drive north from Colstrip for 0.5 mile and turn west on a county road—look for the rod and gun club sign.

Locals fish here regularly, and Castle Rock is gaining regional fame as a largemouth bass and bluegill fishery. The bluegills average about 0.5 pound and are an easy catch, good fun for even the youngest angler.

Through fingerling planting, walleye has become abundant and offers excellent fishing. Largemouth and Smallmouth bass are also present in good numbers. FWP's Phil Stewart thinks that Castle Rock Lake is the best small fishing in the southeast part of the state.

Many anglers are content to fish from the open, gently sloping shoreline, but boaters should be aware that gasoline outboards are prohibited. Bring your electric motor or paddles for this small lake. The Montana Power Company locks the access gate at night and camping is not allowed at Castle Rock.

23 Clark Canyon Reservoir

Clark Canyon Reservoir, located on Interstate 15 approximately 20 miles south of Dillon in Beaverhead County, produces some great lunker trout. The reservoir is readily accessible from I-15 along the entire length of the east side. Montana Highway 324 on the northwest offers visitors ready access to much of the west side of the reservoir.

This is a large, 6,600-acre reservoir that was created by construction of Clark Canyon Dam on the headwaters of the Beaverhead River. Red Rock River to the southeast and Horse Prairie Creek to the northwest combine to form the waters of the reservoir.

Apart from a couple of rock islands toward the middle of the reservoir on the east side, Clark Canyon is a wide, open foothills reservoir. Fishing access sites and picnic areas are scattered around the northwest and east shores. Clark Canyon Reservoir is primarily a rainbow trout fishery, although there are sizeable brown trout and burbot or ling populations, and a fair amount of suckers and other nongame species. In 1989, FWP stopped stocking the Arlee rainbow and concentrated instead on two wild strains, the DeSmet and Eagle Lake rainbow. Though slower growing, these strains show better staying power and a stronger proclivity to reproduce in the wild.

Springtime is the most popular time of year for fishing, with spring activity culminating at the Dillon Rotary Club's Fish Derby held on Father's

Day. This event attracts out-of-state as well as local anglers. The competition and the fishing are fast and furious.

As soon as the ice comes off the reservoir in March or April, you'll find anglers out on the water. Both brown and rainbow trout are active at this time. Trolling has long been popular all over the lake, although many anglers concentrate on the eastern shore from the dam down to the mouth of Red Rock River. And with the DeSmet and Eagle Lake trout, anglers are switching to smaller lures and flies. Some rainbow trout anglers report good success fishing near the mouth of Horse Prairie Creek. Although rainbow trout comprise up to 80 percent of the spring catch, 3- to 5-pound brown trout are fairly common. Browns up to 16 pounds and rainbow up to 10 pounds have been hauled ashore, evidence that there are some lunkers in this reservoir.

Many trollers use large Daredevles, sinking Rapalas, and large Thomas Cyclones on 8-pound monofilament line, usually trolling within 8 feet of the surface. Bait anglers generally stick to worms and marshmallows, using lightweight spin casting gear. Most bait fishing is done from the shore at one of the numerous public access sites. If the traditional gear doesn't do the trick, try smaller flies—and maybe a float tube. Fly fishers report good success in spring and late summer.

During the summer, fishing pressure increases and the success rate declines. This is the time of year when many visitors from Utah and Idaho make their way north to try their luck in Montana. Try trolling deep during the summer months to increase their chances of success. Shoreline fishing tends to increase during the warm months.

The southern end of the reservoir, near the mouth of Red Rock River, is the most popular spot for fly fishing. Weighted flies, sometimes including a small bobber attached to the leader, seem to get the best reviews. Late evenings towards sundown is the best time to try using dry flies. Even at that time it gets pretty tricky, and matching the hatch is a must.

In the fall, pressure drops off (it's usually lighter in the fall than the spring), and success picks up; again the emphasis is on trolling with a trend toward smaller hooks.

The reservoir comes alive again in the winter as anglers head out onto the ice. Since this is an open reservoir, with very few natural obstructions to the wind, it can get mercilessly cold out on the ice. Ice anglers here fish primarily for burbot; there are comparatively few trout taken. Popular locations include near the dam, the northwest shore, and around the islands on the east side. Most anglers use worms, marshmallows, and corn as bait. Some open water rainbow fishing takes place in the winter near the Red Rock River inlet, with most anglers using bait.

A good day's catch at Clark Canyon Reservoir should yield a 2- to 4-pound burbot in the winter, your limit of 2- pound rainbow, and if you play your cards right perhaps some 3- to 4-pound (up to 10-pound) browns. Fishing looks good for both the short and long term at Clark Canyon, as FWP has initiated a program to develop a self-sustaining wild trout fishery at the reservoir.

Clark Canyon Reservoir on the Beaverhead River near Dillon has some trophy rainbows for lucky anglers. AL TROTH PHOTO

The Bureau of Land Management and the Beaverhead National Forest offices, both in nearby Dillon, have maps available of their respective public lands which border the reservoir. For fishing information, stop in at the Hitchin' Post Sporting Goods store in Dillon.

24 Cooney Reservoir

Located in Carbon County 9 miles west of Boyd on a county road, Cooney Reservoir is a heavily fished state recreation area. There are two public campgrounds at the reservoir, one on the west side and the other on the east. Besides camping facilities, there are public toilets, picnic areas, boat access sites, and beach areas for swimming. Since this reservoir is located near Billings, the largest metropolitan area in Montana, the summer season is fast becoming a potential recreation nightmare because of conflicts between water-skiers, swimmers, and anglers. FWP is working to resolve most of these problems before they reach the critical stage of having to restrict any one activity. Facilities have been expanded and improved in recent years.

Cooney Reservoir was once primarily a rainbow trout fishery, stocked annually by FWP with over 250,000 rainbow. But beginning in 1984, FWP annually introduced walleyes and reduced rainbow plants to 150,000 fish. Biologists hoped to create a two-tiered trout and walleye fishery and at the same time control the burgeoning population of suckers. Although the walleye are not reproducing on their own, some fish from the original stocking have grown to 16 pounds.

While most nonangling recreationists use the reservoir heavily only during the summer, anglers ply their trade year-round. The best fishing takes place in the early spring as soon as the ice breaks up. At this time, both shorefishing (where there's open water) and still-fishing while anchored offshore near the ice break-up can be very productive. Bait fishing with worms, grubs, and corn is popular; and lures such as Mepps, Triple Teaser, and Thomas Cyclone seem to work well.

Later in the spring and in the early summer, trollers hit the water before the crush of boaters, jet skiers, and swimmers picks up during the warmer months.

Trollers use a single line of 8-pound monofilament, usually on a spinning rod. Daredevles, small sinking Rapalas, and other medium-sized spoons are popular lures for trolling. Cooney Reservoir is not very deep, 68 feet at the deepest, so trollers should stay in the upper 8 feet of water. During the summer, angling success drops drastically because of the presence of other recreational users and because of rising summer water temperatures.

When the cooler fall weather begins to move through the area, fishing picks up again; trolling, still-fishing, and bank-fishing all bring out lots of enthusiasts. Anglers use the same methods in the fall as they do in the spring.

Winter ice-fishing at Cooney Reservoir attracts a sizeable group of devoted anglers. Corn, marshmallows, and worms are standard bait choices.

Cooney is an open reservoir in prairie and rolling hill country, so bring a good windbreaker and a bucket of charcoal.

The Big Bear Sporting Goods store in Billings is good place to stop and get up-to-date information on the conditions at Cooney. In addition, the FWP regional office in Billings has information on fishing, swimming, camping, and boating at Cooney Reservoir.

25 Deadmans Basin Reservoir

Located in Wheatland County about 15 miles east of Harlowton and 2 miles east of Shawmut on U.S. Highway 12, Deadmans Basin Reservoir is a designated fishing access site. It is a 1,900-acre Musselshell River bottom reservoir that reaches a depth of 64 feet at its deepest point. This is a rather bleak spot, but excellent for rainbow and big browns. It is generally a fairly open body of water. Nearby are extensive recreational facilities, including boat access, toilets, campground, picnic area, and shelters. Nonetheless, Deadmans Basin receives only limited use. Because this open reservoir lies in a wind swept prairie area, sudden storms do pose a hazard to anglers, swimmers, and boaters, so be watchful.

Deadmans Basin is primarily a trout and kokanee fishery, with rainbow predominating. Some brown trout do migrate from the Musselshell River, so anglers should be able to pick one up every once in a while. FWP has planted rainbow trout for the past eighteen years. In 1972-1973, FWP planted some Coho salmon. The rainbow have flourished in the reservoir, but the Coho seem to have disappeared. In 1984, FWP switched to kokanee and still plants about 100,000 each year.

In the summer most anglers fish from the shore, although some extensive trolling occurs in a small area at the upper end of the reservoir about 20 to 30 feet from shore. Rainbow prefer the 8-to 10-foot depth, so trollers should not go too deep. Shore anglers should be careful about bottom fishing, as this reservoir contains its share of suckers. Standard spinners, spoons such as the Thomas Cyclone, and bait work best for rainbow. Please note that use of live minnows is strictly prohibited on this reservoir.

In the fall, browns make their way out of the Musselshell and up to the inlet to Deadmans Basin. Local anglers report that fishing is great for browns between 1.5 and 12 pounds. Wintertime brings out some of central Montana's best ice fishers, and they hit the ice with a fury. Most of these folds come every year and would be more than happy to help newcomers catch their limit. Corn, mealworms, and marshmallows are standard fare through the ice, but you might have to try several types of bait before hitting on the right one. Bring your long underwear, because the wind really howls along the Musselshell River.

A good day's catch, in the summer, should yield a limit of 0.75- to 1.25-pound rainbow and an occasional 2-pound brown trout. You're probably going to get a few carp and suckers from this reservoir, but you also might pull in a nice 2-pound rainbow too. In the winter most anglers are easily able to catch a limit of rainbow, and because most fishing is not on the bottom, anglers usually don't get any rough fish.

Stop in at Ray's Sports and Western in Harlowton to get the latest tips on baits, lures, and places to fish.

Also, FWP reports that in recent years a very popular snagging for kokanee fishery has developed during ice fishing season.

26 Duck Lake

On the Blackfeet Indian Reservation just east of Glacier National Park, Duck Lake is one of Montana's most famous lakes for big rainbows. Located 30 miles north of Browning on the Duck Lake Road, it is popular especially with fly fishers in the summer and ice fishers in the winter.

Duck Lake is the pride of the Blackfeet Fish and Game Department stocking programs, producing rainbows often over 10 pounds and occasional larger browns. The lake is stocked with up to 50,000 3-inch rainbows yearly, adding to an existing population of large browns and rainbows. You may also catch a rare bull trout from a one-time stocking. Wet flies take most fish during the summer months from float tubes. It is a big lake and access around the shoreline is subject to tribal and private jurisdiction.

Anglers commonly stay at the Duck Lake Campground or drive over 100 miles from either Great Falls or the Flathead Valley to fish this pristine lake. Views of Chief Mountain and the eastern peaks of Glacier National Park

An ice house with a good wind anchor is a must for ice fishing on Duck Lake. RUSS SCHNEIDER PHOTO

welcome the angler along with high winds that can often cause whitecaps. The wind can make fly fishing virtually impossible and in the winter can make an icehouse anchor a lifesaver.

Most anglers bring a float tube and sinking line. Popular flies include Damsel Fly Nymphs, Wooly Worms, and Leaches. Large rainbows will also take dries but are more selective on top. For spinners, consider yellow rooster tails, Mepps, and Panther Martins. When ice fishing, strive for small yellow rubber-band flies and grubs. However, the key to ice fishing is to sit in your icehouse and peer down in your hole for cruising fish. Often a little motion will bring a strike to a passing fish.

Be sure to check current regulations. In addition to a reservation fishing permit you also need a float tube permit, icehouse permit, and boat permit if you intend to use them.

27 Flathead Lake

All of Montana's other lakes and reservoirs, natural or man-made, pale in comparison to western Montana's famed Flathead Lake, called by many the "jewel of the Northwest." It is the largest natural freshwater lake in the western United States, with over 200 square miles (or 125,250 acres) of surface area and 185 miles of shoreline.

Flathead Lake is still a tremendous fishery but the dramatic changes in the lake after the introduction of Mysis shrimp and the collapse of the Kokanee fishing. The loss of spawning kokanee should provide a real lesson for those who advocate the introduction of non-native species. Introduced lake trout ate all the stocked kokanee and the introduced mysis shrimp outcompeted other food sources for kokanee. In addition, lake trout have decimated migratory populations of bull trout by outcompeting them for their food source. Lake trout just seem to be a better predator than bull. The only healthy populations of bull trout left in the Flathead system are separated by dams. The Swan River population is doing well, cut off from Flathead Lake by Bigfork Dam. Unfortunately, in 1998 a large lake tout was caught in the Swan River system above the dam. Lake Trout in the Swan River could threaten one of the last vestiges of bull trout. The South Fork population of bull trout is healthy, because it is cut off from Flathead Lake by Hungry Horse Dam. Flathead is still renowned for lake trout and lake whitefish fishing; as well as for many other water-based recreational activities such as sailing, power boating, waterskiing, and swimming.

Fishing at Flathead Lake offers trolling, bank-fishing, still-fishing, bait and lure fishing, but not much fly fishing, choice of trout, whitefish, largemouth bass, northern pike, and perch.

In the past, Flathead Lake was a nationally renowned bull trout and cutthroat trout fishery. Both cutthroat and bull trout used to spawn in considerable numbers and rear juveniles in Flathead's remote tributary streams, with some spawning migrations over 100 miles long. Juveniles would then return to

Eric Hanson holds a Flathead Lake lake trout caught off Somers. Russ Schneider PHOTO

the lake to grow and mature. Now the majority of fish caught from Flathead Lake are introduced lake trout and lake whitefish. Spring fishing at Flathead Lake usually begins in April and extends through June. The lake is so large and deep that the water doesn't really warm up until late June and early July. The north half of the lake is the most popular spring fishing area, although there is always some fishing—especially for lake trout— scattered all over the lake. Deep trolling (60 to 100 feet) away from the inlet using steel line, cowbells, downriggers, vertical jigging and large lures works well for lake trout. All bull trout caught must be released immediately without harm.

Summer recreational activity at Flathead Lake is extremely heavy, with power boating, waterskiing, and sailing competing with fishing in popularity. Summer is also a great time for lake trout angling. These big fish, many in the

A boat—preferably a large one—makes Flathead Lake fishing more productive and safer.

20- to 36-inch range, often concentrate along a line near the center of the lake. Submerged near the centerline is a bar—part of the old Flathead River delta—approximately 100 feet below the surface, which slopes off to the sides. Try fishing the edges of the bar for lake trout using down riggers, steel line, and large lures.

Cutthroat fishing is almost nonexistent at Flathead, but lake whitefish are an untapped summer resource. Still-fishing off the bottom, using worms, maggots, or other bait, is one way to reach these 19- to 22-inch tasty whitefish. Jim Vashro, veteran angler and FWP biologist, suggests using chartreuse or green jigs (Fuzzy Grubs, Mister Twister, and Foxee) or quarter- or half-ounce spoons, like Kastmaster Spoons in silver and chartreuse or silver and metallic green or Crippled Herring in perch finish or Rattlesnake Spoon in green and chartreuse. These should be fished in 30 to 50 feet of water off the numerous points along the shore. Vashro says early morning is best and the fastest action comes in July and August and from November through March.

Lake trout begin to move into shallower water to spawn in the fall, and anglers follow them. One choice location is around Wildhorse Island, where many anglers concentrate their efforts on the mainland side. Typical lake trout fishing methods include:

- Steel Line with M-2 on T-50 Flatfish or Kwikfish Red and White, Blue and White, or frog finish are popular lure patterns.
- Downriggers with squid and dodger or a variety of lures. Fish suspended for smaller fish or near bottom for all sizes.
- Vertical Jigging with a variety of jigs with grub-type tail or jigging spoons.

Other popular lures include MacAttack, Leadagator, Tirlobite, etc., made and tested by Dick Zimmerman of Pablo. Generally, fish shallow to 100 feet for smaller fish; fish 100-to-250 feet for chances at larger fish. Concentrations of bait fish like lake whitefish are the key to lake trout location.

In February 1991, two anglers jigged up ninety-nine lake trout, half of which ranged from 8 to 30 pounds. Their one-day catch (all released) weighed an estimated 800 pounds. Despite the population explosion of smaller lake trout, there are still some lunkers in Flathead. FWP has recovered lake trout up to 25 pounds during tagging studies in the fall, and Vashro reports that eight trout ranging from 30 to 36 pounds were landed in 1991. There was a 41-pound lake trout caught in 1995. If it had been weighted 6 hours earlier when first caught it probably would have been a new lake record. The current lake record is 42pounds caught in 1979 by Dave Larson.

During the winter, anglers must key in on a specific species and choose their fishing location and tackle accordingly. Lake trout fishing really comes into its own during the cold season. Trolling off the underwater bars with cowbells and downriggers should yield a hefty fish and plenty of excitement. Many lake trout anglers put in at Yellow Bay in the winter and fish the area out from the bay.

Whitefish, both mountain and lake, are very popular species in the winter. In fact, winter is the best season for catching these delicious fish. Fish about 1 foot off the bottom either from a boat or, where the ice is thick enough, through the ice. Maggots and corn are the most popular bait for these species. During the winter, it's possible to haul in about fifteen lake whitefish, each 19 inches long, and five to ten lake trout from 22 to 26 inches, with an occasional lunker as a bonus.

ACCESS

The east shore drive along **Montana Highway 35**, bordered by the magnificent Mission Mountain Range, is 35 miles of unexcelled beauty. In summer, roadside stands along the east shore offer a variety of locally grown cherries, apples, plums, and other fruits to delight the palate. The lake is accessible on its west shore along U.S. Highway 93 all the way between Polson and Kalispell.

Wildhorse Island, located along the west shore near the Big Arm, is a 2,165-acre state park. The park, accessible only by boat, hosts bighorn sheep, deer, waterfowl, eagles and falcons, and small mammals such as coyotes and ground squirrels. There are public day use and picnic areas as well as hiking trails and public fishing access sites on the island. You can't camp overnight on the island, but there are plenty of public camping areas on the surrounding mainland shore.

The southern half of Flathead Lake falls within the boundary of the **Confederated Salish and Kootenai Tribes Flathead Reservation**. All recreationists must purchase a tribal recreation permit for overnight or day use within the reservation boundary. The permits are good for the entire season at a modest cost. You can pick up a permit at tribal headquarters in Pablo, south of the lake on U.S. Highway 93, or at many of the small businesses in Polson, Elmo, Dayton, Rollins, and Bigfork.

FWP maintains thirteen public access sites around Flathead Lake, sites which the State of Montana has acquired over the years by purchase and donation. These sites include **Sportsmans Bridge, Somers, Big Fork,** and **Ducharme, Walstad** and **Woods Bay** fishing access sites; **Wayfarers, Yellow Bay, Finley Point, Big Arm,** and **West Shore State Parks,** which have toilets, boat launch, camping, swimming, and picnic facilities; and the **West Shore State Park,** located 20 miles south of Kalispell on U.S. Highway 93. With so many sites to choose from, anglers should have no trouble finding a choice spot to fish.

Flathead Lake certainly deserves the accolades that recreationists heap upon it. Whether you're fishing, boating, swimming, picnicking, or just stopping by in late summer for the cherry harvest, you'll find a myriad of interesting and unique outdoor experiences. There are numerous motels and rental cabins in addition to public campgrounds scattered all around the shoreline. The major population centers around the lake are Kalispell, Bigfork, and Polson, all of which offer a complete variety of groceries, supplies, and information.

28 Fort Peck Reservoir

The waters of eastern Montana are often confounding and mystifying to anglers from other states as well as to native Montanans raised near the crystal clear, cold streams west of the Continental Divide. No stream can lay claim to being at once perplexing and rewarding in quite the same way as the Missouri River once it reaches the Fort Peck Dam southeast of Glasgow and spreads out to become the largest body of water in Montana: Fort Peck Reservoir. Created by the construction of Fort Peck Dam in 1940, the reservoir extends upstream over 135 miles and has a surface area of over 250,000 acres. Big Dry Arm, near the dam, extends the reservoir's waters another 40 miles south up Big Dry Creek.

By the time the Missouri River winds its way past Great Falls and heads through the loose shale country of Fort Benton, it has picked up enough silt and soil to look unfit for fish or fowl. But appearances are deceiving, and even though it has slowed down to a crawl by the time it passes under the Fred Robinson Bridge, just west of the defined limit of Fort Peck Reservoir, the Missouri is less like the staid and stolid warm-water fisheries of its midwest cousins than it appears. Beneath the surface of Fort Peck thrives one of the most diverse and challenging fisheries in the northern Great Plains. Northern pike, walleye, lake trout, sauger, channel catfish, paddlefish, burbot, yellow perch, black crappie, white crappie, a few smallmouth bass, and, yes, even an occasional rainbow trout all live here, along with a host of nongame fish such as carp and a variety of suckers.

FWP has also started stocking chinook salmon here, and in 1991 Fort Peck produced the state record-breaker at 31.13 pounds. The lake is famous for producing recent state records including a 4.88-pound coho salmon caught in 1973 by Irven Stohl; a 25.89-pound channel catfish, a tie caught in 1984 by Gordon Wentworth and again in 1988 by Tom Hilderman; a 20.44-pound freshwater drum caught by Richard C. Lee in 1987; a 8.81-pound sauger caught in 1994 by Gene Moore; a 15.66-pound saugeye (walleye and sauger hybrid) caught in 1995 by Myron Kibler; and most importantly, a 16.29 pound walleye caught in 1995 by Randy Townsend. You have a better chance of catching a state record fish in Fort Peck Reservior than any other place in Montana.

Surface area of this northern prairie reservoir is approximately 5,700 acres. Its depth averages around 10 to 20 feet, reaching about 30 feet at the south end near the dam. Because this reservoir is heavily used for irrigation, it suffers severe fluctuations in water level during the summer and has been almost completely drawn down at times. Besides irrigation draw-down, future problems for fish include the possibility of hydro-power development at the dam.

Local anglers who hang out at Masters Sports in Havre report that the reservoir yields good early summer and spring fishing for northern pike, walleye, and perch. A good day's catch, according to these folks, is a freezer full of 1.5-pound to 2.5-pound northerns or a limit of 1.5-pound walleye. In the past FWP has planted smallmouth bass, rainbow trout, and perch, and northern pike were apparently planted illegally. So far, very few trout and bass have turned up in anglers' creels; no one has pulled a trout from these waters since 1974. But be prepared for them just in case they are still in there.

Trolling is the preferred method of fishing in spring and summer. Most anglers use spinners, spoons, or lures such as Rapala. Some anglers prefer bottom bouncers with a nightcrawler attached. Trolling depth should be set between 8 and 20 feet. Of course, if you want to try for bass, any of the standard bass plugs or flies can be used. Please remember that use of live minnows for bait is strictly prohibited on this reservoir; FWP is trying to keep the Milk River drainage from becoming saturated with the small fish.

Winter ice-fishing for northerns and walleye, using tip-ups baited with grubs or worms, is good to excellent. Local anglers report catches of 19- to 24-inch northerns and 15- to 20-inch walleye. If you're trying for perch, any fleshy bait, or even corn, should yield a nice catch. This reservoir is located on the windy Hi-Line, so bring a good windproof parka along and a bucket of charcoal to help keep you warm.

First-time anglers often do well by fishing the reservoir from the dam area near the town of Fort Peck. Lake trout, chinook salmon, northern pike, and walleye all frequent this area and provide plenty of excitement. Many anglers begin fishing at the dam and, as they get more familiar with the water and fish, quickly spread out to other areas on the reservoir.

The face of Fort Peck Dam is a very good place to find lake trout. FWP says anglers looking for lake trout concentrate their efforts in May and June, although fall fishing (October through November) is also good. During

Dinner for two—served at lakes all across Montana. MARK HENCKEL PHOTO

the warm summer months, lake trout tend to head deep to cooler water, so anglers should shift their depths accordingly. Some anglers spincast with lures from shore, but trolling brings the greatest success. In the spring and fall, trolling between 15 and 20 feet of depth is adequate, but during the warm summer months it's best to set your line much deeper, 80 to 100 feet, using a down-rigger. Large spoons and lures such as a red and white or pearl-coated Daredevle are very popular. Fast retrieves and fairly fast trolling seem to attract the most fish.

Lake trout populations show a slight upward trend, so they will continue to be a popular sport fish in the coming years. These fish average about 8 pounds, but there are some lunkers over 20 pounds in Fort Peck Reservoir. Lake trout and some other species have increased in average size in recent years due to the introduction of cisco and shiners as a food source.

Northern pike are also popular sport fish in Fort Peck Reservoir. Most northern pike fishing is done by trolling at fairly shallow depths—8 to 10 feet—starting near the dam and working around the reservoir. Some summer anglers report success from trolling at greater depths, down to 20 feet. Large spoons and flatfish are the most popular lures for trolling, and some anglers use minnows both for trolling and still fishing. The bays of some of the tributary streams around the reservoir provide excellent northern pike holes, good for either concentrated trolling or still-fishing.

Bear Creek Bay, southeast of the dam, is the first large bay and should provide plenty of fishing challenge. Duck Creek Bay, northwest of the dam, is slightly smaller in size but has numerous shoreline fingers for anglers to work. Gilbert Creek Bay, further west on the south side, is another good place to try. The final south side primary northern pike fishing area is the bay at Hells Creek. Hells Creek is also a state recreation area, with public camping, day use areas, toilets, drinking water, boat ramp, and swimming facilities. You can reach the recreation area either by boat or by road. To get there by road, follow the country road north out of Jordan for 24 miles. The bay at Timber Creek is the final north side primary northern pike fishing area. Although most anglers reach these areas by boat from the reservoir, there are roads through the CMR Refuge that will take you to the bays. Be sure to stop somewhere first and pick up a good local map of the area. The Bureau of Land Management publishes several maps that cover the entire area.

Sauger and walleye are different species that look very much alike, behave in much the same manner, and are fished in the same way. Many anglers can't tell the two species apart. Walleye, however, tend to be a bit larger and range up to 9 pounds in Fort Peck. These fish will take a variety of lures and bait with medium to large spoons, preferably plugs and minnows. Walleye and sauger are generally taken by trolling; still-fishing; and set-line, or bank-fishing. Trollers should go deeper for these than for northerns, at least 20 to 30 feet deep. In addition, trolling speed should be cut to a slow speed. Unlike northerns, which tend to stay towards the eastern end of the reservoir, walleye spread out all over the reservoir, some even migrating up into the Missouri River. Sauger stay more towards the western end and up into the river. Walleye move into shallower shoreline areas at night, and many anglers do well then.

Some dedicated local walleye anglers maintain that the Big Dry Arm is the best walleye hole in the West. Still others make the same claim for the area between Hells Creek State Recreation Area and west to Fourchette Bay. In either case, there are plenty of walleye for everyone at Fort Peck.

The smallmouth bass population has grown and now attracts a respectable amount of angling pressure.

For some anglers, paddlefish provide the only reason to come to Fort Peck. This abundant, unsightly fish does not bite a baited hook; it obtains its food by straining water through its gill rakers and extracting plankton (small, floating, animal and plant organisms) as it lolls along the bottom. But there is an important snagging fishery for paddlefish in the upper, or western, portion of the reservoir.

Paddlefish taken in Fort Peck and the adjoining Missouri River are larger than those taken anywhere else in the country. Females average 80 pounds and males just under 40. The state record, and possibly the North American sport record, is a 142.5-pounder that was taken in 1973 in the river above the lake. Most anglers use 30-pound monofilament line on casting equipment, with three to five treble hooks spaced back from a large sinker on the end. Eighty pounds of paddlefish is a lot of fish, so be sure to use a heavy duty reel and rod. Anglers snag both from boats and from the shoreline. From the end of March through June is the prime snagging season, while these huge fish move up the Missouri to spawn. The area from just west of the reservoir up to

Fred Robinson Bridge on the Missouri River is the most popular snagging area. New regulations limit anglers to two paddlefish per season and each fish must be tagged.

The bottom of Fort Peck is also home to channel catfish, which spawn in the Musselshell and upper Missouri Rivers. Catfish up to 30 pounds have been pulled out of the reservoir. They are attracted by many natural and artificial kinds of bait; generally, the smellier the better. The primary fishing area for catfish is the mouth of the Musselshell and the entire UL Bend area. Some channel catfish anglers swear that the upper Big Dry Arm is just as good as the western portions of Fort Peck. Most fish are taken by set-line or bank-fishing, usually in June when the water warms up to 60 degrees.

Another fine sport fish in Fort Peck is yellow perch, prized for its delicious taste. Even though it's not a large fish, a pan full of perch fillets is pretty hard to beat. There is no limit on perch, and they will take worms and maggots. Perch are fished year-round, including through the ice in winter, and they are found throughout the reservoir. Most perch weigh less than 1 pound, and catch rates are down for this species so it may take some work to pull in enough fish for the table.

Burbot, or ling, at Fort Peck are mostly caught by ice-fishing in the winter. This is one of the reservoir's most popular fish, though no one bothers them much from spring through fall. Spearfishing from dark houses on the ice furnishes excellent wintertime recreation. Rock Creek Bay and the upper Big Dry Arm are the most popular burbot fishing areas. Winter ice-fishing is popular not only for burbot, but also for lake trout, northern pike, walleye, sauger, and perch. Besides spearfishing, many winter anglers use tip-ups and lightweight spinning gear. Maggots, worms, and corn are widely used for ice-fishing.

A good day's catch at Fort Peck should yield about three northern pike in the 1- to 30-pound range, your limit of 4-to 5-pound (up to 20-pound) lake trout, four to five channel catfish averaging about 5 pounds, five walleye or sauger averaging 1 to 2 pounds, and a number of perch. In the winter you should be able to haul a few perch and burbot through the ice. Ten-pound lake trout are becoming more common.

Clearly, Fort Peck is one of Montana's prime fishing locations. It is awe-inspiring in its size, rewarding in its catches, and truly unique in the diversity of species which thrive in its waters. The surrounding CMR Wildlife Refuge and the picturesque Missouri River Breaks provide a thrilling backdrop for a quality fishing experience.

ACCESS

Surrounding this large expanse of water is the **Charles M. Russell (CMR) National Wildlife Refuge**, managed by the U.S. Fish and Wildlife Service, which provides over 1 million acres of public land for fishing, hiking, hunting, camping, bird-watching, and almost any other form of outdoor recreation imaginable (excluding golf courses and go-kart tracks). Public access to the reservoir's entire shoreline is restricted only be the dearth of roads, the geography, and the weather. If you notice storm clouds approaching from the west and are planning to travel out of the reservoir area on one of the dirt roads, be quick about it. Many an unhappy stranger to this country has gotten stuck on virtually level ground during a rainstorm. Local people refer to the mixture of shale soils and water as "gumbo." It has the capacity to grab hold of two- and four-wheel vehicles and render them immobile.

There are three state recreation areas nearby, all located on the south side of the reservoir: **Rock Creek, Hell Creek**, and **James Kipp**. There are also four federal public campgrounds: **Devil Creek, Turkey Joe**, and **Nelson Creek** on the south side of the reservoir; and **The Pines** on the north. New fishing access sites, each with a boat ramp, have been added at **Duck Creek, Fourchette Bay, and Spillway Bay**.

You can reach the CMR Refuge and Fort Peck Reservoir from the west by turning off of U.S. Highway 191 northwest of Lewistown at the Fred Robinson Bridge. Travelers from the south can reach it via Montana Highway 200 at Jordan and then north via the county road. The eastern edge of the reservoir is accessible from Montana Highway 24, which parallels the entire length of the Big Dry Arm and passes through the town of Fort Peck and over the dam. The north side of the reservoir is the least accessible from main roads. U.S. Highway 2 between Glasgow and Malta is the closest paved road. There are numerous county roads that take off south from US 2 and wind their way toward the reservoir.

29 Fresno Reservoir

As a part of the Milk River system, Fresno Reservoir provides irrigation storage for nearby farmers and recreational opportunities for anglers. Located approximately 12 miles west of Havre in Hill County, the reservoir has easy access 2 miles north of U.S. Highway 2. Canadian visitors can reach Fresno Reservoir by crossing the border at Port Willow Creek and heading south on Montana Highway 232.

Surface area of this northern prairie reservoir is approximately 5,700 acres. Its depth averages around 10 to 20 feet, reaching about 30 feet at the south end near the dam. Because this reservoir is heavily used for irrigation, it suffers severe fluctuations in water level during the summer and has been almost completely drawn down at times. Besides irrigation draw-down, future problems for fish include the possibility of hydro-power development at the dam.

Local anglers who hang out at Masters Sports in Havre report that the reservoir yields good early summer and spring fishing for northern pike, walleye, and perch. A good day's catch according to these folks is a freezer full of 1.5-pound to 2.5-pound northerns or a limit of 1.5-pound walleye. In the past FWP has planted smallmouth bass, rainbow trout, and perch, and northern pike were apparently planted illegally. So far, very few trout and bass have turned up in anglers' creels; no one has pulled a trout from these waters since 1974. But be prepared for them just in case they are still in there.

Trolling is the preferred method of fishing in spring and summer. Most anglers use spinners, spoons, or lures such as Rapala. Some anglers prefer bottom bouncers with a nightcrawler attached. Trolling depth should be set between 8 and 20 feet. Of course, if you want to try for bass, any of the standard bass plugs or flies can be used. Please remember that use of live minnows for bait is strictly prohibited on this reservoir; FWP is trying to keep the Milk River drainage from becoming saturated with the small fish.

Winter ice-fishing for northerns and walleye is good to excellent. Local anglers report catches of 19- to 24-inch northerns and 15- to 20-inch walleye. If you're trying for perch, any fleshy bait, or even corn, should yield a nice catch. This reservoir is located on the windy Hi-Line, so bring a good windproof parka along and a bucket of charcoal to help keep you warm.

30 Georgetown Lake

Easily accessible by State Highway 1 approximately 18 miles west of Anaconda, Georgetown Lake ranks as one of western Montana's most popular fishing spots. The surrounding mountains: the Flint Creek Range to the north and the Pintlers to the south also see their fair share of recreationists during backpacking season and the fall big game season.

Georgetown Lake is a large (3,000-acre), high (over 6,000 feet) mountain lake that tends to be a bit shallow. It is a very productive lake, as evidenced by the extensive weedbeds and by the excellent fishery.

Kokanee salmon and rainbow trout are the most fished for species in Georgetown Lake, with brook trout somewhat down the scale. Both the salmon and brook trout populations are self-sustaining, while rainbow are planted annually by FWP. The average size of rainbow has been increasing recently, and 4-pound 'bows are not uncommon. FWP also reports a few lake trout are being taken, including a 15-pounder in the summer of 1991. As with most lakes, Georgetown seems to have its share of nongame fish, such as suckers, but they are rarely caught by anglers.

Georgetown has four public boat ramps, and fishing from boats— either trolling or still-fishing—is extremely popular at the lake. Trolling is best done in the spring, early summer, and fall, because weeds really proliferate during the warm months. Jim Vashro, FWP fisheries biologist, suggests that summer trolling success can best be achieved by staying above the weeds, in less than 8 feet of water. Shore-fishing picks up during the summer months because of the trolling problems.

Most anglers use medium to small lures—Thomas Cyclones, Mepps, Triple Teasers—and Wooly Worms while trolling; and worms, corn, and marshmallows for bank-fishing or still-fishing. Local anglers report some success in late August and September using a jig and maggots for kokanee, concentrating their activity in the Pump House region of the lake. Jericho Bay and Piney Point are popular rainbow trout summer hangouts and are best fished by trolling in the weedless areas.

A miniature marshmallow is a real key to bait fishing, according to Vashro. It floats the bait out of the weeds and really increases the bite. Make sure to let your marshmallows dry and harden before using them.

Georgetown Lake is also a popular place for fly fishers to try their luck. Float tubes, waders, and even plain old bank-fishing all get a good workout from fly fishers. The west end of the lake provides a challenge to fly fishers who want to fish by drifting over the weedbeds in either a boat or a float tube. For the nonpurists, a popular method of catching trout is to use a small spinning bubble attached about 4 feet above a wet fly or Wooly Worm, using a slow, twitching retrieve. Dry fly aficionados will have their work cut out for them at Georgetown. Lighter shades of Wulff patterns, including Royals, are a good starting point. The lake also has a great damselfly hatch during summer and both nymph and adult imitations will provide good action. The lake also contains freshwater shrimp so don't forget your scuds.

Winter ice-fishing produces over a quarter of the annual angling harvest at Georgetown. Bait fishing using maggots, worms, marshmallows, and corn is the predominate method, but some anglers trying for salmon use a flourescent red jig or Glo Hook in combination with bait. Rainbow are generally spread out all over the lake in the winter, while kokanee tend to congregate in localized areas. Depending on which species you're after, you may have to try a number of different ice-holes. According to Vashro, the fish don't go too deep here in the winter, therefore he recommends setting your depth at no more than 8 feet.

A good day's catch at Georgetown should yield your limit of 12- to 14-inch rainbow, or three or four 12- to 14-inch brookies. When ice fishing, an average kokanee daily catch should number between sixty and seventy fish; but watch out, because some anglers have reported hauling in 100 kokanee! Georgetown Lake affords the angler breathtaking views of the Pintler Mountains; excellent fishing any season of the year; and a chance to observe many species of waterfowl, including shorebirds; along with a sizeable white-tailed deer population in the Flint Creek drainage. The lake acts as a wildlife crossroads between the surrounding mountain ranges, and it's not uncommon to see an occasional bear doing a little fishing.

There is a Deerlodge National Forest ranger station north of Georgetown Lake, just a few miles south of Philipsburg. There, you can get maps and information on the Anaconda-Pintler Wilderness Area and the Flint Creek Mountains.

31 Hauser Lake

Hauser Lake, just a few miles downstream of Canyon Ferry Reservoir, is perennially one of the most fished lakes in the state. It is mostly a kokanee fishery. The same setups used to fish Canyon Ferry should work here. The odds are a little better at Hauser for hooking a brown trout, and there are plenty of rainbow. Rainbows average about 1 pound in size and browns run 2 to 3 pounds.

There are some smallmouth bass and walleye in Hauser. Try trolling the shoreline for bass using plugs or poppers and work the area near the causeway for 8- to 10-pound walleye. For the big walleye, he slows his trolling way down and lets his bait bounce along the bottom.

There is some shoreline fishing near the York Bridge, and it's only a short distance from there up to the York Bar for a big juicy hamburger and a cold beverage.

Hauser Lake is easily accessible from Helena via State Highway 280.

32 Hebgen Lake

Hebgen Lake, gateway to Yellowstone Park, is fast becoming one of Montana's prized fishing and recreation areas. Located along U.S. Highway 287 8 miles north of West Yellowstone in Gallatin County, this beautiful Madison River Canyon lake was severely battered during the Montana-Yellowstone earthquake of 1959. Near Hebgen Dam, which separates Quake and Hebgen Lakes, is a Forest Service Visitor Center commemorating the event and explaining the geological activity. It's well worth a visit when you're in the area.

Since the earthquake, Hebgen Lake has thrived as a prime recreation area. It's a summer tourist haven for sailing, waterskiing, picnicking, and camping, in addition to fishing. Even though it receives heavy use, Hebgen is increasing in fishing potential, according to FWP's regional fisheries biologist Dick Vincent, who says, "The long-term outlook is up; fishing should continue to get better year-round." The fact that this lake continues to improve even under heavy pressure is excellent testimony to FWP's successful management efforts.

Hebgen Lake is a rather elongated, 16-mile by 3-mile liver-shaped body of water surrounded by the timbered mountains of the Madison Range to the northeast and the Continental Divide to the southwest. Access is relatively easy because of numerous roads which outline most of the lake, including Horse Butte peninsula on the east, which separates the Madison and Grayling arms of the lake.

Browns, rainbow, and mountain whitefish make up the active sport fishery at Hebgen. Early spring as soon as the ice comes off (through May and June) is the best time of the year for catching brown trout. Still-fishing from a boat positioned slightly offshore (as the ice break-up permits) is the ideal approach. Many anglers use worms or marshmallows to entice the hungry browns. There is some rainbow activity during the spring, which usually picks up as the water warms.

While rainbow fishing picks up in the summer, the success ratio for browns declines. Trolling 8 to 10 feet down for rainbow (deeper for browns) is the most popular summer angling technique. Medium-sized spoons and lures such as Thomas, Mepps, and Rapala all seem to work well. Bank-fishing for trout is also very popular in the summer. There are plenty of public access areas from which to choose. Spincasting, with either lures or bait, is popular with bank anglers. Jerry Cobb of West Yellowstone designs and makes what local anglers call a "killer" lure: a two-color spin-jig. Stop in and see him and give it a try—the results may be terrific.

Bait anglers also do well from a boat anchored about 200 yards offshore, fishing deep—just off the bottom. During the summer months, brown trout head down to the cool deeper reaches and loll around near the bottom. A nice 2- to 4-pound brown could be your reward for patience.

During the warmer months, the Madison Arm and the bay area near the mouth of the South Fork of the Madison host numerous fly anglers. Anglers employ float tubes, wading, and still-fishing to get the "gulpers" on the surface. In the fall, when the browns begin migrating, both the Madison and Grayling arms see plenty of activity. In the Grayling Arm, near the mouth of Duck Creek and on up into the streams itself, migrating browns provide fly anglers with plenty of action. Both wet and dry flies seem to work well during the fall, depending on time of day and temperature.

In the fall, fishing for rainbow increases, with most anglers fishing with bait from the shore. The scenery in the Madison Canyon during this time of the year is absolutely spectacular, so pop an extra roll of film into your fishing vest. Also, be on the lookout for early snowstorms in the fall. Fishing and driving can both get pretty nasty when it's cold and wet outside.

Winter ice-fishing has been slow in the past, but it has improved recently because of management efforts of FWP. If you do plan a winter visit, be prepared to shovel snow off the ice. The most popular area for ice-fishing is near the dam on the north end of the lake. Mountain whitefish, rainbow, and a very few browns make up the winter harvest. Maggots, grubs, marshmallows, worms, and corn are the preferred bait for dropping through the ice.

During the winter, don't forget to bring your cross-country skis. Neighboring Yellowstone Park and the surrounding mountains offer some of the most spectacular skiing in all of Montana. Besides being an angler's dream come true, Hebgen Lake provides visitors with an excellent opportunity to observe many different species of wildlife.

Black and grizzly bears have been sighted around the lake, sometimes even sneaking into a campground looking for handouts. (Remember—all bears are dangerous and should be treated with healthy respect and left alone.) In addition, it is not uncommon to see moose feeding at stream inlets early in the morning and late in the evening. Deer and elk abound practically everywhere. Waterfowl, including pelicans, are common; and both bald and golden eagles are frequent visitors. Osprey show the human anglers what fishing is all about.

Each lake has its own fishing patterns, and learning those patterns is part of the fun.

The Forest Service's Hebgen Lake ranger station, located just north of West Yellowstone on U.S. Highway 287, has maps available for visitors. The ranger on duty also can help provide information on camping sites and boat access sites.

33 Hungry Horse Reservoir

Hungry Horse Reservoir is one of the few large Bureau of Reclamation reservoirs that boasts a naturally reproducing trout population; in fact, it produces some of the best "lake" fishing in Montana. Located just off U.S. Highway 2 south of Glacier Park near the towns of Hungry Horse and Martin City, this excellent cutthroat and bull trout fishery was created on the South Fork of the Flathead River with the construction of Hungry Horse Dam. When the dam was completed in 1953, Hungry Horse was the fourth largest and highest dam in the world. Electric power generated at the dam is fed into the Bonneville Power Administration's Northwest Power Grid and shipped throughout western Montana, Washington, Oregon, and Idaho.

Surface area of this 34-mile by 3.5-mile reservoir is approximately 22,000 acres. It has a maximum depth of 500 feet when full.

Since it is located in a river valley, numerous tributary streams flow into the reservoir. These small tributary streams, along with the South Fork and Spotted Bear Rivers, provide the habitat and conditions that make natural trout reproduction possible and that set Hungry Horse Reservoir apart from most other reservoirs in Montana.

Situated in one of the most picturesque wildland areas of Montana, Hungry Horse Reservoir is bounded by Glacier Park on the north, the Great Bear Wilderness on the northeast, and the Bob Marshall Wilderness just 10 miles south. These unique wildland areas provide anglers and other visitors with breathtaking scenery, exciting backcountry challenges, and some of the best fishing in Montana.

Most fishing activity doesn't really get started until the middle of June, when the reservoir nears full capacity, but from then on it continues full steam throughout the summer and on into the fall. Unfortunately, there is virtually no winter fishing because of the extreme draw-down for power generation. But once moderating weather starts to move through in late spring, local anglers get itchy feet and head for the reservoir.

Overall, this is a good to excellent trout fishery, with cutthroat predominating. Most cutthroat anglers try the bay areas near the tributary streams and, because of the steep banks, tend to favor using boats anchored offshore. There is little shoreline fishing. The most popular bay areas tend to be on the north end of the reservoir near the dam; but the bays near Emery, Riverside, and Quintonkon Creeks on the east side and Doris, Lost Johnny, Wounded Buck, Jones, and Forest Creeks on the west side also see their share of eager anglers.

Light spincasting gear is favored by many anglers, with small Daredevles, Kamloops, Mepps, and Thomas Cyclones being the most popular cutthroat lures. Trolling is one of the most popular methods for fishing this large reservoir. Anglers trolling for cutthroat favor using a single line with small Rapalas, Triple Teasers, Swedish Pimples, and Mepps lures, usually working these lures 10 to 20 feet down. A good day's catch should yield your limit of 12- to 16-inch cutthroat.

Hungry Horse Reservoir also supports an excellent bull trout fishery. Despite closure of most fishing for bull trout in the state of Montana, both the South Fork and Hungry Horse Reservoir have remained a viable bull trout fishery. After closing the fishery to taking of bull trout, FWP may decide to allow the taking of one bull trout in the future. Whatever happens, watch for regulation changes if bull trout populations in the lake drop below their current sustainable levels. The south end of the reservoir near the mouth of the South Fork and its tributary, the Spotted Bear River, are the most popular bull trout fishing areas.

Fall at Hungry Horse is one of the most visually spectacular and colorful seasons of the year. The surrounding fir and larch forests become a checkerboard of dark green and bright yellow colors as the larch needles die in preparation for winter. But spectacular vistas are not the only reasons to head to this reservoir in October. This is prime mountain whitefish angling time—a time that allows whitefish anglers a chance to show the rest of us what fishing is all about. Popular tackle includes light spincasting gear or a fly rod using maggots and grubs on very small hooks, sometimes attached to a small fly with red webbing on it. A good day's catch should yield a limit (100 fish) of 9- to 10-inch whitefish, so don't forget to bring a bucket or bag to haul yours home.

Fly fishing aficionados shouldn't stay away from this reservoir because of a dislike for impounded water. Purists may so choose, but if you like to fly fish and want an interesting and challenging piece of water located in a beautiful setting, then try it out. Hungry Horse is mostly a dry fly area, the most popular patterns being Wulff, Mosquito, grey or yellow Bi-visible, and (heaven forbid) a Woolly Worm-bobber combination. Again, most fly anglers stick to the bay areas near stream mouths.

Not only is the fishing at Hungry Horse great from mid-July through August, but the surrounding mountains conceal some of the most prolific and abundant huckleberry bushes in the state. Nothing tops a day of berry picking like a late afternoon expedition to the reservoir for some fresh trout. Steamed or fried trout sprinkled with lemon juice and green onions, baked potatoes and sour cream, and a fresh-baked huckleberry pie—now that's a menu that can't be beat!

If you're planning a trip to this truly spectacular area, stop in at the Snappy Sports Center or The Sportsman in Kalispell for some tips from local anglers on the latest conditions at the reservoir. In addition, the Forest Service's Hungry Horse and Spotted Bear Ranger Stations also have information on camping, fishing, and boating conditions. Both locations should have available maps of the reservoir and the surrounding mountains.

34 Handkerchief Lake

For an interesting change of pace when visiting Hungry Horse Reservoir, consider Handkerchief Lake on Graves Creek about halfway up the west side of Hungry Horse Reservoir. The lake sits a couple yards below the road and has a brushy shoreline so you're well advised to pack in a float tube, or if you have the gumption, a canoe. The grayling can either be finicky or gullible, but a small dark fly or small spinner is usually enough to get a rise. Handerkerchief provided the state record 3.21-pound grayling to Frederick Dahl in 1994.

35 Lake Koocanusa

Northwestern Montana contains some of this nation's most magnificent scenery, ranging from the frosty, snow-laden peaks of the Cabinet Mountains—which contain several species of pine and fir trees, abundant larch, and an impressive grove of western red cedar—to the floor of the Kootenai River Valley and some of Montana's most productive trout waters.

Not only are there natural wonders to explore in this region of the state, but man-made wonders as well. Lake Koocanusa, located in Lincoln County approximately 17 miles northeast of the town of Libby on Montana Highway 37, is one of the largest man-made reservoirs in Montana. The reservoir, which extends 48 miles north to the Canadian border, was created when the United States Army Corps of Engineers completed construction of Libby Dam in 1972.

In order to create a recreational fishery equal or better than the Kootenai River before it was impounded by the dam, FWP instituted an extensive program of cutthroat trout planting in Koocanusa, dumping literally millions of cutthroat trout into the reservoir. In 1973 alone, approximately 1 million fingerlings were planted. Since that time FWP has stabilized its plantings to an annual total of approximately 100,000 planted in the tributaries.

Besides the planted cutthroat trout, the reservoir now contains virtually all of the fish that inhabited the Kootenai River prior to impoundment by Libby Dam. In fact, kokanee salmon that migrated from British Columbia down to the reservoir made up over 40 percent of the game fish caught in Lake Koocanusa by September 1981. In addition to cutthroat trout and kokanee salmon, the reservoir now contains rainbow and bull trout, mountain whitefish, burbot (or ling), suckers, peamouth, and squawfish. British Columbia began planting Kamloops rainbow in the reservoir in 1985 and FWP followed suit in 1988. The nongame fish population has dramatically increased in the reservoir, so anglers should not be surprised to hook a few peamouth and squawfish.

Lake Koocanusa is open for fishing year-round, but most active fishing takes place in the spring, summer, and fall. Like most reservoirs used for hydroelectric production, it suffers from daily fluctuations of surface elevation, as water is released for power generation, and therefore it never freezes over in the winter. The daily and seasonal water fluctuations also wreak havoc on shoreline access sites. Under severe draw-down, most boat launching facilities used to be left high and dry, but now most boat ramps have been extended, allowing season-long access.

Most anglers concentrate on Kokanee with rainbows in second place. Kokanee anglers start out in the clearer south half in spring, then work their way north over summer as the reservoir clears and mature salmon stage before moving into canadian tributaries to spawn. Kokanee anglers use flatline in spring, then go to lead leaders or downriggers as the salmon move deeper. Catch rates for kokanee are good and the fish average a plump 11 to 12 inches. Trolling works well and locally popular lures include cowbells, wedding rings, and kokanee killers. Maggots also get the job done.

Trout anglers should do well with spincasting gear, fishing either from shore or from a boat anchored just offshore, using light hardware tackle, spinners, and spoons such as small Mepps or Thomas Cyclones.

Trolling in Lake Koocanusa can also be a fairly productive way to fish, provided you can get your boat to the water. Once on the lake, trollers do have an advantage over bank anglers, because they can move into areas nearly impossible to reach from the steep side slopes of the shoreline. Depending on water temperature, most anglers troll about 8 to 24 feet deep, using small to medium size lures. Kamloops, red/green Daredevles, Triple Teasers, and Martin Radiants all get heavy use, although experimenting with any heavy-bodied trout lure may produce some nice fish. Rainbow, cutthroat, and kokanee are all fished by trolling. Tipping the lure with maggots or corn really helps.

Mountain whitefish are making a comeback at Lake Koocanusa, and anglers using light spinning gear with small hooks and maggots should be able to haul in some nice 14-inch fish. Local anglers report some success using standard store-bought whitefish flies either on light spinning tackle or on fly rods.

Lake Koocanusa also hosts one of Montana's most interesting (some say ugly) native fish: the burbot, or ling cod. This strange-looking fish has a single chin barbell, or whisker (unlike catfish, which have two), and an elongated, eel-like body with long dorsal and anal fins. Burbot are freshwater codfish that usually grow to 20 or 30 inches long. Many anglers consider them a gourmet delicacy. These fish prefer large rivers and cold, deep lakes and seem to be doing well in the reservoir. The most likely spots to find these strange fish are in the northern third of the reservoir near Rexford. Burbot weighing around 7 pounds have been taken from Lake Koocanusa in the past few years.

ACCESS

Lake Koocanusa is so large that it helps to get some local advice if you're planning your first fishing trip to Lincoln County. If you approach the reservoir from the south end, stop in at the Sport Shop in Libby to find out what's happening on the lake. If you are coming from the north, the FWP fish hatchery at Eureka is a good place to stop and ask for advice. Any of the Forest Service ranger stations in the area should have maps of the Kootenai National Forest available. These maps cover Lake Koocanusa and the surrounding area. Canoe Gulch Ranger Station is located just a few miles downstream from Libby Dam on Montana Highway 37.

Since the reservoir extends 48 miles through a narrow valley, almost all fishing activity, be it trolling, still-fishing, or shore-fishing, takes place along the north-south shorelines, and all access sites are located on either the east or west side of the reservoir. On the west side, beginning at Libby Dam and following Forest Service Road 228, recreation and access sites include the Souse Gulch Picnic Areas (Army Corps of Engineers), McGillivray Campground, and Barren Creek Boat Ramp (Forest Service). On the east side, starting at Libby Dam and following State Highway 37, recreation and access sites include the Cripple Horse Marina (private), Peck Gulch Boat Ramp, Camp 32 on Pinkham Creek, and Rexford Boat Ramp, all maintained by the Forest Service. Since there are only four developed recreation or access sites on each side of the reservoir, most anglers stick to fishing the mouths of tributary streams, either shore-fishing, still-fishing from a boat anchored offshore, or trolling parallel to the shore.

Although much of the shoreline is steep and inaccessible, adventuresome anglers do hike to undeveloped areas, almost all of which are legally accessible because the reservoir is completely surrounded by public lands of the Kootenai National Forest.

36 Lake Mary Ronan

Lake Mary Ronan, located in Lake County 8 miles northwest of Dayton at Milepost 83 on U.S. Highway 93, is one of the few lakes in Montana not open to year-round fishing. The fishing season on this 1,500-acre lake is closed from February 28 through the third Saturday in May in order to allow undisturbed spawning for the lake's self-sustaining rainbow trout population.

This lovely lake, located in rolling timbered hills and mountains, has become a popular summertime recreation spot for anglers, boaters, waterskiers, and picnickers. There are a number of private cottages and cabins situated around the shoreline. The cast side of the lake houses the Lake Mary Ronan State Park. This site provides public camping, boat access, toilets, and a picnic area.

Lake Mary Ronan is a highly popular fishery from June through February for rainbow and cutthroat trout, kokanee salmon, and largemouth bass. With that array of fish from which to choose, the lake is an angler's smorgasbord, although most anglers who visit the area seem to concentrate their efforts on bringing home a creel of salmon. But the lake does have its dedicated trout anglers and hardcore bass fanatics.

The lake has a tendency to get a bit muddy from time to time, but it still provides an easy opportunity for most anglers to catch their limits, according to Bob Schumacher, retired FWP regional fisheries manager. Try using either Triple Teaser, Swedish Pimple, or Mepps lures, almost anywhere in the open water region of the lake. If bait is your preference, then try using maggots in 30 to 40 feet of water. Drop anchor and jig with Glo Hooks.

Winter really brings out the crowds at the lake, so pack your long johns, grubs or maggots, corn and marshmallows, and head on out. A popular method of pulling fish through the ice involves using a jig sweetened with bait. Kokanee, rainbow, and cutthroat all succumb to the jig and bait combination. Twenty-inch, 4-pound rainbow trout have been taken in February, so be on the watch for one of those big rainbow.

Local anglers describe the lake as a three-story affair in the summer, with kokanee found in deep water, rainbow and cutthroat mid-way down or just off the weedbeds, and bass in the shallower shoreline areas. Fly fishing is best during spring and summer using mayflies, caddis, and damselflies. Ten- to 18-inch cutthroat and feisty rainbow up to 22 inches provide some great fishing.

The weedbeds in the shore line areas are prime largemouth bass hangouts and provide a lot of exciting fishing during the summer months. Although a wide variety of bass plugs and poppers is necessary for spincasting gear, some anglers report successful fly fishing using frog and mouse imitations.

A good day's catch here should yield your limit of 14-inch salmon or trout; bass anglers should be able to bring home a few 2- to 5-pound bass.

In the fall, winter, and spring, visitors are likely to see deer near the lake and may even get a chance to see a moose wade out into the water. The warble of a loon can often be heard, and ducks and geese stop during the spring and fall migrations.

Local angling conditions and information can be obtained at either the FWP office in Kalispell or at Camp Tuffett in Proctor on the way to the lake.

Jim Vashro of FWP reports that an illegal introduction of perch is threatening the fishery. If you suspect illegal transplanting in any fishery call 1-800-TIP-MONT to report violations.

37 Lindbergh Lake

Located in the northwest corner of Missoula County, Lindbergh Lake is a rather narrow, long, summer resort lake. A county road 16 miles north of the town of Seeley Lake on Montana Highway 83 provides easy access. Lindbergh Lake, located near the divide between the Swan and Clearwater drainages, is an excellent jumping-off point for nearby high mountain lakes. Crystal, Turquoise, and Glacier Lakes are all within an easy day's hike from Lindbergh Lake.

Because of limited spawning areas and low basic productivity due to low temperatures and lack of food sources, this is not an outstanding angling location, but it is still a very scenic and remote spot. FWP annually plants the lake with 30,000 4- to 6-inch cutthroat trout and about 100,000 kokanee salmon, but there just isn't enough food to sustain a large fish population, and the lake is too remote for more intensive management.

All that aside, the lake does provide good summer fishing for 12-inch cutthroat trout. In addition, kokanee salmon provide plenty of challenge to any angler. Thomas Cyclones and Mepps spinners do well, along with other artificial lures, when trolled about 8 to 20 feet deep. There is virtually no winter fishery here because of the lake's severely low temperatures and remoteness. FWP says that the lake is holding its own as a fishery. The department will continue its present stocking rate and schedule.

Lindbergh Lake is remote enough that your chances of seeing some big game and other species of wildlife are good. Moose, mule deer, white-tailed deer, elk, and black bears frequent the area and usually can be seen early in the morning and late in the evening. There is a Forest Service campground at the north end of the lake, and anglers report waking in the morning and watching a moose gently wade along the shallower edges. And, of course, the late evening lullaby of the loon has put many a weary camper to sleep.

Stop in at the Condon Forest Service Ranger Station, located on Montana Highway 83, for backcountry maps and information on fishing conditions at the lake.

38 Martinsdale Reservoir

Martinsdale Reservoir sits on the county line between Meagher and Wheatland Counties. It is located just outside the town of Martinsdale off Montana Highway 294, 2 miles from the U.S. Highway 12 junction. The reservoir was created by the building of a Works Progress Administration (WPA) dam in the 1930s for the multiple uses of fishing, waterfowl hunting, and irrigation storage. Unlike many irrigation storage reservoirs, Martinsdale is not hampered by severe draw-down and water fluctuations; consequently, fishing is good almost year-round.

Martinsdale is holding its own as a rainbow and brown trout fishery, though it receives heavy fishing pressure all year. FWP has also begun planting Yellowstone cutthroat trout. Trolling and shore-fishing are both popular here, but most anglers use boats, as Martinsdale is a fairly large body of water—1,000 acres. Trollers report good success between 10 and 15 feet deep using standard spoons and artificial lures, although cowbells and worms yield fish too. Local anglers suggest that you should easily catch your limit of 12- to 16-inch rainbows and browns. If you shore-fish and let your bait sit on the bottom too long, you are liable to hook a sucker or two, but currently such rough fish pose no threat to the overall health of the reservoir.

Winter-ice fishing at the reservoir attracts many visitors from Billings, Roundup, and Bozeman. Standard ice-fishing bait such as corn, salmon eggs, mealworms, and marshmallows should do nicely. Most anglers fish fairly close to the surface, no deeper than 10 feet. In general, more larger trout are taken from Martinsdale during the winter months than at other times of the year.

Martinsdale offers better fishing for rainbow and browns year-round than most irrigation reservoirs. FWP plans to continue planting approximately 80,000 rainbow fingerlings per year, so this reservoir should continue to produce exciting trout fishing for the foreseeable future.

There are good public camping facilities around the shore, and boats are easily launched from the rocky shoreline. If you are in a boat, watch the weather, because sudden, furious winds can make it dangerous to be out on the water.

Besides recreational fishing, waterfowl hunting on the reservoir and the nearby canal enjoy a good deal of popularity. Duck hunters can easily bag their limit in the fall by jump-shooting along the canal or by setting out some decoys on the reservoir.

39 McGregor Lake

Just west of Marion in Flathead County, approximately 30 miles west of Kalispell on U.S. Highway 2, lies McGregor Lake.

The best angling at McGregor Lake occurs in spring, early summer, and through the ice in winter. The lake has a good self-sustaining population of lake trout and is stocked by FWP with rainbow trout.

In addition, the 1,500 acre lake sustains a few brook trout and yellow perch. Most anglers concentrate on the lake trout because of their size, fishing for them at depths of 30 to 130 feet.

A mid-lake bar splits McGregor Lake in half; many anglers successfully fish along both sides of the bar. On a good day you should expect to catch your limit of 2- to 4-pound lake trout. Some good-sized lake trout, 36 inches or longer, have been pulled through the ice in mid-winter. Rainbows in the three- to five-pound range can be caught along the shore. Thanks to Mysis Shrimp, these lake trout are some of the tastiest around.

Jim Vashro recommends vertical jigging as the most successful way to pull in lake trout. During the spring and summer, most anglers troll or still-fish from boats using spoons, spinners, and cowbells with worms. When fishing deep for lake trout, many anglers use depth-marked line, which makes it easier to judge how deep you're fishing. Since lake trout are very sensitive to temperature, it is important to find the right temperature regime and depth. If you have a water thermometer, be sure to use it, because in winter and early spring the 40- to 50-degree temperature regime preferred by lake trout may be fairly close to the surface. By summer, however, that same ideal temperature may be 100 or more feet below the surface.

McGregor Lake also offers backpacking anglers a beautiful trailhead for a backcountry trek. Nearby Lolo and Kootenai National Forests provide a number of developed public campgrounds, and Logan State Recreational Area has toilets, drinking water, and camping and picnic areas. If you plan to do any backcountry hiking in the area, pick up either a Lolo or Kootenai National Forest map before heading out. And check with local rangers about bear activities. This is grizzly country, even though they are rare. Take all bear country precautions.

39 Nelson Reservoir

Located in Phillips County approximately 15 miles east of Malta on U.S. Highway 2, Nelson Reservoir provides northern border anglers with ample opportunity to ply their trade. In addition, nearby Hewitt Lake and Lake Bowdoin National Wildlife Refuges provide spectacular waterfowl observation sites. Canada geese are a common sight on Nelson Reservoir as well as at the nearby refuges. Pronghorn antelope and mule deer abound in the surrounding glaciated plains, and upland game birds such as ring-necked pheasant and sharp-tailed grouse are common in nearby grain fields.

The surface area of Nelson Reservoir is approximately 4,500 acres. The reservoir is easily accessible by paved road one mile north of U.S. Highway 2. The Bureau of Reclamation maintains a rather nice campground here, and there are plenty of sandy beaches and shallow shorelines for family water sports.

Fishing for northern pike, walleye, and yellow perch is best April through November, with prime time coming early in spring when the ice breaks up. Late in the fall, just before freeze-up, fishing activity picks up again. In the warm open-water months, most fishing is done by trolling off the bottom over the bars. Some anglers prefer common pike lures.

You should be prepared for good-sized northerns in the 3- to 4-pound range and large perch up to 2 pounds. In past years, a 41-inch, 15-pound northern was taken in July, and a 34-inch, 7-pound northern was taken during September. According to FWP biologists, Nelson Reservoir holds northerns up to 20 pounds, so be prepared for a lunker to hit. Local anglers report a good day's catch to be seven to eight game fish.

Winter ice-fishing on this northern border lake can be fast and heavy, but button up, because the winds get pretty strong along the Hi-Line. Perch and walleye far outnumber the number of northerns hauled through the ice. Corn and marshmallows are used for ice-fishing. Some anglers prefer spearing for northerns and find that this method works best right after freeze-up.

Before heading out to Nelson Reservoir, it's a good idea to stop at a sporting goods store in Malta to see what local anglers are using (nightcrawlers and spinners frequent the list) and what fish are hitting.

Ice fishing on Nelson Reservoir—as always, hoping for a big one.
FRANK MARTIN PHOTO

Nelson Reservoir, one of the most popular fishing holes in Montana.
MARK HENCKEL PHOTO

The walleye, definitely a big warm-water drawing card in a state full of trout fanciers. MARK HENCKEL PHOTO

41 Nilan Reservoir

Located approximately 8 miles west of Augusta in Lewis and Clark County, Nilan Reservoir is a highly popular year-round fishing hole for refugees from nearby Great Falls and Helena. This 500-acre prairie reservoir, which is reached by county road, provides not only recreational opportunities but also irrigation storage for neighboring farms. Because of this multiple use, recreationists should be prepared for late summer draw-down and the resulting loss of fishing and other recreational opportunities. Because Nilan is a prairie reservoir like its neighbor, Pishkun Reservoir, it also serves as a stop-over site for migrating waterfowl of the Central Flyway.

In addition to the spectacular scenery of the Rocky Mountain Front, the nearby Lewis and Clark National Forest also provides something more immediate for visitors: public campgrounds. Another public campground is located about 8 miles north of the reservoir.

Boat launch facilities at Nilan are adequate until mid-summer, when trailer launching becomes a chore. Later on in the summer, when severe draw-down occurs, trailer launching becomes impossible.

Nilan Reservoir is best known as a rainbow trout fishery, though an occasional cutthroat makes its way into an angler's creel. Like many man-made reservoirs with severe water-level fluctuations and subsequent warmer water temperatures, Nilan Reservoir also hosts a significant sucker population.

Most anglers prefer trolling for rainbow, but some also bank-fish, especially during lazy summer days. Local anglers suggest trolling about 10 to 15 feet deep using small spoons, spinners, or cowbells and worms. On a good day, you should be able to catch your limit of 10- to 12-inch rainbow, with some anglers hauling in an occasional 5-plus-pounder.

As with any prairie reservoir, watch the weather to the west for signs of a summer storm moving in. This is not an extremely large body of water, so there is no major hazard, but the quickness of their approach makes prairie storms unsettling and uncomfortable.

Winter ice-fishing draws enthusiastic crowds here. Normal ice-fishing bait—corn, marshmallows, and mealworms—are all popular at Nilan. Experimentation is the only way to select proper bait. Be sure to bring a good windbreaker, because the wind sweeps down from the Rocky Mountain Front and really rages once it hits the flatland.

FWP reports that Nilan Reservoir is doing well under heavy fishing pressure and future management depends on the severity of water level fluctuations due to irrigation demand.

42 Pishkun Reservoir

Situated approximately 10 miles east of the Rocky Mountain Front in open prairie, Pishkun Reservoir is unique among prairie lakes because of its crystal clear water. It provides ample stop-over space for migratory waterfowl of the Central Flyway. Pishkun is located in Teton County approximately 20 miles southwest of Choteau, and several other reservoirs—Nilan, Willow Creek, and Gibson—all lie within 30 miles.

A public campground with boat launch facilities is located at the reservoir. Boat users should be aware that a dangerous whirlpool lurks at the outlet. It should be avoided.

Pishkun ranges in depth from 30 feet on its western end to a maximum of 81 feet near the eastern end, and it's a good prairie fishery because of its high water quality. Northern pike, rainbow trout, and yellow perch all provide the most sophisticated angler with plenty of excitement. At one time, Pishkun held a thriving kokanee fishery—in fact, Montana's record kokanee salmon weighing 5 pounds, 15 ounces, was taken out of Pishkun in 1976. But the salmon have declined in recent years and kokanee stocking was discontinued in the early 1990s.

Northern pike are active both in the summer and winter at Pishkun. In warm water, still-fishing from a boat around the brushy areas using spoons and large flies is a good bet. Pishkun grows very large rainbow trout, but numbers are kept low by heavy predation from northern pike. FWP experimented with different sizes and strains of stocked rainbows the mid 1990s but none were able to avoid pike predation. Attempts will probably be made to re-establish the kokanee fishery which declined in the 1980s for unknown reasons.

As with any reservoir that has fluctuating water levels, recreational fishing at Pishkun is always subject to change depending on the irrigation demand in any one year. Spring and fall usually provide a spectacular show of many different kinds of geese and ducks. Canada, Ross', and snow geese have all been known to sojourn here, along with hundreds of ducks. Mule deer and upland game birds inhabit the surrounding coulees and plains, so keep your eyes open as you drive in and out of the reservoir.

43 Rainbow Lake

Rainbow Lake, or Dog Lake, as it is known locally, is located on the western boundary of the Flathead Indian Reservation along Montana Highway 28, equidistant between the towns of Plains and Hot Springs in Sanders County. It is situated on a ridge that divides the Clark Fork and Flathead River drainages, surrounded by pine and fir forests.

Facilities at the lake include toilets, campgrounds, picnic areas, and boat access. These facilities are maintained by both the Hot Springs Lions Club and the Confederated Salish and Kootenai Tribes.

Many species of big game can be seen around the lake and the surrounding forest. Moose, mule deer, bears, and even elk frequent the area. In addition, ducks and geese migrate through in the spring and fall, and whistling swans often stop off here. Beaver, muskrat, and other furbearers also abound. Nearby springs have attracted wild turkeys and many species of nongame wildlife.

Anglers and hunters should note that a tribal recreation permit is required for all fishing. Hunting of big game and other native wildlife is strictly prohibited. Tribal recreation permits are readily available in Plains or Hot Springs and at tribal headquarters in Pablo. The Flathead Indians welcome nontribal people to their reservation to camp, fish, and picnic but have reserved big game for the preservation of their traditional ways.

Rainbow Lake was once a 100 percent rainbow trout fishery, with a handful of sunfish in the lake, but trout fishing dropped off after northern pike were illegally introduced in the mid-1980s. The northern reach 10 to 18 pounds, but heavy fishing pressure is leveling off their size and numbers. Still-fishing from boats in the preferred method for trout, although both trolling and shore-fishing will yield some nice fish. Rainbow Lake still produces good numbers of 5- to 10-pound rainbow.

In winter, many anglers enjoy Rainbow's excellent ice-fishing. Corn, worms, maggots, and marshmallows all seem to work fine, although corn is definitely preferred. You should be able to catch your limit and have a great time doing it. Since it can get rather chilly, bring a bucket with charcoal or something comparable to keep your hands warm.

If you are able to get to Rainbow Lake in the spring, be sure to scout the surrounding forest for edible mushrooms. Local anglers tell tales of secret morel stashes hidden along the nearby bogs. Be sure to consult a good identification book before eating any wild plants to prevent eating potentially fatal poisonous plants.

44 Seeley Lake

Seeley Lake, at 1,300 acres, is another of western Montana's prized recreation spots. Located just 55 miles northeast of Missoula on Montana Highway 83, near the confluence of the Clearwater and Blackfoot Rivers, this heavily used summer resort is surrounded with cabins, beaches, and picnic and camping areas.

The lake sits in a beautiful setting of larch, fir, and pine forests with vegetation reaching right down to the water's edge. It is a rather long, narrow lake with little shoal area and a fairly rapid drop-off. The bottom plunges to 110 feet within a few feet from shore. As the lake sits at approximately a 4,000-foot elevation, the nights cool down quite rapidly in the summer, and the water in the lake stays cool all summer.

Cool temperatures don't deter recreational activities, however, and it's likely you'll see plenty of waterskiers on the lake, especially on the weekends. There are occasional conflicts between young ski enthusiasts and anglers, so be prepared to assert your right to fish. Usually a word of caution or warning will suffice, and most skiers will leave you undisturbed.

Fishing at Seeley Lake is usually good. The lake contains kokanee salmon; northern pike; cutthroat and rainbow trout; and a few perch. Salmon-snagging off the docks in the fall is a popular way of hauling in a bunch of nice, mature fish. Snaggers use large treble hooks with 2 to 3 inches of pencil lead wrapped around the top and 20-pound test line. The technique is pretty simple; success depends entirely on finding a school of fish. You just toss the hook 20 feet or so out and retrieve it by a series of quick, hard jerks, hopefully snagging a salmon in the process.

In the summer, anglers troll deep for kokanee salmon, using cowbells, spinners, and spoons. If you want to try for trout, don't troll as deep, only about 10 to 15 feet, and use similar spoons or spinners. There is some still-fishing for trout using worms, but keep an eye out for waterskiers.

Winter ice-fishing, primarily for perch and rainbow, is fair to good at Seeley Lake. Although you might hook some cutthroat and kokanee, they usually are too small in the winter to be of much use. This is another mountain lake, and winter temperatures dip pretty low, so bring your longjohns if you plan to be out on the ice.

45 South Sandstone Reservoir

South Sandstone Reservoir is located 7 miles south of Plevna in Fallon County. The town of Baker is only 12 miles to the west via U.S. Highway 12. The dam and reservoir, built in 1975, are fairly recent additions to the Montana State Recreation System. Facilities at the site include boat access, toilets, drinking water, camping and picnic areas, and shelter.

FWP has planted northern pike, perch, and walleye; they appear to be doing well. Highest fishing success is reported in the spring and fall. Trolling and bank-fishing are both popular at this eastern Montana water hole. If you have a boat and want to troll, don't go too deep, because all you'll get is the bottom. Worms and minnows are used extensively as well as standard pike lures, spoons, Rapalas, and jigs.

FWP also planted largemouth and smallmouth bass, and crappie, here, and the largemouth population has fared well, producing good numbers of 1- to 2-pound bass. The smallmouth bass and crappie are less abundant.

A good day's catch in the spring and fall should yield three or four 2- to 5-pound northerns and two or three 2- to 4-pound walleye. South Sandstone Reservoir is welcome relief from the dry surrounding countryside. But just because the area is dry does not mean there's no wildlife. Visitors should expect to see mule deer and pronghorn antelope as well as upland game birds on the surrounding native grasslands. Waterfowl use the reservoir in the spring and fall as a stop-over during their annual migrations. Nearby in the Long Pines area, wild turkey hunting is an annual event. Nongame wildlife such as turtles (including snapping turtles) inhabit the reservoir.

This reservoir is one of Montana's most recent recreational additions and shouldn't be missed if you're traveling across eastern Montana. It is a splendid example of a prairie ecosystem, and the fishing is good.

46 Spar Lake

Lincoln County is blessed with many excellent trout streams and lakes, but none is prettier than Spar Lake. Situated in the Cabinet Mountains south of Troy, west of Montana Highway 56 on the Lake Creek Road, Spar Lake ranks as one of western Montana's most picturesque mountain lakes.

Spar Lake is primarily a summer trolling fishery for cutthroat, lake and brook trout, and kokanee salmon. Anglers should be able to catch some 3- to 10-pound lake trout here. Thirteen- to 15-inch brookies have been pulled out of the lake, also. FWP has been stocking the lake heavily with kokanee salmon for the past few years, and Spar now produces some of the largest salmon in the area, ranging from 16 to 18 inches.

As Spar is a 400-acre, cold, clear, deep mountain lake, fish productivity is not exceptional. However, the surrounding terrain and the nearby Cabinet Wilderness Area provide ample incentive for anyone seeking spectacular scenery and peace and quiet.

The Kootenai National Forest maintains camping facilities at the west end of the lake, and there are marked trailheads for backcountry enthusiasts. The ranger station in Troy can provide you with maps of the lake area and the designated wilderness area. The area is full of wildlife, including mule deer, elk, moose, and black bears, along with a few grizzly bears. Since this is bear country, please take precautions in storing and disposing of foodstuffs and fish remains.

47 Swan Lake

Swan Lake, located in Lake County right on Montana Highway 83 near the town of Swan Lake, is one of northwestern Montana's crown jewels. The lake provides a quality fishing experience worthy of acclaim, even though it may not make the list of Montana's blue-ribbon hot-spots.

The Swan Mountains to the northeast and Mission Mountains to the southwest surround this picturesque lake. This is a fairly large lake, about 10 miles long and 1 mile wide, with a surface area of about 2,680 acres.

There is a waterfowl refuge, a Forest Service campground, and the lake's only public boat ramp at the south end. Scattered around the lake shore are a number of private summer homes and several private resorts.

Currently, FWP is trying to establish some cutthroat trout spawning runs in the lake's tributaries, and so far they have been moderately successful. The lake is home to rainbow and cutthroat trout, kokanee salmon, yellow perch, northern pike, sunfish, and bull trout. The pike have largely wiped out the once resident bass population. Besides these game fish, the lake supports an abundant northern squawfish and peamouth population.

Anglers do well trolling for salmon and trout in the summer using Mepps spinners, Thomas Cyclone spoons, cowbells, dodgers with a glo-hook, wedding rings, and anything tipped with maggots or corn. There is some nightcrawler use in conjunction with a bottom bouncer. Shoreline and tributary inlet areas are good for rainbow and cutthroat during spring and fall. Summertime plugging for northern pike, using standard plugs and flatfish or Rapala lures, should yield 4- to 18-pound northerns.

Fly anglers should not neglect this beautiful lake. Beginners should stick to either the north or south end at the river's inlet and outlet, using Wooly Worms or nymphs. In late summer, Joe's Hopper works well on the river stretches. There is some dry fly fishing on the lake itself, but it is not easy, and matching the hatch is a must. Try a very small caddis fly imitation in one of the lighter shades.

Winter ice-fishing often yields cutthroat and rainbow trout, kokanee, plus a smattering of perch. For bait, try corn and marshmallows.

Local anglers tend to hang out at the Elm Court and Swan Village Market in Swan Lake, so stop in and get the lowdown on how to fish this lake.

During the spring and fall, Swan Lake attracts abundant waterfowl, including a lot of Canada geese. During the evenings, loons break the mountain quiet with their eerie call. Bald eagles and osprey make the rounds of this fishing hole just as much as human anglers. Mule deer, elk, bears, and many species of nongame wildlife abound in the surrounding forests. In fact, wintertime driving near the lake on Montana Highway 83 can be hazardous because of the many deer crossings.

One word of caution: be careful when boating across the lake. Parts may be shallow. Locals may tell you that the shallowest parts are in the middle of the lake. Go slow until you know the lake.

One of the famous Montana pan-sized trout. MARK HENCKEL PHOTO

48 Tongue River Reservoir

In the heart of the northern plains coal country is one of southeast Montana's finest recreational jewels, the Tongue River Reservoir, a state record-winning fishery. Because this reservoir is located a few miles north of the town of Decker in Big Horn County and 5 miles north of the Wyoming state line, it is heavily used by citizens of both states.

Tongue River Reservoir, a prairie fishery widely used by boaters, swimmers, picnickers, and anglers, is a long narrow channel, approximately 5 miles by 0.8 mile. Although this is a prairie reservoir, there are a few trees around the shoreline. The reservoir was created on the Tongue River when the State of Montana built an irrigation storage dam. In past years, high water has done serious damage to the dam. Repairs may result in much better water levels after 1999, but the reservoir will remain low during repairs.

The big story at the Tongue River Reservoir is crappie fishing. Crappie are not caught all season and catch rates are good at times. Feathered and plastic lead-head jigs are popular patterns. Mealworms, angleworms, corn, and small spinners also work well against these feisty fish.

Sharpen your knives and your patience and head for the Tongue River. Fishing is good from late June throughout the summer. Most anglers fish by casting out and then bouncing the lure or bait along the bottom. Bottom bouncers work well, but some people prefer to do it naturally.

A good day's catch on the Tongue River Reservoir should yield four to five walleye around 3 pounds, but an occasional lunker in the 9- to 12-pound range does turn up. The Montana state record northern pike was taken from the reservoir in 1972—it weighed 37.5 pounds—but few of these big fish remain. If you spend any time fishing the bottom, you probably will turn up some channel catfish around 18 to 22 inches long.

The nearby Tongue River Breaks offer some spectacular prairie scenery and provide habitat for many species of wildlife. Mule and white-tailed deer, pronghorn antelope, and many species of migrating waterfowl and shorebirds frequent the area. Human anglers are not the only ones to flock here: white pelicans are a common sight on the river.

If you look closely at the soil in the Breaks you should be able to spot a dark, black layer or seam running through the soil. It's coal, and it's both a bane and a boon to the region. Nearby strip-mining of coal poses a constant threat to wildlife, fish, groundwater, and the Tongue River itself. In addition, there is renewed interest in coal slurry pipelines to ship the black gold out of the region. Opponents to slurry pipelines argue that they would deplete the region's precious supply of clean water and wreak havoc on the state's major industry, agriculture. Needless to say, the export of water from the Tongue River would have a devastating impact on the fisheries both in the reservoir and in the mainstream of the river.

Alpine Lake Fisheries

Even more so than the blue-ribbon rivers and broad valley lakes, Montana's alpine lakes offer an angling experience unique to the Big Sky. Regardless of which high-country fishing hole you choose for a particular trip, spectacular scenery is guaranteed. Most of Montana's mountains also provide good opportunities for solitude, wildlife watching, and a wide palette of colorful fish—rainbow, browns, goldens, lake trout, cutthroat, brookies, and grayling.

For all that, fishing mountain lakes can be unpredictable, uncomfortable, and even hazardous. Winter freeze-outs may wipe out a lake's fishery until new recruits move in or are planted. Stocking cycles also change, which is an important factor in determining the number and size of fish in lakes that cannot support a permanent, self-sustaining fishery. And even lakes with thriving fisheries run hot and cold—one day the trout hit on every cast, and the next day brings nary a nibble.

Mountain weather can be even more fickle than fish, changing from sun to rain to sleet or snow and back to sun within an afternoon. Snow can fall any day of the year at higher elevations. Always be prepared for wet weather and colder temperatures—ideal conditions for inducing hypothermia (low body temperature). Loss of body heat is as potentially lethal in July as it is in January. Remember that many alpine areas are remote and little-traveled; help may be days away.

The best safeguards for mountain travel are planning, common sense, and experience. If you're new to backcountry expeditions, go with a group of experienced friends or hire an outfitter. You'll have more time to enjoy the fishing and plenty of chances to gain valuable skills and knowledge.

Many of the lakes listed in this section are in designated wilderness areas and are accessible only on foot or horseback. Always check with the local Forest Service or the Montana Fish, Wildlife, and Parks office before hitting the trail. Ask about trail conditions, stocking schedules, and special regulations governing fishing, camping, or livestock use.

District and wilderness area maps are available at Forest Service offices. Maps in the wilderness series are particularly useful, showing elevational contours, forest coverage, property ownership, access roads, trails, and detailed physical features.

To protect fragile shoreline soils and vegetation, pitch your tent at least 200 feet from the water's edge and picket livestock on higher, well-drained ground. Practice no-impact camping—use a campstove instead of an open fire, bury human waste far from any water source, and pack out all garbage. A clean camp is particularly important in bear country.

Most important of all, fish gently. Growth rates are slow in these high-country lakes, and trout work harder to survive here than in more hospitable waters. Some tarns hold the last remaining pure strains of native

The Absaroka-Beartooth Wilderness contains hundreds of backcountry lakes, including Rainbow Lake in the East Rosebud drainage, as shown here. CHRIS CAUBLE PHOTO

grayling and westslope cutthroat. You can help preserve this precious resource by practicing catch-and-release, using barbless hooks, and working your catch quickly so as not to exhaust the fish. For eating, keep only as many fish as you need for the next meal, and take only small fish. Two 9-inchers are as filling as one lunker, and probably tastier.

The following are brief overviews of Montana's major wilderness areas, with a couple of lake fishing suggestions on each. Refer to USFS Recreation Maps and USGS 7.5 Minute Quadrangle Maps to plan your outing.

49 Absaroka-Beartooth Wilderness

Montana's highest mountains rise in a vast complex of peaks, plateaus, and lake-studded stream drainages along the northeast border of Yellowstone National Park. This windy, rugged landscape contains more than 1,000 lakes, 435 of them harboring fish. A trip in the Beartooths offers outstanding scenery and solitude, a genuine wilderness experience, and excellent alpine fishing. A select handful of lakes are described here, and anglers wanting more comprehensive information on the Beartooths should pick up a copy of *Fishing the Beartooths* by Pat Marcuson. It describes more than 1,000 lakes and streams in the Beartooth Plateau, detailing the location and size of each lake, access, stocking frequency, and successful fishing strategies.

Some good places to try fishing include: Pine Creek Lake, Knox Lake, Fish Lake; Rainbow Lake on the Lake Plateau, Horseshoe, Fish, Mirror, and Blue Lakes; Fourmile and Speculator Creeks; Silver Lake, Speculator, West Boulder, and Kaufman Lakes; Bridge Lake at the base of Crow Mountain; Flood Creek and the Middle and North Forks of Wounded Man Creek; Goose Lake and other lakes at the head of the Stillwater; Mystic Lake in the West Rosebud; East Rosebud Lake, Rainbow Lake, Lake At Falls, and Fossil Lake; Black Canyon Lake, Sliderock Lake, the Hell Roaring Chain of lakes and Moon Lake.

The Forest Service has special regulations on party size and livestock use within the Absaroka-Beartooth Wilderness—check at the ranger districts in Gardiner, Livingston, Big Timber, and Red Lodge for more information.

50 Anaconda-Pintler Wilderness

With Georgetown Lake to the north and the famed Big Hole River to the south, the Pintler Mountains serve as a spectacular backdrop to many a successful fishing trip. The Anaconda-Pintler Wilderness follows the Continental Divide here, helping to protect the headwaters of three of western Montana's premier trout streams: Rock Creek, and the Bitterroot and Big Hole Rivers. The wilderness area also boasts a number of respectable fishing holes in its own right.

Some good places to try fishing include: Carpp and Lower Carpp Lakes; Upper Carpp Lake; Tamarack and Edith Lakes; Johnson, Martin, Rainbow,

An exposed lake in the Bob Marshall Wilderness. DARRIN SCHREDER PHOTO

and Phyllis Lakes; Edith Lake; Ripple, Kelly, and Hidden Lakes; South of the Divide are Mystic, Crystal, and Lion Lakes; Mussigbrod Lake northwest of Wisdom; and Lower Seymour Lake and Upper Seymour Lake.

51 Bob Marshall Wilderness Complex

The Great Bear, Bob Marshall, and Scapegoat Wilderness Areas together comprise one of the largest remaining expanses of roadless land in the contiguous United States. From the southern boundary of Glacier National Park to Montana Highway 200, the Bob Marshall complex runs along both sides of the Continental Divide, unbroken by roads and crossed only by horse and foot trails. Most of the fishing concentrates around the lakes and streams of the Sun River drainage and the Middle and South Forks of the Flathead River basins.

Some good places to try fishing include: Sunburst and Olor Lakes; upper Necklace, Woodward, and Lena Lakes; To the southwest, Lick, Koessler, and Doctor Lakes; Pyramid Lake; Big Salmon Lake; upper Middle Fork of the Flathead; Stanton, Dickey, Almeda, and Marion Lakes; Tranquil Lakes; Castle Lake; Flotilla Lake; Gibson Reservoir; and the Sun River.

52 Crazy Mountains

The Crazy Mountains were named, so one story goes, after a lost pioneer woman wandered out of them alone and half-crazed. Cross-country hikers can easily experience the poor woman's plight in the Crazies' compact jumble of peaks and canyons, but well-beaten trails lead to the best fishing lakes in this range.

Some good places to try fishing include: Rock and Smeller Lakes; Cottonwood; Campfire and Moose Lakes; Granite, Thunder, and Blue Lakes; Pear or Druckmiller Lakes; and Twin Lakes; and Swamp Lake.

53 East And West Pioneers

Nearly encircled by the renowned Big Hole River, it should come as no surprise that the Pioneer Mountains contain more than their share of fine trout fishing. After all, a riverine trout fishery lives and dies on the quality of the surrounding watershed. Fully 33 percent of the Pioneer's lakes hold trout, the highest occupancy rate of any mountain range in southwest Montana. Thanks to good road access and a well-developed trail system, most of these lakes are comparatively easy to get to.

Some good places to try fishing in the West Pioneers include: Ferguson and Foolhen Lakes; Sand and the two Stone Lakes; Baldy Lake; Lake of the Woods and Odell Lake; and three Bobcat Lakes.

Some good places to try fishing in the East Pioneers include: Estler Lake; the trio of Pear, Boot, and Anchor Lakes; Browns Lake; Lake Agnes and Rainbow Lake; Waukena and Tahepia Lakes; Crescent, Grayling, Lion, and Canyon Lakes, and Lake Abundance; Hidden and Sawtooth lakes; Schulz, Lower Boatman, and Grouse Creek Lakes; and Lower Elkhorn and Gorge Lakes.

54 Gallatin Range

When the Gallatin and Madison Rivers are swarming with the latest hatch of drift boats and hip waders, Bozeman anglers head for the hills, to the lakes of the Gallatin Range. Hyalite Reservoir, 18 miles south of Bozeman, tops the list of multiple-use recreation areas in the Gallatins.

Some good places to try fishing include: Hyalite Lake; Emerald and Heather Lakes; Rat Lake; Hidden Lakes and the trio of Golden Trout Lakes; and Ramshorn Lake.

55 Madison Range

Most of the alpine lakes in the Madison Range are clustered in two areas—the Spanish Peaks unit to the north, and the Taylor-Hilgard unit to the south. Unfortunately, both areas have received heavy fishing pressure for decades and many lakes are scarred by innumerable campsites, trees hacked for firewood, and trampled, devegetated shorelines. When the Spanish Peaks and Taylor-Hilgard units were added to the national wilderness system in the mid 1980s, word of their natural beauty and resources spread, attracting even more visitors.

Some good places to try fishing include: Lake Cameron; No Man Lake; Lost Lake and Shadow Lake; and Albino Lake.

56 Mission Mountain Wilderness

Just west of Montana Highway 83 between Seeley Lake and Swan Lake, the Mission Mountains rise as a wall of soaring peaks, shining glaciers, and dense forests. The Missions are studded with clear, cold lakes, many of which harbor good-sized trout. Most of the range is designated as wilderness, and the west slope lies within the Flathead Indian Reservation. Access is often restricted on tribal lands for non-tribal members. At the least, you may have to buy a permit to hike or fish.

Some good places to try fishing include: Cedar Lake; Piper Lake; Upper and Lower Cold Lakes; and Crescent Lake basin including Crescent, Glacier, Heart, and Island Lakes.

57 Tobacco Root Range

Though scarred from heavy mining activity for more than 100 years, the Tobacco Roots still offer good trout fishing. More than thirty-seven lakes contain fish—brookies, cutthroat, rainbow, and a scattering of grayling. But with the exception of Branham Lakes and Noble Lake on the west, angling here is often an exercise in perseverance.

Some good places to try fishing include: Three paternoster lakes—Hollowtop, Deep, and Skytop; and Albro Lake; Bell Lake; Twin lakes; Cliff, Lupine, Alpine, and Lily Lakes; Branham lakes; and Noble Lake.

Other Montana Lake Fisheries

As a bonus feature, we have included in the following table seventy-seven more outstanding or very popular lakes, ranked in order by their sizes.

The codes used in the last column of this table are as follows: **A**—abundant, **B**—abundant with a proportion of large fish, **C**—common, **D**—declining, **E**—presence expected, **R**—rare, **U**—uncommon, **V**—uncommon with large fish and **Z**—abundance unknown.

	Lake	Drainage	County	Size (Acres)	Depth (Ft.)	Species	Abundance
58.	LAKE ELWELL	Marias River	Liberty	17,000	150	rainbow	U
						perch	C
						pike	C
						walleye	A
						burbot	U
59.	NOXON RAPIDS RESERVOIR	Clark Fork River	Sanders	8,800	250	cutthroat	V
						rainbow	V
						whitefish	V
						brown	V
						bull trout	V
						perch	A
						largemouth bass	A
						smallmouth bass	A
						pike	R
60.	LIMA RESERVOIR	Red Rock River	Beaverhead	7,413	32.8	burbot	C
61.	LAKE FRANCIS	Dry Fork, Marias	Pondera	5,536	45	northern pike	C
						rainbow	R
						walleye	A
						perch	C
						burbot	U
62.	BYNUM RESERVOIR	Miller Creek	Teton	4,120	45	walleye	C
						perch	A
63.	CABINET GORGE RESERVOIR	Clark Fork River	Sanders	3,800	220	rainbow	U
						cutthroat	U
						brown	U
						northern pike	U
						whitefish	U
						bull	U
						largemouth bass	U
						perch	A
						smallmouth bass	R
64.	ENNIS	Madison River	Madison	3,780	18	rainbow	A
						brown	A
						grayling	C
65.	LITTLE BITTERROOT	Bitterroot Creek	Flathead	2,925	260	kokanee	A
						cutthroat	C
						rainbow	V
						perch	C

	Lake	Drainage	County	Size (Acres)	Depth (Ft.)	Species	Abundance
66.	UPPER RED ROCK	Red Rock River	Beaverhead	2,206	6	grayling cutthroat burbot brook	D V C V
67.	LAKE HELENA	Missouri River	Lewis & Clark	2,100	14	brown perch rainbow largemouth bass	R V U U
68.	PABLO RESERVOIR	Flathead River	Lake	2,040	39	largemouth bass perch rainbow	 A A C
69.	NINEPIPE RESERVOIR	Flathead River	Lake	1,852	27	largemouth bass perch	 A A
70.	DUCK	Milk River	Glacier	1,398	60	rainbow	B
71.	TALLY	Logan Creek	Flathead	1,326	250	kokanee bull rainbow cutthroat lake pike	A C C C U C
72.	GIBSON RESERVOIR	Sun River	Lewis & Clark Teton	1,282	90	rainbow cutthroat brook	U R R
73.	BULL LAKE	Lake Creek	Lincoln	1,249	64	cutthroat kokanee largemouth bass rainbow brook perch bull northern pike	C U C V U A C Z
74.	PLACID LAKE	Swan River	Missoula	1,110	90	perch rainbow largemouth bass cutthroat brook kokanee brown bull	A U U C R C R R
75.	WARHORSE LAKE	Buffalo Creek	Petroleum	1,000	12	largemouth bass	 R
76.	RUBY RESERVOIR	Ruby River	Madison	970	66	brown cutthroat rainbow	U Z U
77.	WILLOW CREEK (HARRISON RES.)	Willow Creek	Madison	868	74	rainbow brown	C C
78.	PAINTED ROCKS RESERVOIR	Bitterroot	Ravalli	803	180	cutthroat rainbow bull brook	C C R R

	Lake	Drainage	Size County	Depth (Acres)	(Ft.)	Species	Abundance
79.	KICKING HORSE RESERVOIR	Flathead River	Lake	800	28	largemouth bass perch rainbow	A A V
80.	FRENCHMAN RESERVOIR	Frenchman Creek	Phillips	790	23	perch	C
81.	LOWER GLASS LINDSEY	Sweetgrass Creek	Sweet Grass	768	22	perch rainbow brown	A C C
82.	COMO	Bitterroot River	Ravalli	753	100	rainbow cutthroat	C U
83.	WILLOW CREEK	Lodgegrass Creek	Big Horn	750	95	rainbow brown	A A
84.	GAFFREY	Lake Creek	Sheridan	637	15	northern pike largemouth bass	Z Z
85.	UPPER STILLWATER	Stillwater River	Flathead	630	74	rainbow cutthroat northern pike brook perch largemouth bass	V D A V A E
86.	CLIFF	Madison River	Madison	620	125	rainbow	C
87.	HYALITE RESERVOIR	Hyalite Creek	Gallatin	618	125	cutthroat grayling brook	A A Z
88.	SALMON	Clearwater River	Missoula	613	70	rainbow bull cutthroat kokanee brown perch	C R C A U A
89.	MIDDLE THOMPSON	Thompson River	Lincoln	601	160	rainbow kokanee brook largemouth bass cutthroat lake	V C U B A V
90.	QUAKE	Madison	Gallatin	600	80	rainbow brown cutthroat	Z Z Z
91.	DICKEY	Kootenai River	Lincoln	579	74	kokanee brook cutthroat northern pike rainbow	C V V V V
92.	ECHO	Flathead River	Flathead	546	70	whitefish northern pike brook perch largemouth bass	V A V A B

229

Lake	Drainage	Size County	Depth (Acres)	(Ft.)	Species	Abundance
93. PETROLIA RESERVOIR	Flatwillow Creek	Petroleum	514	42	perch burbot walleye pike	U R C U
94. HELENA REGULATING RESERVOIR	Missouri River	Lewis & Clark	499	67	kokanee perch	C U
95. SWIFT RESERVOIR	Birch Creek	Pondera	498	60	rainbow	U
96. HUBBARD RESERVOIR	Little Bitterroot & Flathead Rivers	Flathead	483	62	rainbow brook salmon	A U E
97. LAKE 12	Lake Creek	Sheridan	474	12	northern pike	V
98. SMITH	Ashley Creek	Flathead	443	13	perch cutthroat brook rainbow	B V V C
99. HOLLAND	Holland Creek	Missoula	427	155	bull kokanee cutthroat rainbow perch	V V V V C
100. EUREKA RESERVOIR	Teton River	Teton	400	25	rainbow brook brown	C Z Z
101. SILVER	Storm Lake Creek	Deer Lodge	394	72	bull lake rainbow kokanee cutthroat	V R V C R
102. BLAINE	Flathead River	Flathead	372	140	brook northern pike cutthroat lake largemouth bass whitefish kokanee perch	U C C V C V C A
103. GLEN	Glen Creek	Lincoln	340	38	bull kokanee rainbow brook whitefish	D A A V A
104. GREY WOLF	Swan River	Missoula	228	200	cutthroat	A
105. SMITH RIVER RESERVOIR	Smith River	Meagher	327	60	rainbow brook burbot	C U C
106. LEBO	Spring Creek and Big Elk Creek	Wheatland	314	14	rainbow brown tigermuskie	C C U
107. MORONY	Missouri River	Cascade	300	60	rainbow brown perch walleye	U U C U

Lake	Drainage	County	Size (Acres)	Depth (Ft.)	Species	Abundance
108. Alva	Clearwater River	Missoula	292	95	cutthroat	C
					bull	V
					perch	A
					kokanee	C
109. Upper Aero	Skytop Creek	Park	291	95	cutthroat	C
110. Mission Reservoir	Mission Creek	Lake	289	70	cutthroat	A
111. Inez	Clearwater River	Missoula	286	69	cutthroat	C
					bull	U
					kokanee	U
					perch	C
112. Newlan Creek Reservoir	Newlan Creek	Meagher	280	100	rainbow	U
					brook	U
					cutthroat	U
113. St. Mary	Dry Creek	Lake	272	272	cutthroat	A
					brook	C
					rainbow	C
114. Coopers	Blackfoot River	Powell	274	55	cutthroat	C
					brook	U
					rainbow	U
					bull	V
115. Bair Reservoir	Musselshell River	Meagher	271	60	rainbow	C
					brook	C
116. Foy	Ashley Creek	Flathead	270	133	rainbow	A
117. Big Creek 1&2	Big Creek	Ravalli	269	140	rainbow	C
118. Egan Slough	Flathead River	Flathead	266	27	northern pike	A
					perch	A
119. Lower Stillwater	Stillwater	Flathead	248	52	northern pike	A
					rainbow	V
					perch	A
					cutthroat	V
					bull	U
120. Loon	Kootenai River	Lincoln	238	115	rainbow	C
					cutthroat	V
					brook	V
					largemouth bass	A
					smallmouth bass	C
121. Rogers	Sickler Creek	Flathead	237	19	perch	C
122. Elk Lake	Elk Spring Creek	Beaverhead	235	66	grayling	D
					burbot	U
					cutthroat	C
					lake	C
123. Granite	Lake Creek	Carbon	238	125	rainbow	C
					brook	U
124. Sophie	Kootenai River	Lincoln	214	60	bull	V
					largemouth bass	A
					cutthroat	C
					rainbow	V
					perch	A

Lake	Drainage	Size County	Depth (Acres)	(Ft.)	Species	Abundance
125. BEAN	Dearborn River	Lewis & Clark	206	30	rainbow	C
126. ISLAND	Pleasant Valley Creek	Lincoln	205	55	largemouth bass cutthroat brook	A E E
127. CHURCH SLOUGH	Flathead River	Flathead	205	35	largemouth bass perch northern pike whitefish	C A C U
128. FENNON SLOUGH	Flathead River	Flathead	200	20	largemouth bass perch northern pike	C C C
129. YELLOWTAIL AFTERBAY	Bighorn River	Bighorn	200	25	rainbow brown	C U
130. MCDONALD	Post Creek	Lake	188	106	rainbow brook cutthroat bull	U U C D
131. CRYSTAL	Swan River	Missoula	174	66	cutthroat	A
132. HIDDEN	Madison River	Madison	156	50	rainbow brown	C C
133. LAKE FIVE	Mud Creek	Flathead	156	62	largemouth bass cutthroat brook perch	C E U U
134. BLANCHARD	Flathead River	Flathead	147	32	perch northern pike largemouth bass	A A A

Glacier National Park

Glacier National Park is best known for its spectacular scenery, wildlife, and backcountry hiking opportunities. Nearly 1.5 million visitors come to the park each year to experience its grandeur. Straddling the Continental Divide in northwestern Montana along the Canadian border, Glacier Park features rugged mountain peaks and some fifty glaciers. Wildflowers blanket the high mountain valleys and grassy meadows. Wildlife abounds—mountain goats, bighorn sheep, elk, moose, deer, black bears, and, most notably, grizzly bears. Glacier Park is one of the grizzly's few remaining strongholds in the lower United States.

Thus, for most people, fishing is a secondary attraction to Glacier Park. But the park offers good fishing opportunities, highlighted by the chance to catch a variety of native species from Glacier's pristine waters. In many sections of the park, fish are small due to cold and nutrient-poor waters that limit insect populations and fish growth. However, some lakes provide anglers a chance to catch trophy fish. And almost anywhere anglers go in Glacier, they'll be surrounded by extraordinary beauty.

Waters from the park flow into three oceans. The west side of the park drains into the north and middle forks of the Flathead River, eventually reaching the Pacific Ocean. East of the Continental Divide, park waters drain north into the St. Mary River and south via the Missouri River, eventually reaching the Arctic and Atlantic oceans, respectively.

Fish management in Glacier Park has changed during the last fifteen years. Emphasis has shifted away from consumptive fishing for stocked fish to sport fishing for native species. Creel limits have been reduced for native species; and several streams, particularly along the Middle Fork of the Flathead, have been closed to fishing to protect important cutthroat and bull trout spawning waters. Lakes and streams are no longer stocked because introduced species proved detrimental to native species. Park management efforts are now directed at preserving natural aquatic systems.

Native species of concern to park management programs include the westslope cutthroat trout and bull trout. Historically, westslope cutthroat trout were found throughout the waters of the Columbia River system, but they were eliminated in many areas. Populations remain strong in Glacier Park, however, providing the main catch for anglers today.

Lake trout, native only to lakes east of the Divide, were introduced into several lakes on the west side of the park. These fish get very large, often exceeding 15 pounds in some park lakes, but the introduction of lake trout has decimated bull trout population on the west side by out-competing bull for their cutthroat food source.

Bull trout are native to the Columbia and Saskatchewan River drainages of Glacier Park. Bull trout are known for their remarkable spawning runs, and many "park" fish are spawners from Flathead Lake, more than 30 miles to the south. All bull trout caught must be immediately released.

Glacier National Park

Kokanee salmon were introduced throughout Glacier Park during the early 1930s and continue to thrive in several park lakes. Kokanee from Flathead Lake once spawned in large numbers in lower McDonald Creek each fall, attracting a spectacular concentration of bald eagles. But this kokanee population collapsed and now the eagles gather in lesser numbers at Lake Koocanusa and along the upper Missouri River.

Grayling is another introduced species that now receives special management consideration. The grayling survives only in a few isolated waters in Montana and is considered in need of special support. Experts believe Glacier is within the grayling's historic range, and the park provides needed grayling habitat today.

Bears also have an interest in the fish of Glacier. They are attracted by fishy odors and may potentially cause trouble for a careless angler. Park regulations concerning the handling of fish in the backcountry are designed to minimize these encounters and should be judiciously heeded. Occasionally, authorities must close an area to fishing to avoid conflicts between humans and bears.

Anglers should pick up a copy of Glacier's fishing regulations before wetting a line. Available at ranger stations and visitor's centers, the regulations detail various seasons, closed waters, and limits.

Fishing pressure in Glacier Park is light compared to Yellowstone National Park. Approximately 10 percent of park visitors fish, and few of them spend more than a couple of hours at it.

The main threats to the park fishery are from activities outside the park boundaries. Extensive clear-cutting on forested lands outside of the park may cause sedimentation problems for bull trout and cutthroat trout in the Flathead River System. Most importantly, introduced native fisheries suffer from interbreeding with intoduced fish and increased predation and competition from introduced fish.

Even more threatening is the potential for acid rain in the park's mountain lakes. With little buffering capacity, these lakes could easily acidify, eliminating aquatic insects and other fish food sources. Ultimately this could impact fish populations through productive failure and/or starvation. Friends of the park will need to raise their voices in the coming years.

Strategies: In Glacier, almost all of the fishing action takes place in the fifty or sixty lakes that support fish. As in most high mountain lakes, the fishing in Glacier can be very temperamental—dead at some times, fast and furious at others.

What makes for hot or cold fishing has puzzled anglers for years, but two factors seem relatively clear. First, low light levels make fish feel safer from their predators, and therefore fish tend to be more active in the early morning and late evening hours. Heavily overcast or stormy times also seem better. Secondly, hatches of insects on a lake's surface often galvanize the fish into action. Once one fish begins to feed on the bugs, the others are likely to join in and dimple the lake's surface with their rises.

Russ Schneider, author of *Fishing Glacier National Park,* recommends getting away from areas easily accessible by roads. "A short hike can mean the difference between catching fish and beating the water," he says.

When anglers arrive at a lake ready to fish, they should look the lake over for special features where fish tend to congregate. Inlets and outlets are often hot spots. Prospect near promontories, fallen trees, steep dropoffs, and shoals. Anglers should approach lakes carefully to avoid spooking fish along the edge. Most of the insect life is along the shoreline, thus bringing cruising trout in to feed. The first casts should be in close; later the angler can work further out in the lake. And generally speaking, anglers do better when they move away from the most heavily used and easily accessible part of the shoreline.

Flies, lures, and bait all catch fish in Glacier. In fact, some of the fish are so hungry and unsophisticated, at Ole or Isabel Lake for instance, that they will take almost any fly. At other times, the fish seem much more choosey about what they ingest. Fish in certain lakes—such as Hidden and Oldman—have reputations for being quite discerning.

Whether cast with a fly rod or with a bubble on spinning gear, flies often prove most effective at catching fish. Staff at The Sportsman in Kalispell, recommend long leaders and small flies. When the fish are rising to the surface, use dry flies; if there is no surface action, try a small nymph, such as a hare's ear.

Schneider agrees with this strategy, but notes that especially large mayflies come off of some of the park's lakes. Three patterns he especially likes are the Yellow Humpy, Olive Elk Hair Caddis and Parachute Adams. Larger flies work when fishing wet, such as #6-10 Wooly Worms, #8-10 damselfly nymphs, #6 leech patterns, and #6-8 Marabou Muddler.

For spinning lures, the Thomas Cyclone probably ranks as the most popular hardware. The original red and white Daredevle catches more than its share. Also, the various types of Mepps and Panther Martins fool plenty of fish. Try spinning with an ultra-light rod, which makes great sport out of fighting even a 10-inch brook trout.

The most widely used bait is the nightcrawler (which cannot be dug up in the park), but some anglers prefer, grasshoppers, grubs, marshmallows, cheese, or maggots. The regulations strictly prohibit the use of live fish for bait as well as the use of set lines.

Fishing for lake trout generally requires special techniques. Having the use of a boat is usually an advantage, because lake trout summer in the deep parts of lakes. Bank anglers have their best chance at a lake trout either in spring, just as the ice comes off, or in late fall, when lake trout come into the shallows to spawn. Early season anglers may have trouble gaining access to a particular lake due to snow on the trail. In some places, the trails do not clear until July.

Fishing Waters

The following is an alphabetical list of fishing waters in Glacier, with a brief description of the angling possibilities. Anglers headed into the backcountry must have a camping permit. All anglers must obtain and carry a copy of current fishing regulations.

Akokola Lake offers good fishing for small cutthroat. Easily fished from shore and about 23 acres in size, Akokola is a 6-mile hike from Bowman Lake.

Arrow Lake is a steep, 6.5-mile hike from Lake McDonald into dense bear habitat. Also easily fished from the shore, this 60-acre lake grants excellent fishing for some nice westslope cutthroat and Yellowstone cutthroat trout.

Avalanche Lake is an easy 2-mile hike from the Avalanche Creek Campground and subsequently gets fairly heavy fishing pressure. A lovely, small cirque lake lying below several waterfalls, Avalanche has a good population of 8- to 10-inch cutthroat. Fly anglers may wish to take their waders or float tube with them to reach the deeper water for unhindered backcasts. The water is extremely cold.

The Belly River is one of the better streams in the park. Accessible by trail from the Chief Mountain Customs Station, the stream holds 7- to 10-inch rainbow as well as some grayling close to either end of Elizabeth Lake.

Bowman Lake has westslope cutthroat trout, kokanee, and some lake trout, but it requires skill and knowledge to fish for them successfully. A boat helps, although the north shore has some good bank-fishing. Bowman has road access.

Bullhead Lake, a fairly level, 4-mile hike from Many Glacier Hotel or Swiftcurrent Motel, has good fishing for 8- to 12-inch brook trout.

Camas Lake offers very good fishing for Yellowstone cutthroat, but requires a 10-mile hike from Lake McDonald.

Cerulean Lake has no trail or road leading to it and probably is the most difficult lake on this list to reach. The handful of anglers who do find this spot find very good fishing for westslope cutthroat trout. However, the angler may also find grizzly bears.

Cosley Lake is a fairly large lake about 8 miles by trail from Chief Mountain Customs Station. While fishing is only fair for 8- to 12-inch rainbow, it can be very good for lake trout, the predominant fish in the lake. In 1982, an angler caught one over 17 pounds from the shore.

Cut Bank Creek offers challenging fishing in heavy brush and timber for 8- to 10-inch brook and rainbow trout.

Elizabeth Lake is a popular backcountry lake 9 miles from Chief Mountain Customs Station. The open shoreline makes bank-fishing a pleasure. Sometimes wind-swept, sometimes placid, the lake has excellent fishing for grayling and rainbow from 12 to 18 inches.

Lake Ellen Wilson provides very good fishing for brook trout up to 15 inches long. Situated in mountain goat country, the lake is reached only after a 9- or

10-mile hike either from Lake McDonald of the Jackson Glacier Overlook. With either route, the angler faces a vertical gain of about 3,600 feet.

Lake Evangeline is another great spot for fishing away from civilization. Yellowstone Cutthroat 12 to 15 inches swim in this beautiful cirque lake at the top of the Camas Creek drainage.

Fish Lake can be good for westslope cutthroat early in the season, when anglers can reach the deep water beyond the lily pads. This swampy but beautiful little lake is a steep 1.9-mile hike from Lake McDonald Lodge.

Fishercap Lake is rather slow fishing for pan-sized brookies in a beautiful area 1.5 miles from Many Glacier.

Francis Lake has good fishing for 10- to 18-inch rainbow. Six miles up the trail from the U.S. end of Waterton Lake at Goat Haunt Ranger Station, this lake also features a dramatic waterfall above its southwestern side.

Glenns Lake is long and narrow with a shallow shoreline. Anglers should look for the deeper spots to fish for 14- to 18-inch lake trout.

Grace Lake is a relatively easy 9-mile hike from the trailhead past Logging Lake. As it is difficult to cast with a fly rod from shore, anglers might favor spincasting for 12- to 15-inch cutthroat.

Grinnell Lake is an easy 1-mile hike from the Lake Josephine boat dock. In addition to incredible beauty, anglers often find 9- to 12-inch brook trout in the turquoise glacial flour-colored lake.

Gunsight Lake is a phenomenally spectacular spot to fish for 10- to 14-inch rainbow as well as a few lunkers. Anglers must hike about 6 miles from the Jackson Glacier Overlook.

Harrison Lake harbors westslope cutthroat, and kokanee. Anglers need to take a lengthy hike from West Glacier to get here, except possibly late in the season when fording the Middle Fork of the Flathead cuts the trip down to 4 miles.

Hidden Lake contains 12- to 16-inch wily Yellowstone cutthroat. An up-and-down 3-mile hike from Logan Pass, the lake is good for fly fishing and wading. The lake has recently been made catch-and-release only. Check current regulations.

The Howe Lakes are a short hike from the trailhead along the dirt road from Fish Creek Campground to Polebridge. Best early in the season before the water warms up, both lakes are good for westslope cutthroat trout fishing. The upper lake is the deeper, but smaller, of the two.

Isabel Lake supports some nice 9- to 13-inch trout. The don't see a lot of pressure so your favorite lure should work. Depending on which trail the angler chooses, Isabel is 12 to 17 miles from road access.

Josephine Lake is just over a small rise no more than 1 mile from the Many Glacier Hotel. Some small brookies and kokanee provide the sport.

Katoya Lake has excellent fishing for nice cutthroat—when grizzly bear activity has not closed the 7-mile trail from Cut Bank Campground.

Kintla Lake is a 6-mile-long, narrow lowland lake with westslope cutthroat trout, kokanee, lake trout, and some bull trout. Fishing in this scenic lake is best done from a boat, but the bank angler willing to walk away from the road and campground can find some good fishing.

Lincoln Lake, an 8-mile hike from Lake McDonald, has good fishing for pan-sized westslope cutthroat.

Logging Lake is an 8-mile-long, narrow, lake with 9- to 12-inch westslope cutthroat. The best fishing is reached by walking the shoreline to deeper water. Fly fishing is difficult due to the timbered banks. From the North Fork Road, anglers need to hike 4.5 miles.

McDonald Creek has sparse numbers of small westslope cutthroat and lake trout. Above the lake, the stream is beautiful to behold but disappointing to fish.

Lake McDonald is the largest and most used lake in the park. This 9-mile-long lake holds lake trout, kokanee, and westslope cutthroat. Trolling for lake trout averaging 15 inches probably is the best bet for action. Boats are available for rent at Apgar. Fishing here may test the patience; most serious anglers go elsewhere.

Medicine Grizzly Lake, a 5-mile hike from Cut Bank Campground, has good fishing for rainbow.

Mokowanis Lake has very slow fishing.

Oldman Lake is home for some large, crafty Yellowstone cutthroat that cruise the shoreline in plain view of sometimes-frustrated anglers. Wet flies may be the ticket. This lake, which requires a 7-mile hike from Two Medicine Campground, also harbors some big beavers.

Ole Lake is a small, remote lake with good fishing for mostly pan-sized cutthroat.

Otokomi Lake, 6 miles from the Rising Sun Campground, has some 10-to 14-inch fat cutthroat which are elusive but sometimes fall for wet flies.

Quartz Lake is a very good spot for large cutthroat. However, the lake has no trails around the shoreline, and anglers must hike in from Bowman Lake over a ridge.

Red Eagle Lake can be good for large, 2- to 4-pound rainbow-cutthroat hybrids. In 1955 the new state record cutthroat, a 16-pounder, was taken from this lake, but it was probably a hybrid. An easy 8-mile hike from St. Mary, the lake is better to those that can bring in a float tube and fish wet line.

Redrock Lake offers fair fishing for 9- to 12-inch brookies 3 miles up the trail from Many Glacier.

Lake Sherburne is actually a reservoir with fluctuating water levels controlled by a dam just outside the east boundary of the park. Sherburne is the only lake in the park with northern pike, feisty fish averaging 18 inches and ranging up to enormous.

Snyder Lake is a cold lake with little food for the multitudes of 7- to 9-inch cutthroat that greet anglers who have made the 4.5-mile hike from Lake McDonald.

Saint Mary Lake is an extraordinarily beautiful roadside lake renowned for its scenery and its fishing. Trolling from a boat rewards anglers with white-fish, rainbow, or lake trout.

Early morning on one of the many hidden lakes of Glacier Park.

Swiftcurrent Lake, just out the back door of Many Glacier Hotel, has proven good fishing for 9- to 11-inch brook trout plus some kokanee. Boats can be rented to paddle around this beautiful, 99-acre gem of a lake.

Trout Lake is another of the specially regulated lakes in the Camas Creek drainage. Unfortunately, the brushy banks make fly fishing difficult, but those who solve this problem find good fishing for pan-sized cutthroat plus. Anglers must make a 4-mile hike into bear country to reach this lake and should be alert.

Two Medicine Lake, along with its upper and lower sister lakes, offers fair fishing mostly for rainbow and brook trout. The vast majority of the trout in these lakes measure under 15 inches, but in 1983 an angler caught an eastern brook trout that weighed almost 9 pounds even after it had been cleaned. Had the angler left the guts in the fish, it would have easily broken the state record. These lakes make beautiful places to fish and contemplate the mountains on quiet days.

Waterton Lake is a large, scenic, often wind-swept lake spanning the U.S.-Canada border. Best fished by boat, the lake surrenders a few 30-pound lake trout among the predominant catch of whitefish.

For more detailed information on fishing the waters of the park, see *Fishing Glacier National Park* by Russ Schneider, (Falcon).

Yellowstone National Park

Although Yellowstone Park owes its world-fame to its spectacular geysers, abundant wildlife, and unique scenery, the park also offers exceptional angling opportunities. Over 160,000 anglers a year take advantage of its high quality fishing. Yellowstone is richly endowed with over a hundred superb trout streams and subalpine lakes.

Despite the tremendous and ever-increasing pressure from anglers, fishing in the park has actually been improving over the past ten years. Regulations aimed at protecting the fishery and the complex food chain of this extraordinary ecosystem were extensively revised in 1970. Today, Yellowstone Park has some of the most restrictive and successful regulations in the country. They include local and seasonal closures to protect spawning fish, the elimination of bait fishing, size and creel limits, catch-and-release for most of the park, and fly fishing only waters.

The results have been more fish, a greater diversity of fishing opportunities, and more anglers taking advantage of these opportunities. The percentage of successful anglers has risen, and in many waters, average fish size is increasing.

Park policy has shifted away from consumptive fishing toward a fish-for-fun philosophy that seems to be working. The large variety of regulations make it essential for the angler to read the park's fishing regulations carefully to avoid violations.

Yellowstone Park is divided into six fishing zones, each with unique fishery characteristics and regulations. Opening day is generally July 15, depending on the zone. Creel and size limits vary from zone to zone, as do catch-and-release or fly fishing only waters, so check and carry the regulations. No matter where in the park they fish, however, all anglers must pay for a fishing permit, which is available at any visitor center or ranger office.

Fishing in the park is limited to single-hook, artificial flies and lures. Fish mortality, particularly in the catch-and-release waters, has significantly declined with the elimination of bait fishing.

A wide variety of flies and lures are effective in the park. Standard dry flies used on lakes or smooth-surfaced streams include the Adams, Blue Dun, Ginger Quill, and Light Cahill. Royal Wulffs, Humpies, elk hair caddis, and hoppers bring the best dry fly action in the fast, broken water stretches. Salmon fly patterns are good in season on the Yellowstone River. Wet flies worth trying include Woolly Worms, Yellow Muddler Minnows, and a variety of dark-colored streamers. In the park, Hamilton Stores has helpful clerks and supplies of fishing gear. Outside the park, West Yellowstone and Gardiner are amply supplied with fishing shops that can provide up-to-date information for specific waters. They also have guide services for park fishing.

Lures are particularly successful in the park's lakes but can be used effectively in many rivers and streams as well. A selection of red-and-white spoons, Mepps, Panther Martin, and Bolo spinners should provide good action. On

Yellowstone National Park

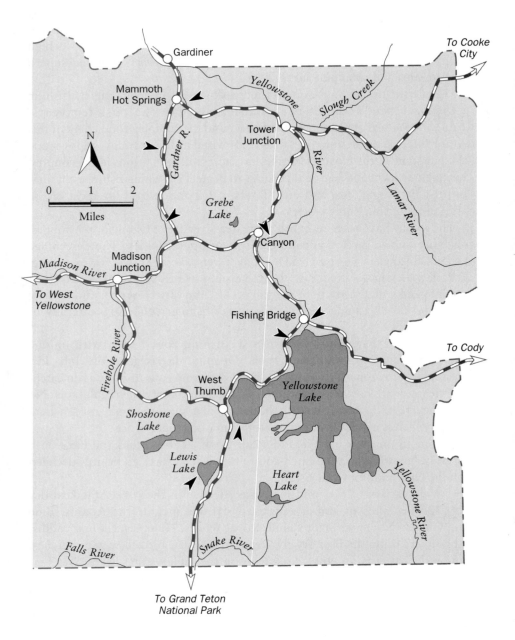

Bringing in a fat cutthroat from Slough Creek, only one example of the excellent stream fishing found in Yellowstone Park.

rivers, a fly and bubble on spinning gear may prove the most successful for the spin angler.

The fishing potential in Yellowstone Park is almost limitless. The kind of fishing preferred or the species of fish desired will influence where one chooses to fish. Yellowstone Park fisheries biologist Bob Gresswell believes that "the best fishing in the park is found in catch-and-release areas for Yellowstone cutthroat trout. There are good populations of nice-sized fish in these waters, and the fish are catchable."

By comparison, brown and rainbow trout fisheries in the park, such as the Madison River, provide tough fishing for the average angler, with a substantially lower average catch rate. Brook trout fishing is fast and hot, but the fish are small. The percentages of fish caught per species reflect these conditions: 70 percent cutthroat, 10 percent rainbow, 7 percent brown, and 7 percent brook trout. An amazing 50 percent of the fish caught in Yellowstone exceed 14 inches.

Some twenty-four waters receive over 95 percent of angler use in Yellowstone Park. These provide the best combination of good fishing and easy access. Most are accessible from park roads and require little or no walking. However, many backcountry lakes are barren because of no natural reproduction and no stocking.

Backcountry lakes and streams require permits (readily available at any ranger station) for overnight camping. Remember that Yellowstone is home to black bears and grizzly bears, both of which can be dangerous. The park service has an information pamphlet on how to avoid bear trouble that is definitely worth reading.

Fishing Waters

Yellowstone Lake and River are cited first in this list because together they account for 50 percent of the park's fishing use. The remainder are presented alphabetically for easy reference.

Yellowstone Lake is the most popular fishery in the park, and with good reason. Whether fishing from shore or by boat, anglers enjoy amazingly consistent results.

The pure native Yellowstone cutthroat fishery in the lake has had its ups and downs over the years. In 1975, the park service established a regulation which allows anglers to keep fish only up to a maximum of 13 inches. Since the advent of this rule, the fishery has responded magnificently. The average Yellowstone cutthroat now measures 14.6 inches and, for the first time in many years, a few go over 20 inches. "Now, its hard to catch a cutthroat under 13 inches," says Bill Schneider, author of *Hiking Yellowstone*.

The latest threat to the native Yellowstone cutthroat population is an introduced strain of lake trout, which competes heavily for available food. While park biologists are studying the problem, they have enlisted anglers' help by asking folks to keep any lake trout they catch and show their catch to a ranger. The fish make good eating, and any reduction in their numbers is good for the cutthroat.

Anglers hoping to enjoy trout for dinner sometimes have a happy problem—the fish they catch measure over the 13-inch limit. Richard Parks, author of *Fishing Yellowstone*, who operates Parks Fly Shop in Gardiner, has a solution—for boating anglers at least. He has observed that the bigger fish tend to hang out closer to shore in the shallow water. To catch legal keepers, he advises, "move away from shore and fish deeper—that's where the little ones are."

A huge body of water with a surface encompassing 88,000 acres surrounded by over 100 miles of sandy beaches, rocky breaks, and forested shorelines, Yellowstone Lake has a general weather pattern anglers should heed. The early morning hours usually find the lake's surface wonderfully smooth, but by late morning, the breezes have started up at least a light chop. Afternoons often see violent thunderstorms and sudden high winds with large waves that can swamp small craft. Even during the hottest days of summer, these bone-chilling waters pose the immediate threat of hypothermia—survival time is short. Anglers should keep constant watch on the weather and stay within easy reach of the shore. And be sure to check boating regulations.

Virtually the whole lake offers excellent fishing. The south and southeast arms have reputations for even better angling, but they are miles from the nearest road and have some restrictions on boat motors. The whole north shore parallels park roads, while hiking trails reach remote sections on the east and south. Public boat launches and marinas at West Thumb and Bridge Bay offer convenient services.

As to what lure or fly to use, Parks says that "almost anything catches fish—the standard brands and patterns all work." Flies work well early in the season when cast to rising fish. Spoons and spinners brings results almost any time. Parks notes that the most popular lure is Jake's Spin-a-Lure, a heavy metal lure about the size of a domino with red spots on its side. Small to medium sizes work best. Lures with more than one cluster of hooks are illegal.

The Yellowstone River ranks as one of the nation's premier trout streams. Thousands of anglers annually wade into the river and think they have discovered heaven right here on earth.

The river actually begins in wilderness to the south of the park and flows down to Yellowstone Lake through the Thoroughfare, a wild section of the park far removed from civilization. When it flows into the Southeast Arm of the lake, it is already a river of substantial size. People who value wilderness experiences trek to the Thoroughfare to enjoy these trout-laden waters in the solitude they treasure.

Now much more conveniently available to the angler, the river gently flows back out of Yellowstone Lake through several miles of pines and meadows, past the Sulphur Cauldron, and across the tranquil, wildlife-rich Hayden Valley before cascading violently into the picturesque Grand Canyon of the Yellowstone.

Some of the Hayden Valley portion is closed to all fishing, but anglers can ply the waters at either end provided they release any fish they catch. The upper end, between Fishing Bridge and the Sulphur Cauldron, draws the most anglers and has been called the most intensively fished stretch of wild trout water in the United States.

The fishing begins spectacularly on opening day when the resident river cutthroat and some of their lake cousins are just concluding their spawning. Stacked along the banks, behind logs and rocks and across the gravel bars, the thousands of fish are readily visible to even casual observers. Although not in the best condition after their recent strenuous activity, these beautifully colored fish readily take flies and lures in the first days after opening. Landing rates are sometimes fantastic; some anglers consider this cutthroat fishing at its finest.

As the weeks pass, the fishing becomes progressively more difficult. Parks suggests that the lake's cutthroat have moved back to the lake, leaving the resident river fish more room and less urgency about feeding. He also thinks the fish get smarter after being caught several times. "There's a learning curve situation here," Parks says. "They are in much better shape and much more wary by the end of the summer." Parks caught one fish which had plainly been caught seven times before. This is recycling at its finest.

Except briefly at LeHardy Rapids, the river is one smooth glide from the lake outlet to the bridge just above the Upper Falls. Bank fishing is very good along this stretch; wading is even better. Floating is prohibited.

Though spinners and spoons catch fish here, most anglers tie on flies, even if they have only a spinning rod and reel. With a bobber, spin anglers who have never used a fly before often surprise themselves by catching plenty of fish.

This section of the river has an inconsequential salmon fly hatch about July 15, mostly in the LeHardy Rapids. Plentiful mayflies and some caddis and baetis round out the hatches. Experienced angler Mike Brady watches especially for a big grey mayfly, the grey drake. He also notes that some fine hatches of small mayflies come off the water during and after stormy weather. For attractor flies, Brady singles out the house and lot fly, sometimes known as the hair wing variant, as a must to keep on hand.

From the Lower Falls down through the Grand Canyon, past Tower Junction, through the Black Canyon, and on to Gardiner, the river continues to offer outstanding fishing. Except at a bridge near Tower Junction, anglers must be willing to hike several miles down to the river, then climb steep trails back out.

Still, there are several attractions to the fishing here. Because the river is more remote and anglers must expend considerable effort just to reach it, the crowds do not fish here. Incredible as it may seem to some, an angler could walk an hour to the river, fish all day in one of the finest trout fisheries in the country, and hike out without seeing another angler.

This section of the river has some of the best fast water fishing in the park. For example, anglers can fish Seven Mile Hole ("Seven miles down and a hundred back up," in the words of Maury Leach, author of *The Yellowstone Angler*), or the bottom 3 miles of the canyon. The remainder of the Grand Canyon is off limits due both to the dangers of climbing in the canyon and to bear management closures.

A big brown making a spawning run up the Gardner River.

This section of the river has the attraction of a late and often very good salmon fly hatch. In Parks's experience, fishing salmon fly patterns produces excellent results in July and sometimes early August, even after the hatch is over. Thereafter, the fishing "holds up very well through the season," the best bets for success being caddis imitations, attractors, grasshoppers, and little streamers.

From Knowles Falls to Gardiner, the river has a more varied population of game fish. In addition to the predominant cutthroat, anglers can also find a few brookies, good numbers of browns and rainbow, and some rainbow-cutthroat hybrids with interesting color variations. Since the trout are not fished much, they tend to be less selective and sophisticated than most, but Parks observes that, once on the hook, they are scrappy fighters.

The Bechler River, located in Yellowstone's southwest corner, runs its course in an area of beautiful waterfalls and large meadows far from the sight of most of the fishing public. A road well off the usual tourist routes runs from Idaho into the Bechler Ranger Station, with a spur to the Cave Falls picnic area near the mouth of the Bechler. Because mosquitoes by the zillions use the Bechler's soggy meadows for their breeding grounds, most anglers avoid wetting a line in the Bechler until the end of the summer.

Most of the larger trout in the Bechler swim in the lower end of the river, from its junction with the Falls River up to Bechler Falls. Most of the rainbow and cutthroat average 10 to 12 inches, but a few of the rainbow grow considerably larger. Especially in the meadow sections of the stream, deep pools and undercut banks provide excellent cover. Anglers use a wide range of flies and lures effectively, but trying a grasshopper imitation can be dynamite.

The Falls River runs along the southwest border of the park. The river can be reached by road from Idaho into the Cave Falls picnic area. Fishing is excellent for rainbow and cutthroat averaging 10 to 11 inches. Trails provide some access to the upper reaches.

The Firehole River is one of Yellowstone's nationally famous trout streams. It is also the fourth most popular fishery in the park. The river's 30 miles are restricted to fly fishing, with a stretch through the Old Faithful geyser basin and above the water intake closed to fishing. The Firehole is one of the most picturesque rivers in the park as it winds its way through meadows dotted with geysers. Some geysers erupt literally into the Firehole. Bison and elk are commonly seen grazing along the river.

Unless the weather has been unusually cold, anglers should try other waters in July and August. As Parks says, "the fish go on a hopeless hunger strike" during the heat of the summer. As much of the Firehole's water comes from thermal features along its course, summer water temperatures sometimes reach 85 degrees, which puts trout into a feeding funk.

Instead, local anglers save the Firehole for early and late in the season. In June, provided the river is not too turbid, modest-sized nymphs and streamers generally work best. Toward the end of June, Parks sometimes has good luck with dry flies—perhaps mayfly imitations, but more likely caddis.

In autumn, most experienced anglers regard the Firehole as a spring creek and fish accordingly. With long, fine leaders and size 18 flies such as Quill Gordons and blue wing olives, anglers stalk the spooky trout, which Parks describes as having "Ph.D.'s in fisherman avoidance." There rainbow and browns average about 1 foot in length, but a few large fish haunt the Firehole. Parks fooled one of these, a 5.75-pound brown, on a Woolly Bugger in 1983. This seems like a phenomenally large fish for a relatively small trout stream, but then the Firehole in the fall has magical qualities.

From Biscuit Basin downstream to the mouth is the most popular fishing stretch and has the best fish habitat. Wading is easy on the Firehole, but watch for occasional deep pockets. Geyser activity keeps the water warm, further enhancing the wading. There is good road access along the entire length of the river.

The Gallatin River has its beginnings in the park, but most of the fishing takes place outside park boundaries. (This book devotes a full chapter to the Gallatin.)

The upper reaches of the Gallatin in the park run through big meadows. Undercut banks and deep holes punctuate the meandering, easily wadable stream. With no trees to hinder backcasts, the upper Gallatin is an excellent place to teach kids how to fly fish. Lots of aggressive pan-sized trout and whitewater fishing keep the attention level high.

The Gardner River runs almost its entire course within the park, joining the Yellowstone River just outside the border at the town of Gardiner on the north edge of the park. This is a classic pocket-water stream. The fast current is broken by an abundance of rocks that provide terrific holding water for fish.

Osprey Falls in Sheepeater Canyon divides the river in two. The upper 8 miles above the falls has mostly 9- to 10-inch brookies and a few small rainbow. The lower 23 miles has brown, rainbow, and brook trout averaging 9 to 12 inches. Almost all the larger trout caught in the Gardner come from the lower end of the river, which is warmed by the runoff from Mammoth Hot Springs. Most of the lunkers here have migrated out of the Yellowstone River. The park service protects some of the spring and fall spawning with seasonal closures. But when the season is open, this beautiful rushing trout stream provides some excellent fishing.

The Gibbon River is another of Yellowstone's famous and scenic fishing streams. Much smaller than the Madison or Yellowstone, the Gibbon provides superb fly fishing. The Gibbon flows for 37 miles from its headwaters at Grebe and Wolf Lakes to Madison Junction, where it joins the Firehole to form the Madison River. The river above the exquisite 84-foot Gibbon Falls was originally barren of sport fish, but now supports a good population of brook, brown, and rainbow trout. The meadows around Elk Park, Gibbon Meadows, and Norris Basin feature fine fishing when a hatch is on and the fish are rising.

Below the falls, the river provides fairly good fishing for brown trout and some rainbow and brook trout. There are lunker browns in here, but they're not easy to catch. This water is restricted to fly fishing only. Attractor flies work very well in the broken water. The river provides ideal trout habitat as it meanders through meadow.

Park roads run along most of the Gibbon's length, providing easy access. This is one of Yellowstone's more heavily fished waters, although the success rate is only fair compared to most of the park's fisheries. It just takes a little more skill to outwit the Gibbon River trout.

Grebe Lake, about a 3.5-mile, level hike near Canyon, provides good catch-and-release fishing for beautiful pan-sized and larger grayling. Cutthroat-rainbow hybrids, running from 10 inches on up in size, provide another attraction. Unfortunately, Grebe Lake is also a virtual mosquito factory.

Anglers have a very good success rate here and consider Grebe Lake one of the most satisfying fisheries in the park. Remember the possibility of encountering a grizzly here. The big bears occasionally graze on the area's succulent meadows in the early summer.

Heart Lake is a backcountry lake about 8 miles in from the trailhead on the south entrance road. Though not a difficult hike, the lake receives only moderate pressure, especially considering its attributes. Spectacular scenery, interesting vegetation, and geyser activity add significantly to the pleasures of fishing this beautiful lake, the fourth largest in the park.

Both the native cutthroat and the introduced lake trout grow to large sizes here. The lake trout average 18 to 20 inches, but sometimes much large individuals are caught. The cutthroat average 16 to 18 inches, but John Varley and Paul Schullery, in their beautiful book *Freshwater Wilderness* note that a few monsters in the 2- to 8-pound category swim in this lake and suggest that, before the introduction of lake trout, these lunker cutthroat were probably more plentiful.

Heart Lake has special restrictions protecting the cutthroat. Best fishing for lake trout is in the fall, when they are in shallow waters for spawning.

Indian Creek is a small stream flowing northeast for 13.5 miles to join the Gardner River. The stream has very good fishing for 7- to 10-inch brookies. Indian Creek is remarkably popular for its size.

The Lamar River flows for 66 miles across the northeast section of the park to its junction with the Yellowstone River. One of the longest rivers in Yellowstone Park, the Lamar also provides some of the best fishing. The Lamar has stated a remarkable come back since fish population slumped in the 1960s. However, current populations are down slightly and the river stays sediment laden much longer than other rivers, so fish accordingly. The lower third of the river, easily accessible, is now catch-and-release only for cutthroat trout.

The Lamar features excellent fishing for cutthroat; rainbow (including a few large rainbow in the lower reaches); and occasional, beautifully colored rainbow-cutthroat hybrids. Anglers heavily pressure the obvious, easily accessible spots, but much of the Lamar sees very few hooks. Angler Bill Schneider notes that even a short, mile-long hike increases the success rate considerably.

Parks regards the Lamar as one of the premier terrestrial waters in the park. From mid-July through August, Parks fishes hopper imitations along the banks and at the riffle-corners. He finds that by early September, the water has dropped, the fish are spooky, and the fishing slumps badly.

The Lamar reacts to rainstorms in just the wrong places with a shot of muddy water that makes the river unfishable.

Lewis Lake, near the south entrance, is the third largest lake in Yellowstone. This popular fishing lake features road access, a boat launching ramp, and a 100-unit campground on its shore.

Originally barren, Lewis Lake now supports a good population of brown trout, lake trout, and a rare big brook trout, but these fish are hard to catch. Like Shoshone Lake, Lewis Lake has a reputation for trophy-sized trout. During the summer, boat anglers have significantly better success than the shore anglers. The best times to try for lake trout are just as the ice comes off in June, and in the fall, when they are in shallower water for spawning. At other times, anglers must get their lures very deep.

The Lewis River flows south out of Shoshone Lake through Lewis Lake to its junction with the Snake River just inside the park. Marshy swamplands along the river below Lewis Lake provide excellent habitat for moose. Downstream from Lewis Falls there are turnouts with good views of the steep Lewis Canyon.

The most popular section of river is the catch-and-release water below Lewis Falls. Since the advent of catch-and-release fishing, the landing rate has improved, providing good fishing for 10- to 12-inch brook trout. Some lunker brown trout in the Lewis River prove very hard to catch. The river through the canyon is mostly inaccessible. Steep walls make walking treacherous and hiking in most areas is prohibited.

The channel between Shoshone and Lewis Lakes has become a popular fall fishing spot, despite the requisite 5-mile hike and unpredictable weather. A broad, slow-moving stream that can be canoed during the summer, this channel is normally only a moderate fishery. But in the fall, the upper half of the river is a major spawning ground for large brown trout averaging 18 inches and ranging up to huge. The river is shallow and crystal clear at this time, making fishing difficult but spectating fabulous.

Only 14 miles of the famed **Madison River** flow in Yellowstone Park (Montana claims the vast majority of this superlative river, and the nonpark Madison is treated in its own chapter in this book.) Nonetheless, the 14 miles of river that flow through the park catch more fishing pressure than any other waters in the park except Yellowstone Lake and Yellowstone River. Part of this attention is due to the location of a major campground at Madison Junction, where the union of the Firehole and Gibbon Rivers gives the Madison its beginnings. Another reason for this attention is its national reputation in sporting magazines and trout fishing books.

Without a doubt, the Madison in the park is a superb trout stream. But anglers new to this section of the Madison should keep in mind two qualifications: First, stating that the river is superb does not mean it is easy to catch fish. In fact, fully half the anglers who try the Madison do not catch any fish. The river and its wily fish prove stern taskmasters even for expert anglers who long ago graduated from Basic Fishing 101. The entangling weed beds, glassy water, and shaky banks swing the odds in favor of the trout.

Secondly, because roughly a quarter of its water comes from thermal areas along the Gibbon and the Firehole, Madison trout suffer from heat stress in July and August. Parks suspects the fish feed on a midnight to 4:00 a.m. shift, but otherwise the fishing action is usually desultory except during a cold spell.

As with the Firehole, most knowledgeable anglers trek to the Madison either in June, when the water is still cool (and sometimes turbid), or in September and especially October. And like the Firehole, the Madison has a fly-fishing only restriction. Again, most anglers use either small dry flies or modest-sized nymphs and streamers. Mike Brady recommends mostly nymphs in the spring; perhaps pale morning duns from June 15 to July 7, soft hackle flies in September, and Marabou Muddlers and Spuddlers in October. Parks claims that "the faith of the fisherman matters about as much as the pattern." If you're unsure about the difference between gold-ribbed hare's ear nymphs and elk hair caddis, and therefore have little faith, check with the friendly, informative tackle shop keepers in West Yellowstone.

Due to conducive water temperatures, prodigious amounts of food, excellent cover, and protective restrictions, the Madison supports a large number of trout. Varley and Schullery suggest that were it not for the influxes of spawning fish from Hebgen Lake and the resulting multitudes of fish fry, the river might support even more resident trout. Instead, it gives up some of its resources in order to serve as a nursery or rearing area for fish ultimately destined to head downstream to Hebgen Lake.

Still, the fall spawning runs of rainbow and browns add excitement to the already extraordinary experience of fishing the Madison. Anglers return year after year to try their skills again. During the runs, fish in the 15- to 20-inch range become quite common. Nice as these fish are, what really buzzes through some anglers' minds is the knowledge that a true monster trout might be the next to take the hook. Brady cites the example of the night Montana Fish, Wildlife, and Parks Department (FWP) biologists set four gill nets in Hebgen Lake and the next day found a brown of at least 10 pounds in each net. Also, he remembers a 20-pounder caught in June 1982 in Hebgen Lake. While any trout over 5 pounds is probably a one in 10,000 fish, and while not all Hebgen Lake browns spawn in the Madison, just the possibility of tying into the fish of a lifetime puts zest in one's waders.

Anglers can easily reach most of the Madison from the road that closely parallels the river. Some incredibly mucky bogs guard the river in spots above the Seven-Mile Bridge. The music of bugling elk often accompanies fall fishing here.

Nez Perce Creek flows for about 15 miles from Mary Lake into the Firehole River. It is bordered by forest and meadows and is a popular area to see bison. The Mary Mountain Trail follows the creek most of the way to Mary Lake.

Nez Perce Creek has 10- to 11-inch brown and rainbow trout, but the fishing is only fair. The most popular area of river is the lower end, accessible by car.

Obsidian Creek is a small stream bordered by the road between Mammoth and Norris. It flows for nearly 16 miles, ending in the Gardner River. There is good fishing for pan-sized brook trout that provide great action for kids of all ages.

Pelican Creek extends for 52 miles from its mouth on Yellowstone Lake east of Fishing Bridge. Pelican, a broad, slow-moving creek, flows through willowy swamplands at its lower end. This is a likely area to see moose. The road crosses Pelican Creek, but you can reach the fishable portions of the creek only by trail. This area is subject to special regulations and grizzly bear closures. Check current regulations.

Pelican is the second largest tributary to Yellowstone Lake and provides critical spawning grounds for the lake's cutthroat trout. There is also a sizable population of resident cutthroat. Because of spawning, the lower end of the creek is closed to fishing. The remainder is catch-and-release. The season does not open until July 15.

Pelican Creek offers some of the finest fishing in Yellowstone Park. The cutthroat run 14 to 16 inches and are very catchable. Anglers give Pelican Creek the best overall rating for quality of fishing. This is also good bear country, so be on guard.

Riddle Lake is located just south of Grant Village. A 2-mile hike is necessary to reach the lakeshore, which is bordered by large meadows west and south. Riddle Lake has good fishing for foot-long cutthroat. Check the regulations for special restrictions.

Shoshone Lake is the second largest lake in Yellowstone, covering 12 square miles, and reportedly the largest lake in the U.S. without road access. Restricted to motorless craft, the lake provides excellent canoeing. It is also easily accessible by trail either from the north via the DeLacy Creek Trail (3.1 miles) or from the south at the north end of Lewis Lake. Despite the hike, this is a rather popular fishing spot.

Originally barren of fish, today Shoshone has a good population of big lake trout, some brown trout, and a few brook trout. These browns are lunkers averaging a tremendous 16 inches, with brook trout only slightly smaller. Boat anglers get most of the lake trout, while bank anglers do better for browns and brookies. The lake trout generally hang out in deep water (requiring special rigs) until October and November, when they move into shoals to spawn.

Slough Creek, in the northeastern corner of the park, is one of the most highly rated fisheries in Yellowstone. Approximately 16 miles of the stream are within the park, but this stretch is accessible only by trail for all but the lower end, where a campground provides access. Since the introduction of catch-and-release-only regulations in 1973, cutthroat size has increased, and the trout now average a healthy 13 to 14 inches, with a respectable number exceeding 16 inches. Slough Creek also has a small population of rainbow and rainbow-cutthroat hybrids in its lower reaches. Anglers frequently use terrestrial patterns such as Joe's Hopper and attractors such as the Royal Wulff, as well as the usual nymphs, small streamers, and small mayfly and caddis imitations, but you might have to try the smallest of tippets and decrease to size 18 flies to catch fish.

Despite its limited access, this is one of the more popular fishing streams in the park. It provides outstanding fishing in a pristine setting. In its lower end, Slough Creek has a rocky bottom and riffly water interspersed with large boulders. Upstream a few miles, it opens into the meadows of Slough Creek Valley, where the water is exceptionally quiet.

The Snake River extends for 42 miles along the southeastern boundary of the park before leaving Yellowstone at the south entrance. This is a moderate fishery for cutthroat, brown, rainbow, brook, and lake trout.

Much of the Snake River has limited access. There is road access at the south entrance, but the majority of the river requires some hiking.

The Snake is a deep river with wide gravel streambeds. It runs through scenic canyons intermixed with peaceful meadows.

Soda Butte Creek is bordered by the park road from the northeast entrance near Cooke City. It is a popular stream, providing good fishing for 10- to 11-inch cutthroat and a few rainbow trout amidst a valley of magnificent scenery.

Sylvan Lake is a popular roadside fishery, complete with picnic tables, located on the road between Fishing Bridge and the park's east entrance.

Anglers do well hooking 10- to 12-inch cutthroat trout. Due to the heavy pressure this small, 28-acre lake was receiving, it has been designated catch-and-release fishing only. Sylvan Lake now has one of the highest catch rates in the park.

For more detailed information on fishing the waters of the park, see *Fishing Yellowstone National Park* by Richard Parks, (Falcon.)

About the Author

Michael Sample has been photographing and writing about Montana since the 1970s. As co-founder of Falcon Publishing in 1979, Sample, with his photography and writing has helped Falcon become one of the premier outdoor publishers. And, as Montana's best known photographer, he has shared his love of the state in numerous publications, including the immensely popular gift book, *Montana On My Mind*. His works include the following photo books: *Montana: The Last Best Place*, *Bison: Symbol of the American West*, *Glacier On My Mind*, *The Montana Calendar*, and his most recent work, *Yellowstone On My Mind*. He currently fishes out of Billings, where he lives with his family.